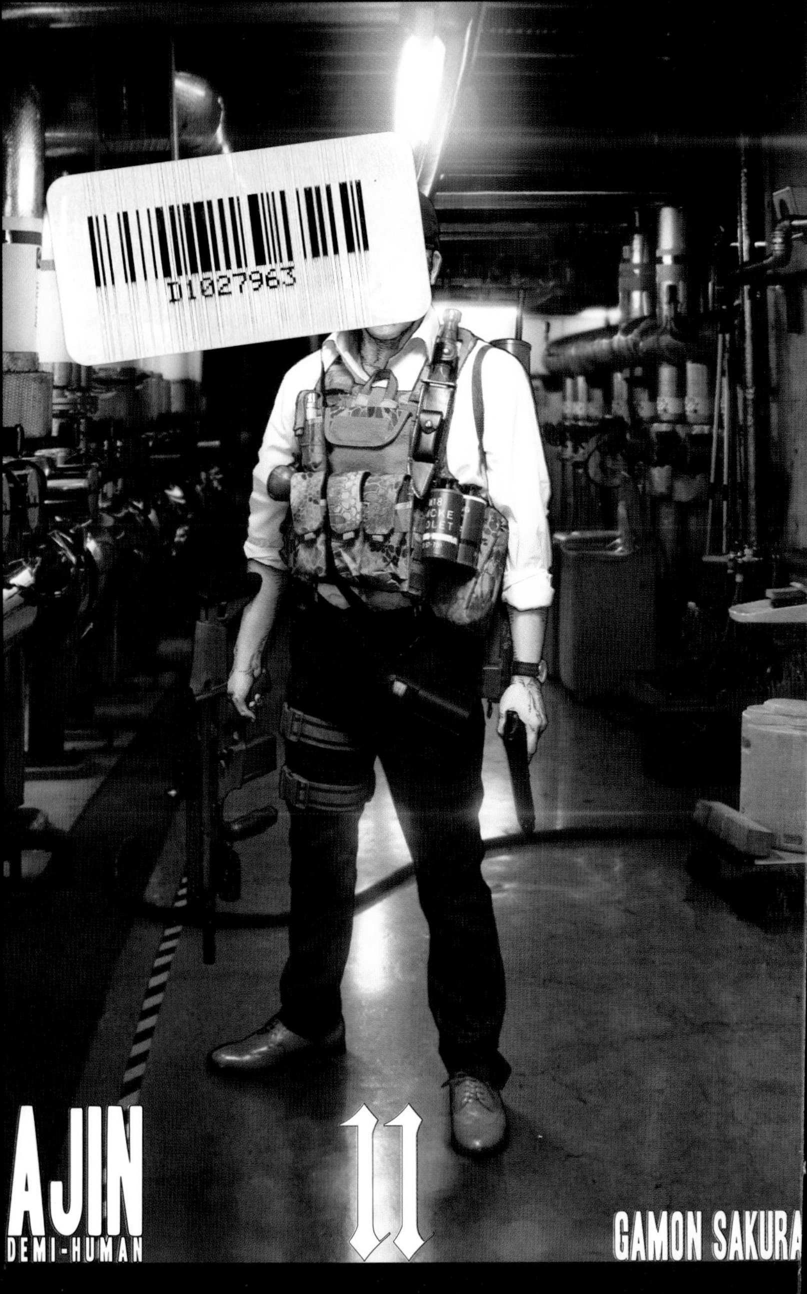
AJIN
DEMI-HUMAN
11
GAMON SAKURA

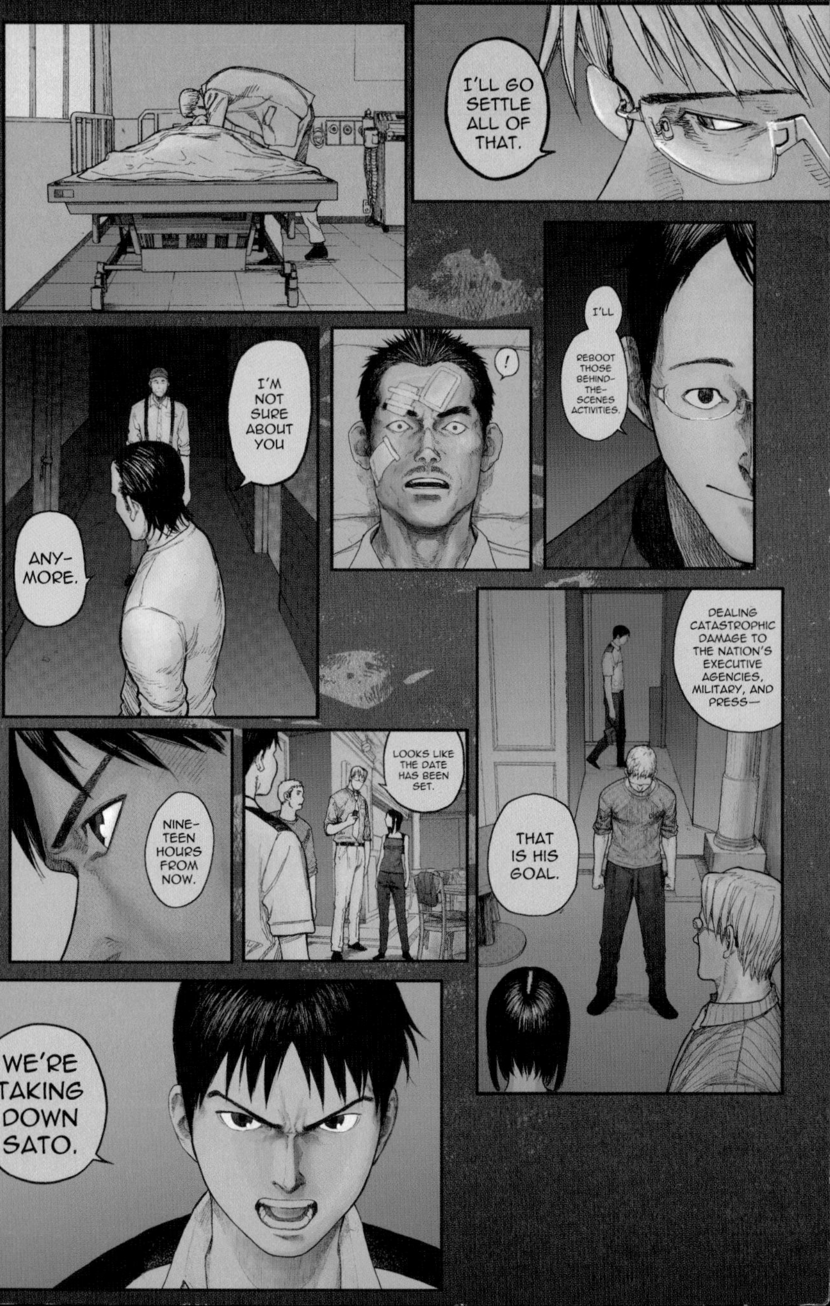
I'LL GO SETTLE ALL OF THAT.
I'LL
REBOOT THOSE BEHIND-THE-SCENES ACTIVITIES.
!
I'M NOT SURE ABOUT YOU
ANY-MORE.
DEALING CATASTROPHIC DAMAGE TO THE NATION'S EXECUTIVE AGENCIES, MILITARY, AND PRESS—
THAT IS HIS GOAL.
LOOKS LIKE THE DATE HAS BEEN SET.
NINE-TEEN HOURS FROM NOW.
WE'RE TAKING DOWN SATO.

DRAMATIS PERSONAE

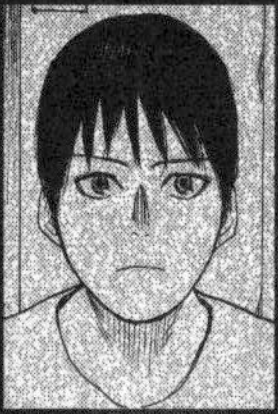

KEI NAGAI

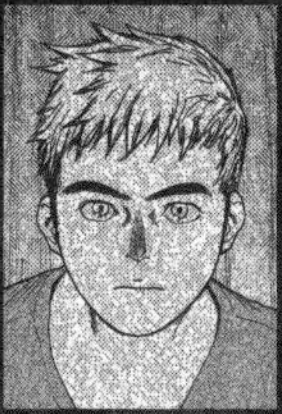

KO NAKANO

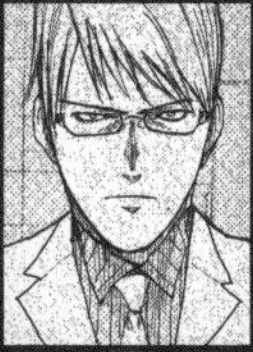

YUU TOSAKI

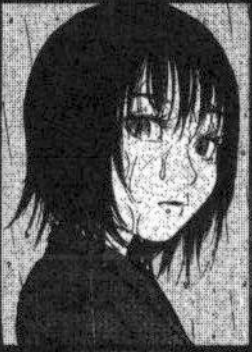

IZUMI SHIMOMURA

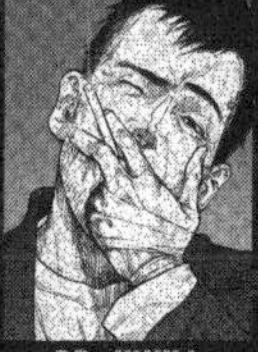

DR. IKUYA OGURA

THE FOUR BLACK SUITS

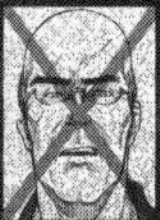

HIRASAWA

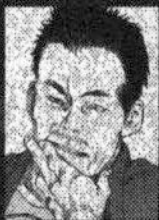

MANABE

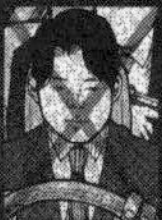

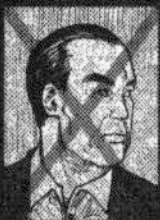

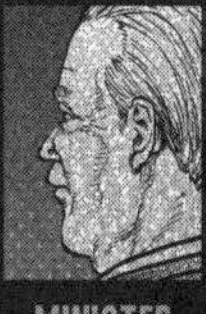

MINISTER

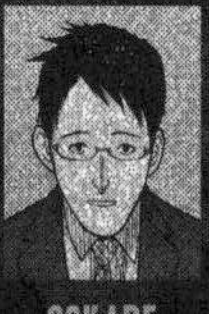

SOKABE

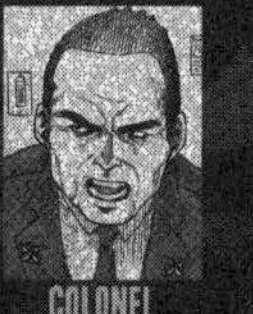

COLONEL KOUMA

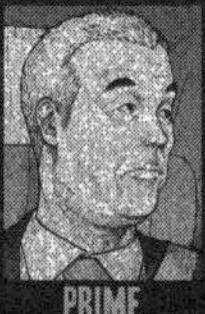

PRIME MINISTER

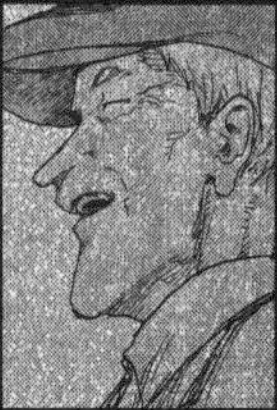

SATO

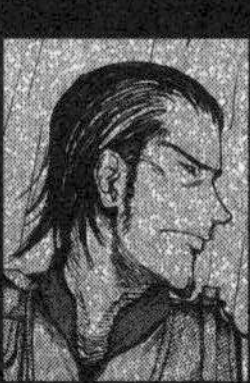

TANAKA

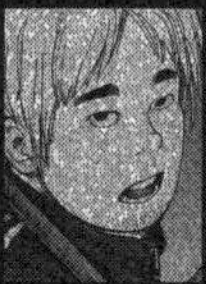

OKUYAMA

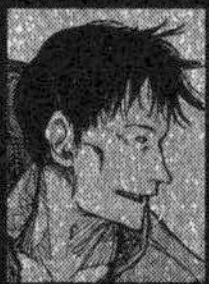

TAKAHASHI

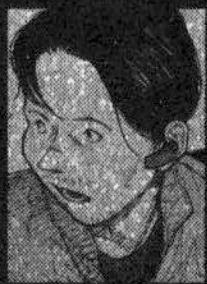

GEN

File:49

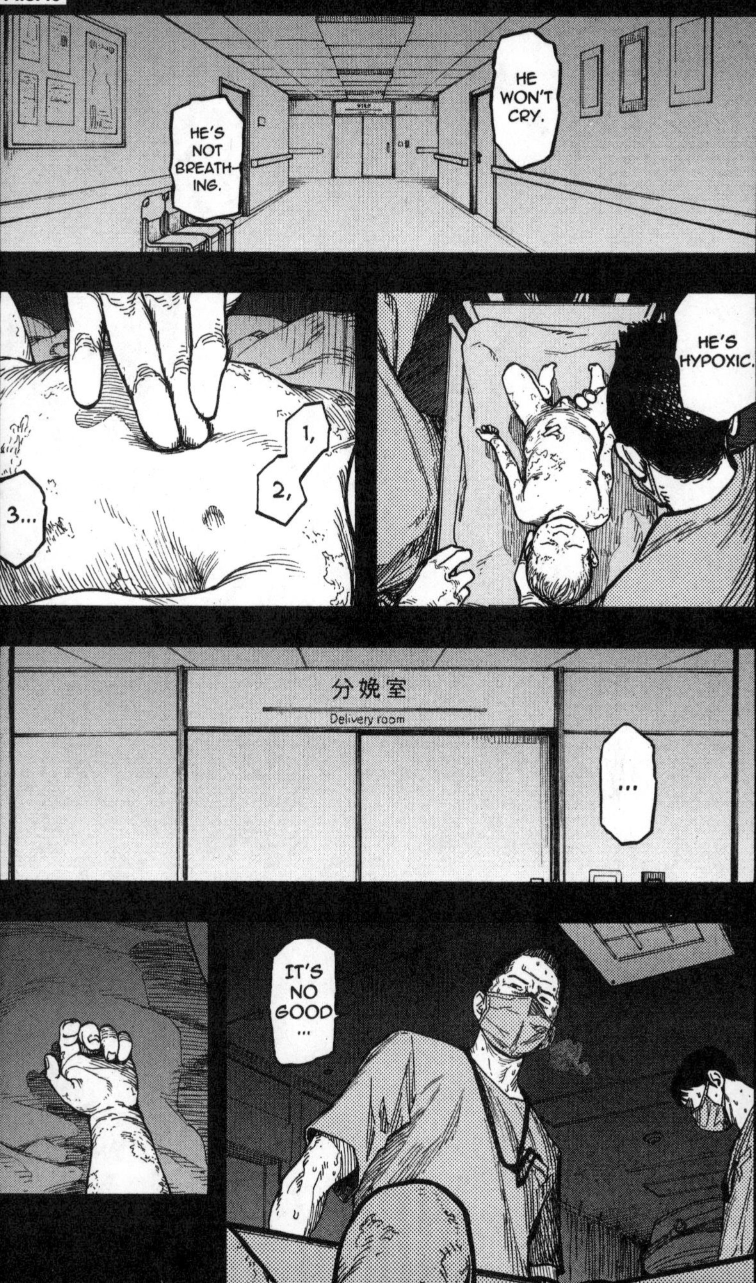
HE WON'T CRY.
HE'S NOT BREATH-ING.
HE'S HYPOXIC.
1,
2,
3...
分娩室
Delivery room
...
IT'S NO GOOD...

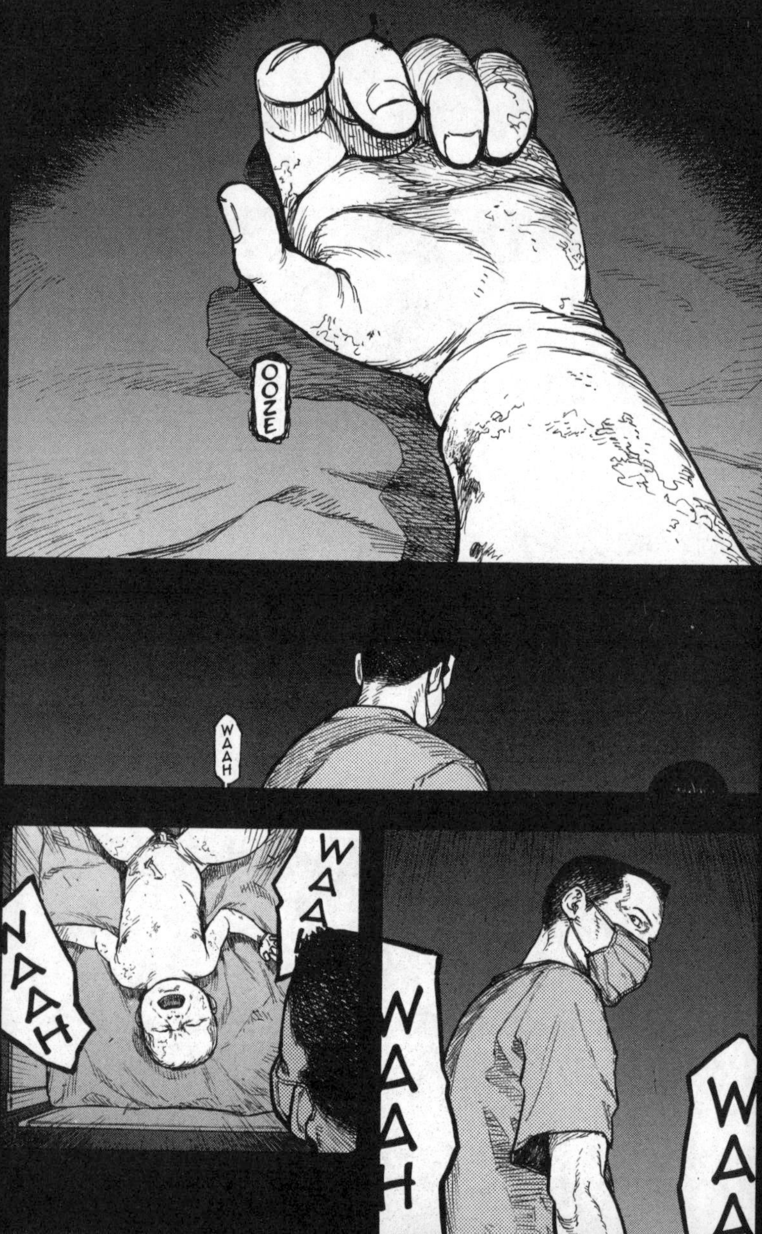
OOZE
WAAH
WAA
WAAH
WAA
WAAH

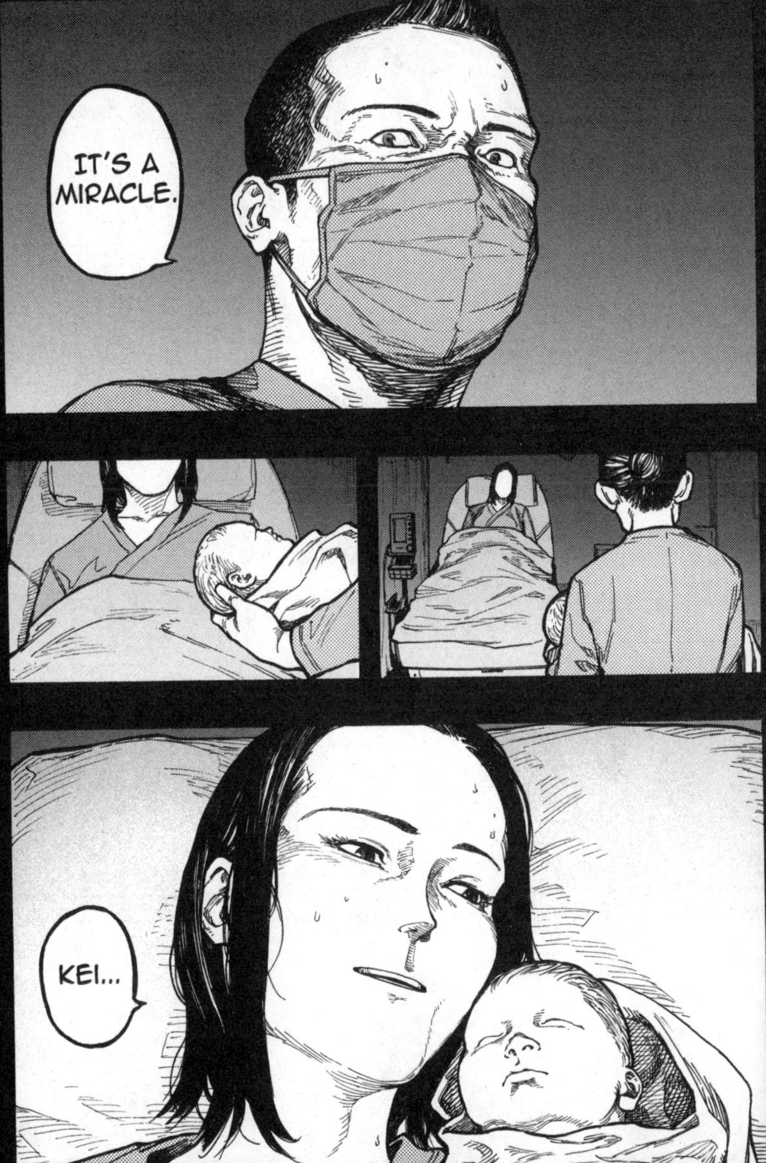
IT'S A MIRACLE.
KEI...

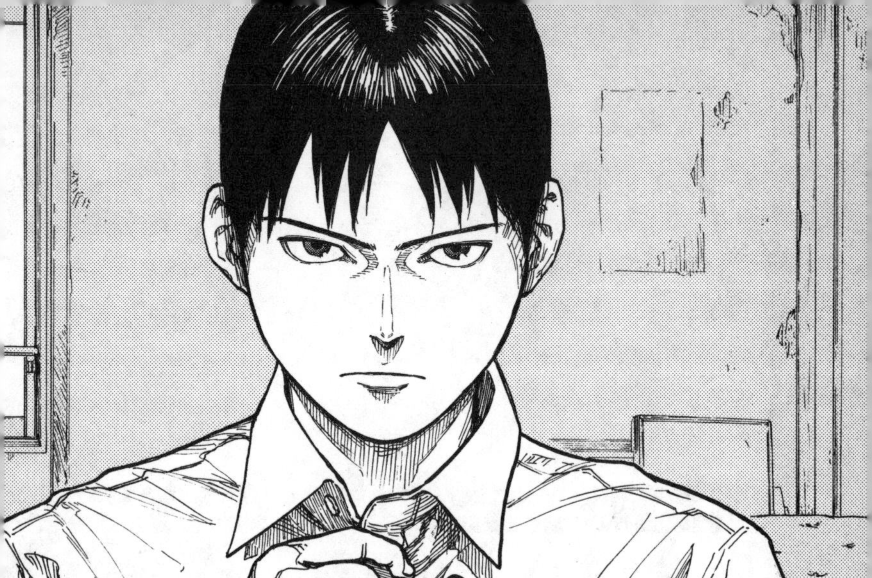

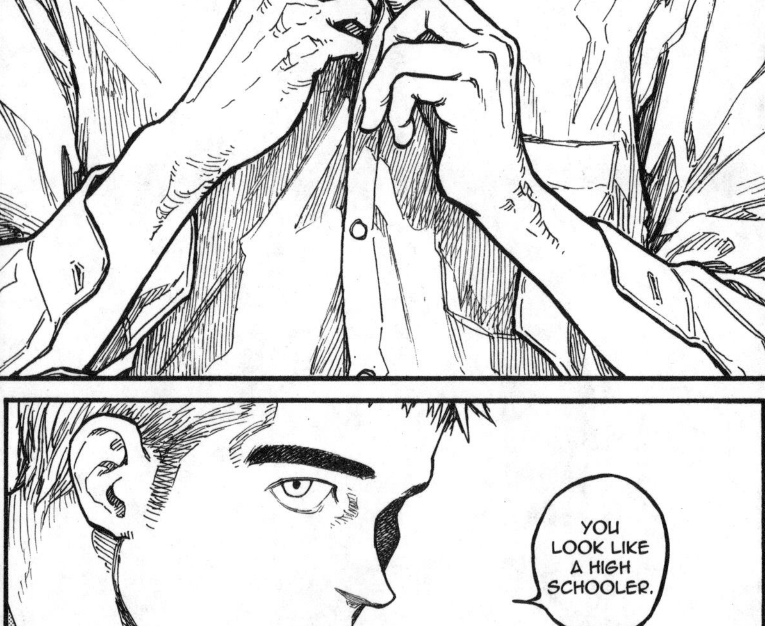
YOU LOOK LIKE A HIGH SCHOOLER.

File 49: Steep Road

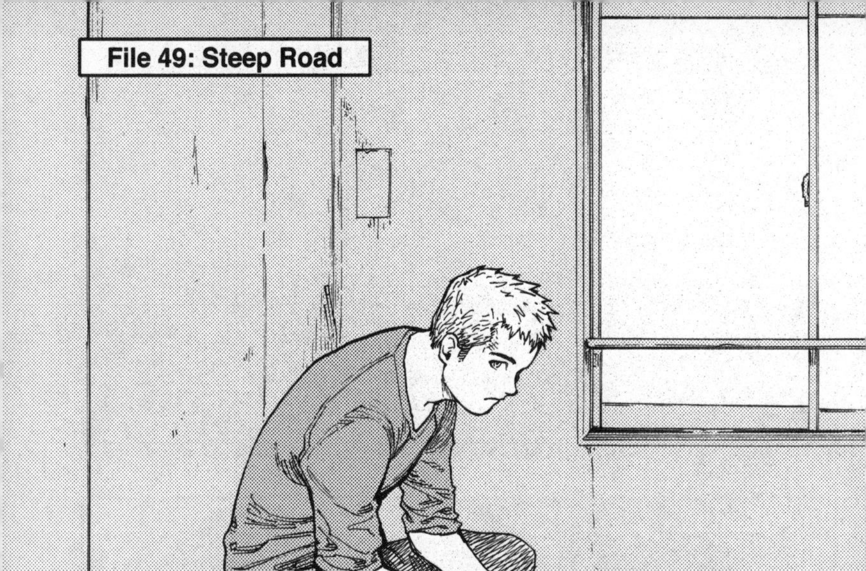

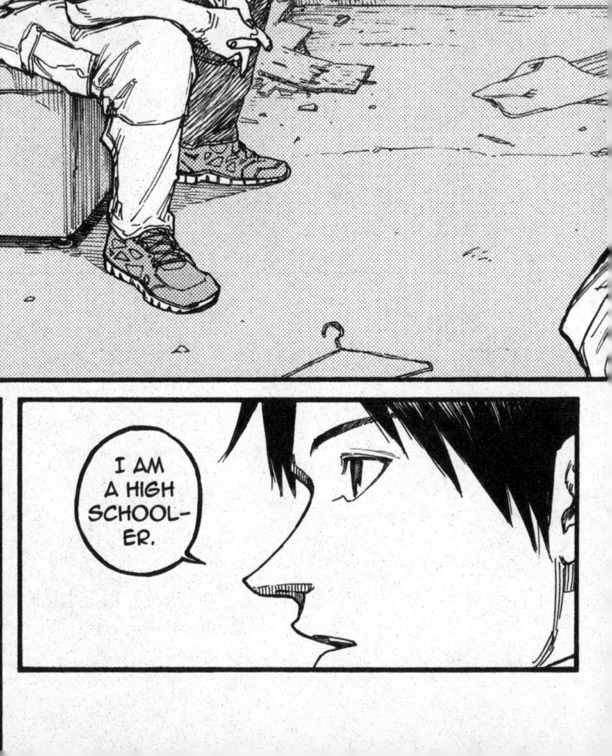
I AM A HIGH SCHOOL-ER.

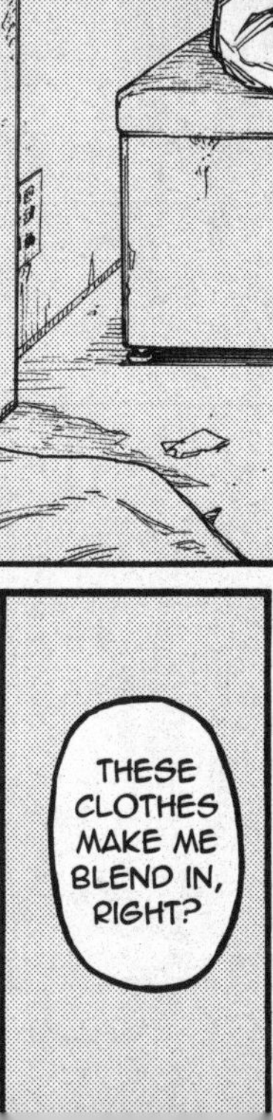
THESE CLOTHES MAKE ME BLEND IN, RIGHT?

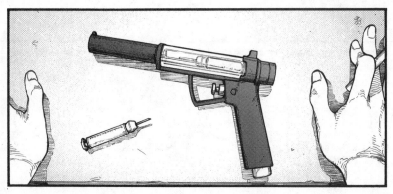

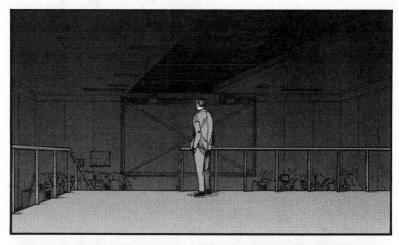

IT'S THE TOWER OF BA-BEL...

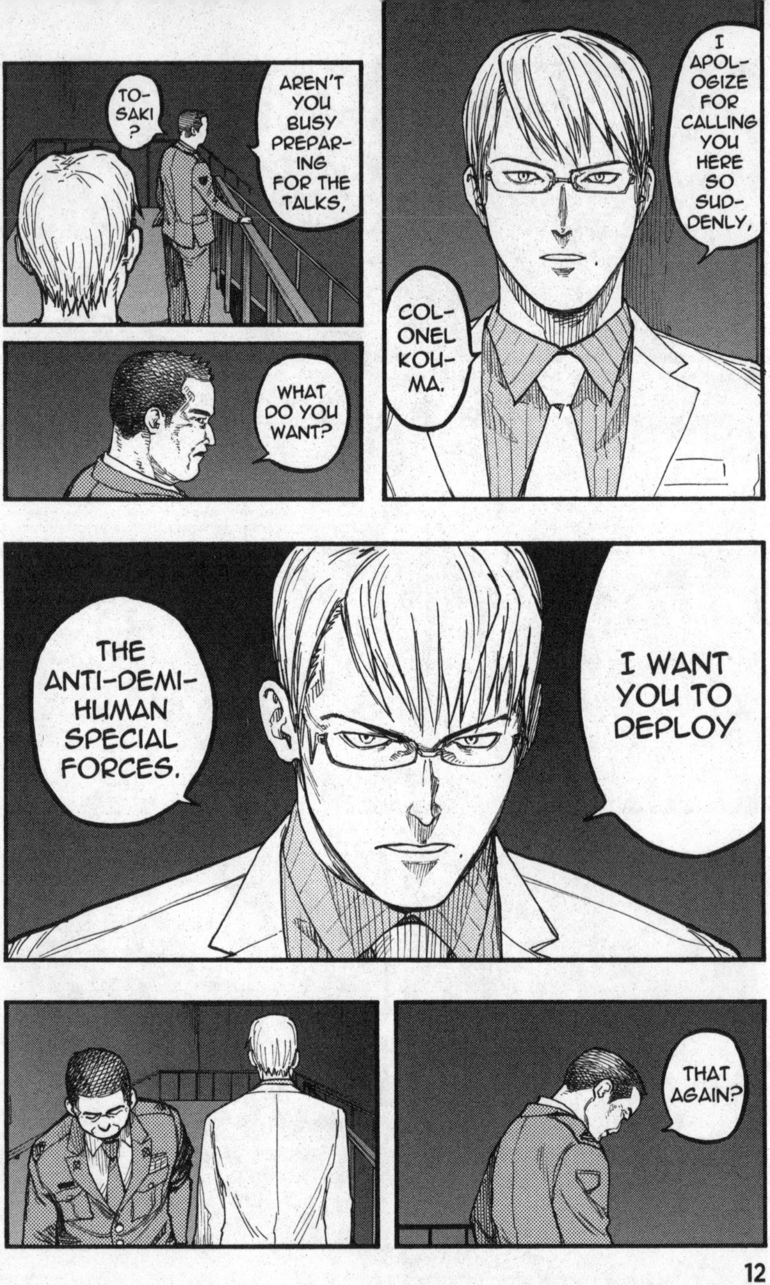
I APOLOGIZE FOR CALLING YOU HERE SO SUDDENLY,
COLONEL KOUMA.
AREN'T YOU BUSY PREPARING FOR THE TALKS,
TO-SAKI?
WHAT DO YOU WANT?
I WANT YOU TO DEPLOY
THE ANTI-DEMI-HUMAN SPECIAL FORCES.
THAT AGAIN?

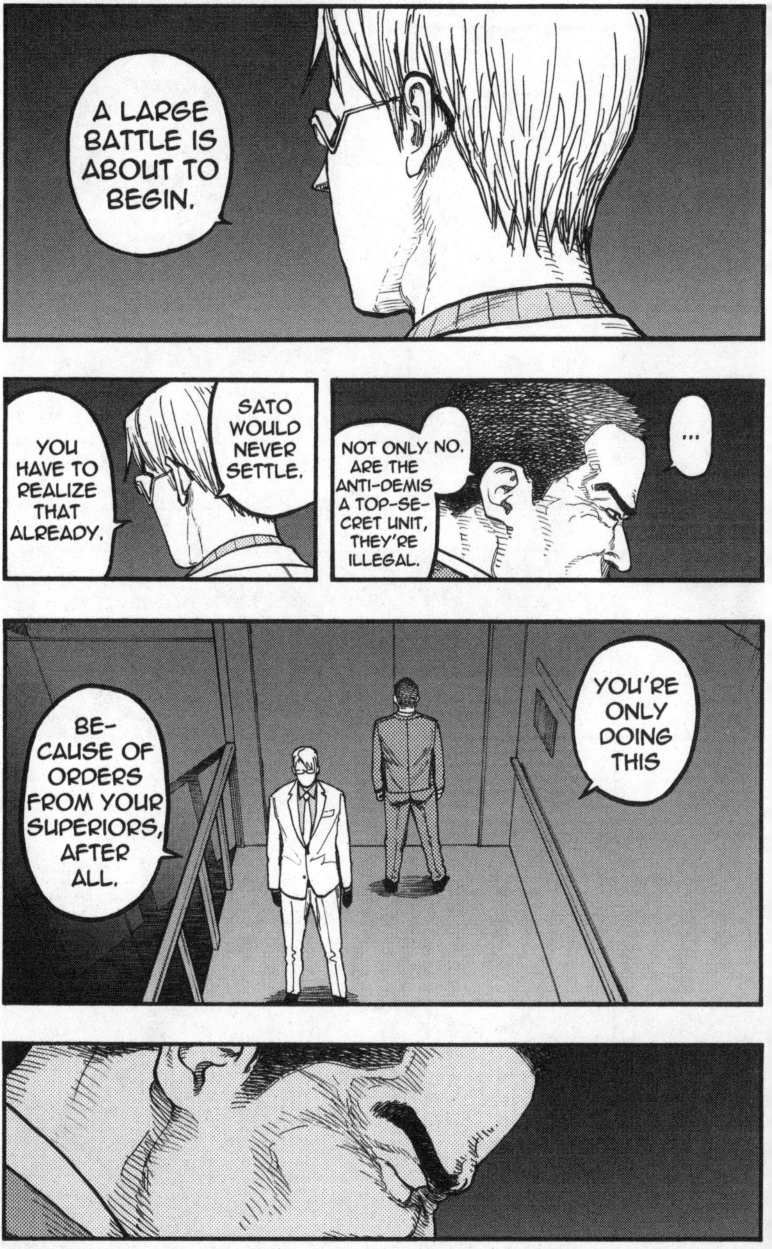
A LARGE BATTLE IS ABOUT TO BEGIN.
...
NOT ONLY NO. ARE THE ANTI-DEMIS A TOP-SECRET UNIT, THEY'RE ILLEGAL.
SATO WOULD NEVER SETTLE.
YOU HAVE TO REALIZE THAT ALREADY.
YOU'RE ONLY DOING THIS
BECAUSE OF ORDERS FROM YOUR SUPERIORS, AFTER ALL.

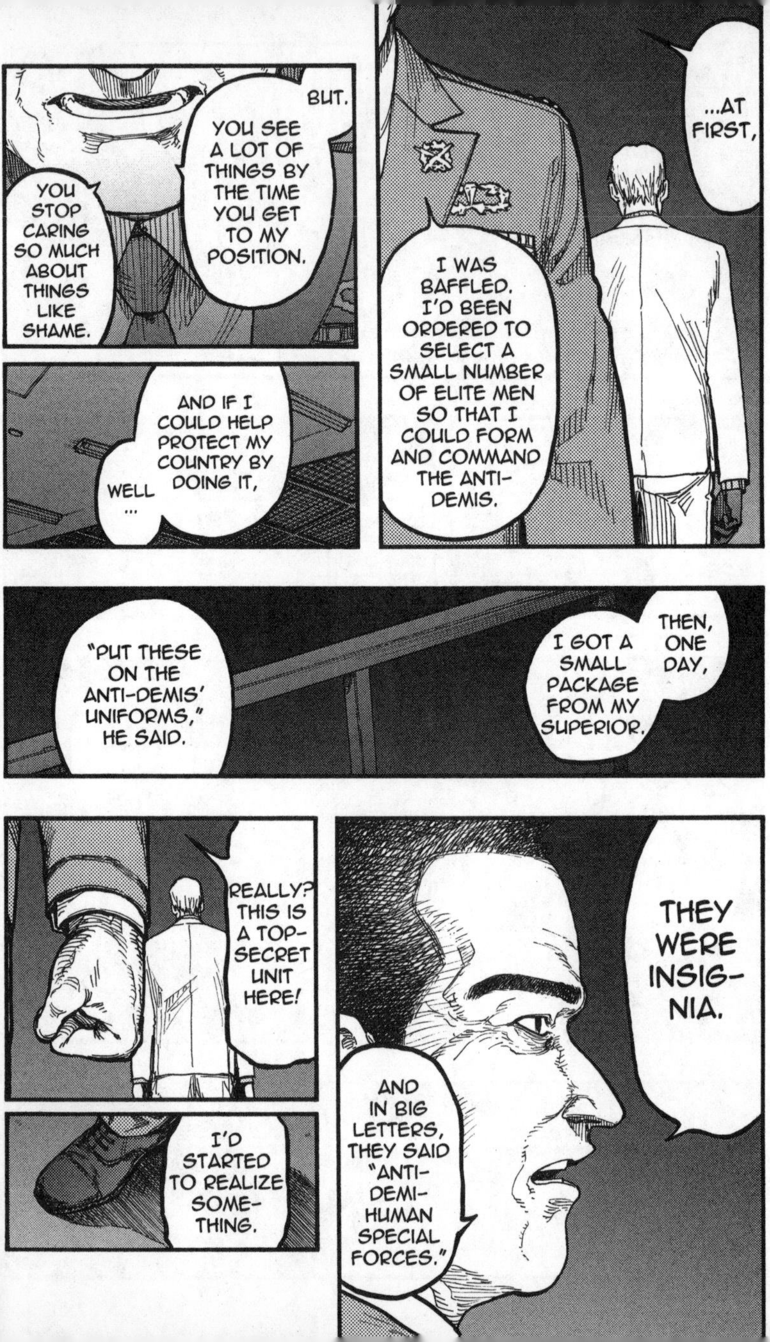
...AT FIRST,
I WAS BAFFLED. I'D BEEN ORDERED TO SELECT A SMALL NUMBER OF ELITE MEN SO THAT I COULD FORM AND COMMAND THE ANTI-DEMIS.
BUT.
YOU SEE A LOT OF THINGS BY THE TIME YOU GET TO MY POSITION.
YOU STOP CARING SO MUCH ABOUT THINGS LIKE SHAME.
AND IF I COULD HELP PROTECT MY COUNTRY BY DOING IT,
WELL ...
THEN, ONE DAY,
I GOT A SMALL PACKAGE FROM MY SUPERIOR.
"PUT THESE ON THE ANTI-DEMIS' UNIFORMS," HE SAID.
THEY WERE INSIG-NIA.
AND IN BIG LETTERS, THEY SAID "ANTI-DEMI-HUMAN SPECIAL FORCES."
REALLY? THIS IS A TOP-SECRET UNIT HERE!
I'D STARTED TO REALIZE SOME-THING.

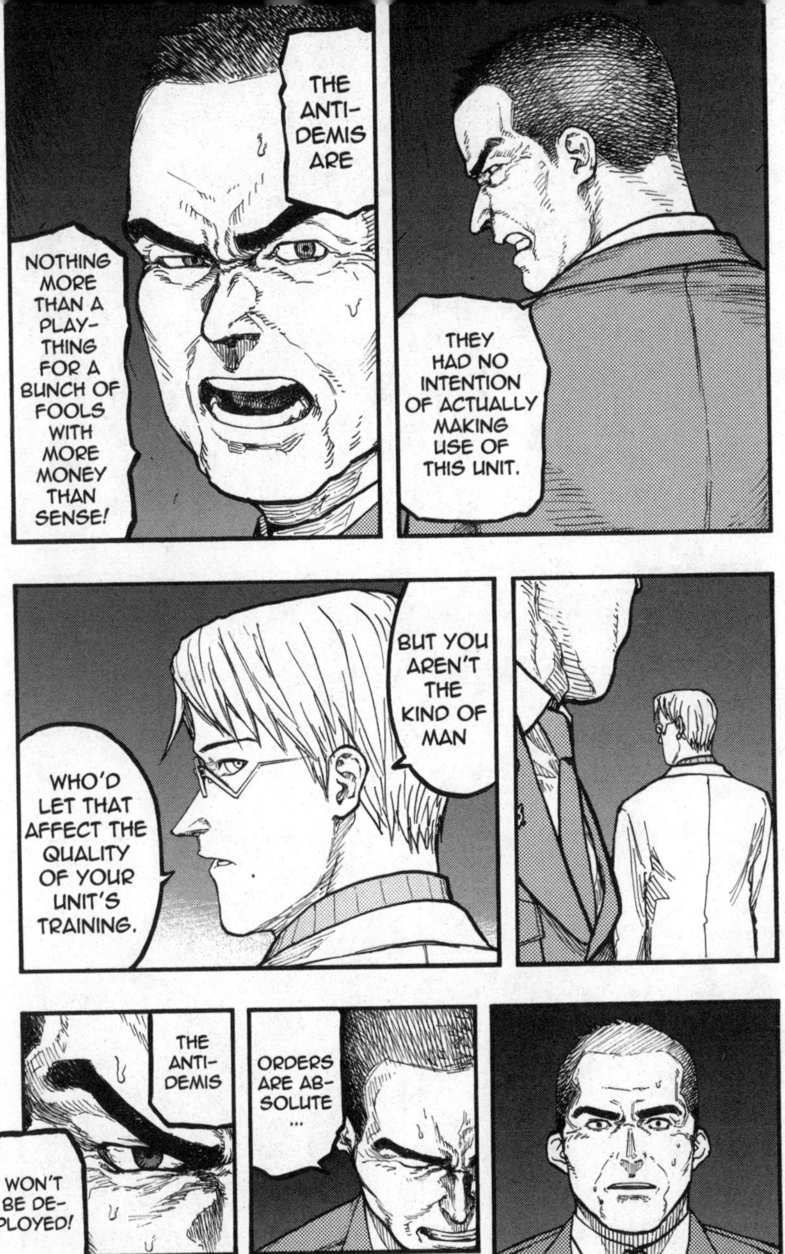
THEY HAD NO INTENTION OF ACTUALLY MAKING USE OF THIS UNIT.
THE ANTI-DEMIS ARE
NOTHING MORE THAN A PLAY-THING FOR A BUNCH OF FOOLS WITH MORE MONEY THAN SENSE!
BUT YOU AREN'T THE KIND OF MAN
WHO'D LET THAT AFFECT THE QUALITY OF YOUR UNIT'S TRAINING.
ORDERS ARE AB-SOLUTE ...
THE ANTI-DEMIS
WON'T BE DE-PLOYED!

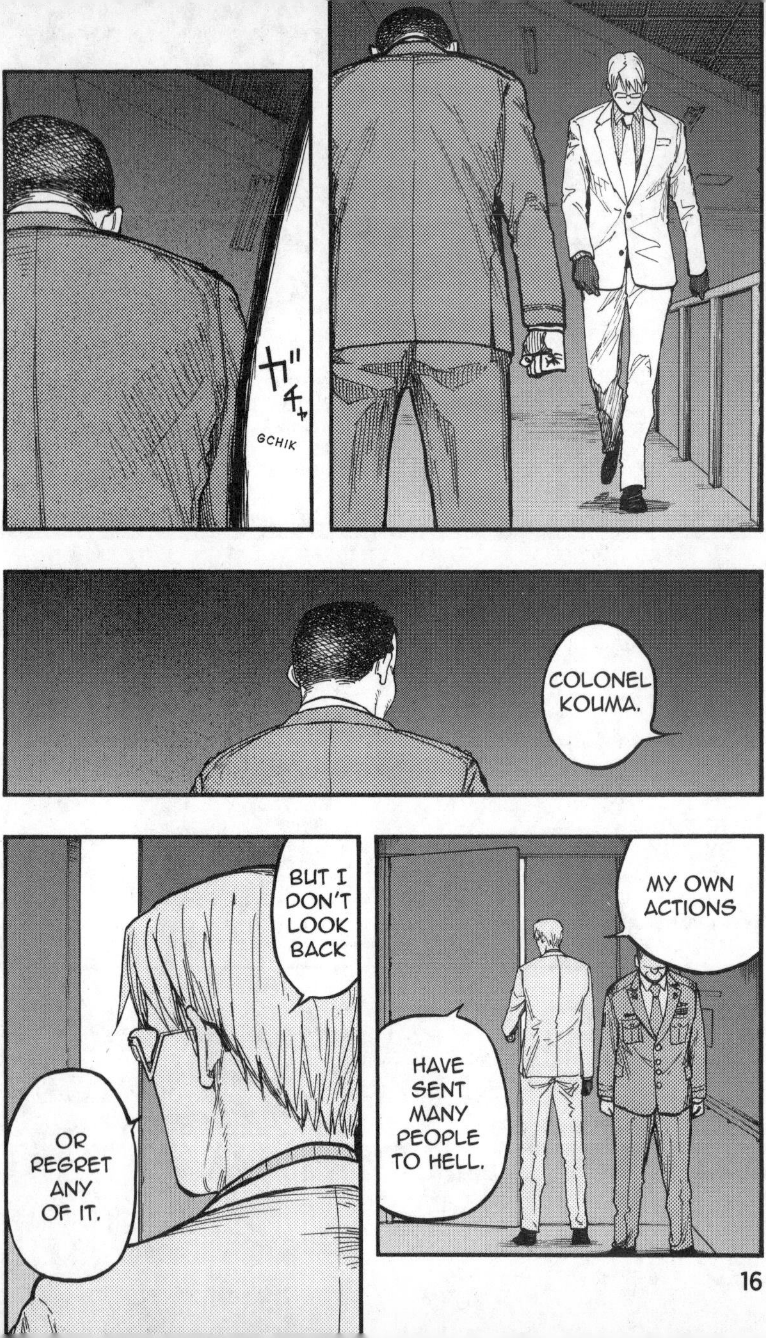

ガチャ
GCHIK
COLONEL KOUMA.
MY OWN ACTIONS
HAVE SENT MANY PEOPLE TO HELL.
BUT I DON'T LOOK BACK
OR REGRET ANY OF IT.

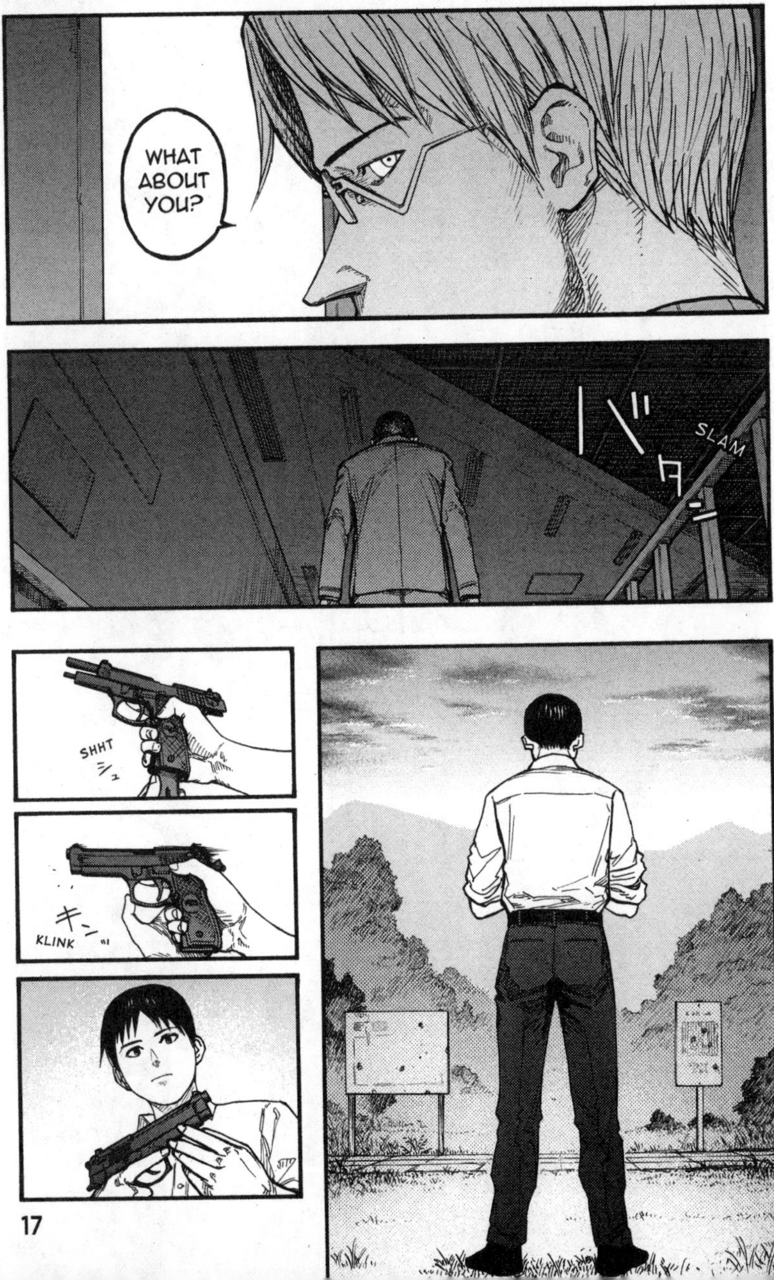
WHAT ABOUT YOU?
バターン
SLAM
SHHT
シュ
キン
KLINK

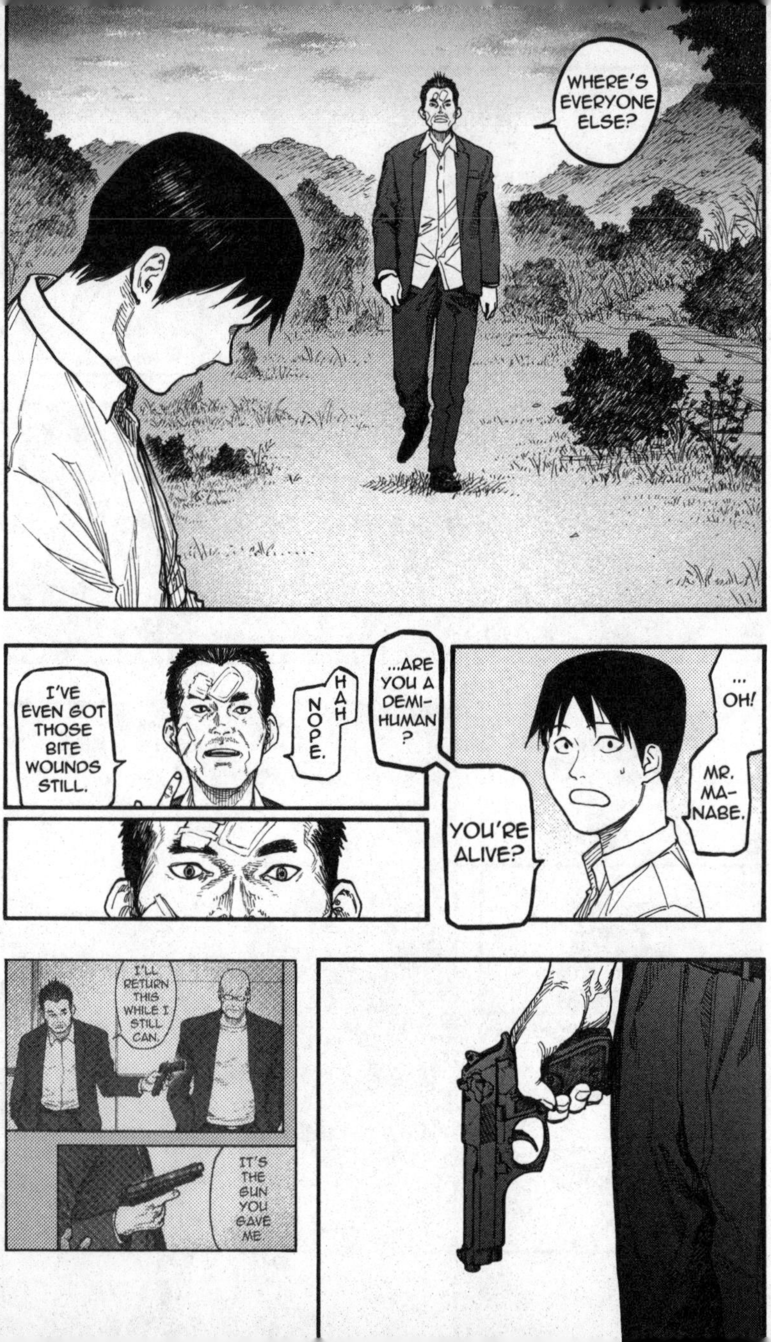
WHERE'S EVERYONE ELSE?
...OH!
MR. MANABE.
YOU'RE ALIVE?
...ARE YOU A DEMI-HUMAN?
HAH NOPE.
I'VE EVEN GOT THOSE BITE WOUNDS STILL.
I'LL RETURN THIS WHILE I STILL CAN.
IT'S THE GUN YOU GAVE ME

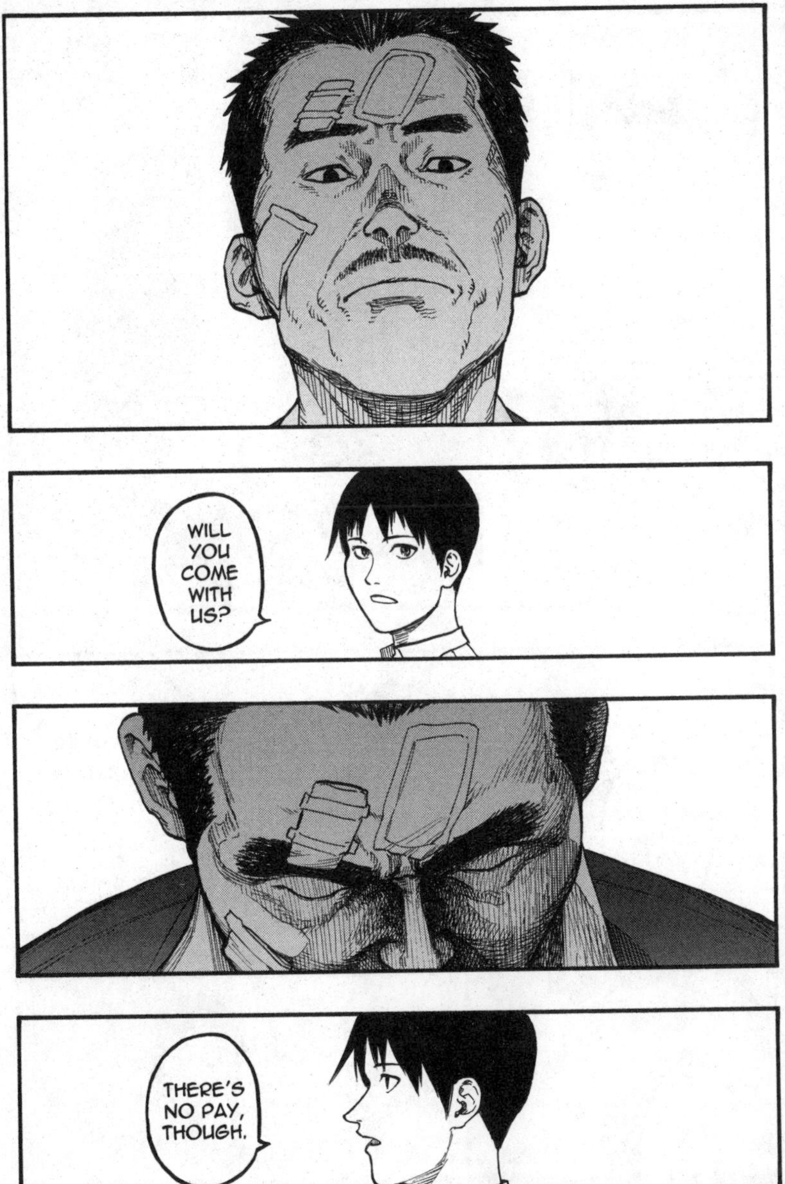
WILL YOU COME WITH US?
THERE'S NO PAY, THOUGH.

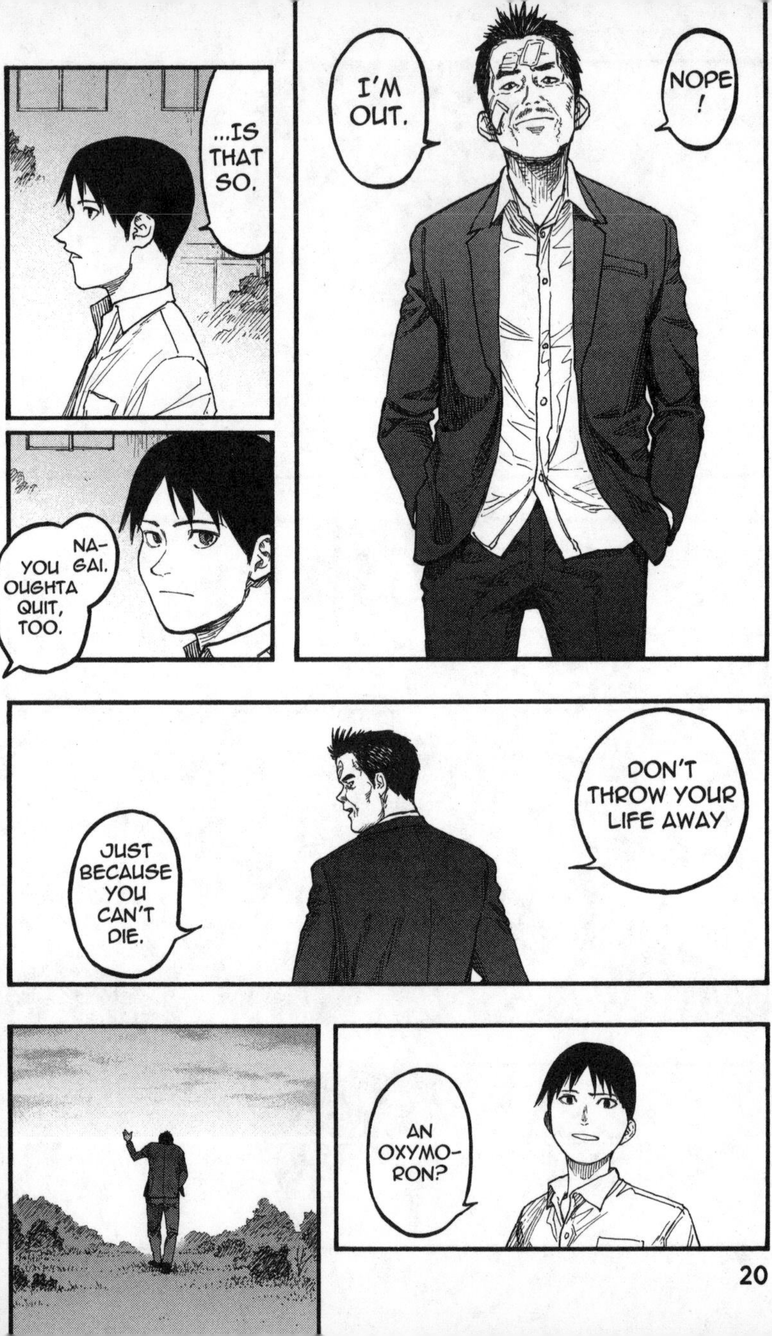
NOPE!
I'M OUT.
...IS THAT SO.
NA-GAI. YOU OUGHTA QUIT, TOO.
DON'T THROW YOUR LIFE AWAY
JUST BECAUSE YOU CAN'T DIE.
AN OXYMO-RON?

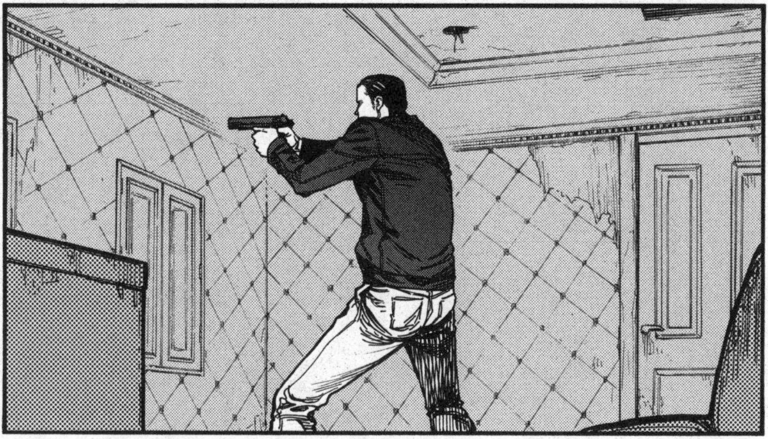

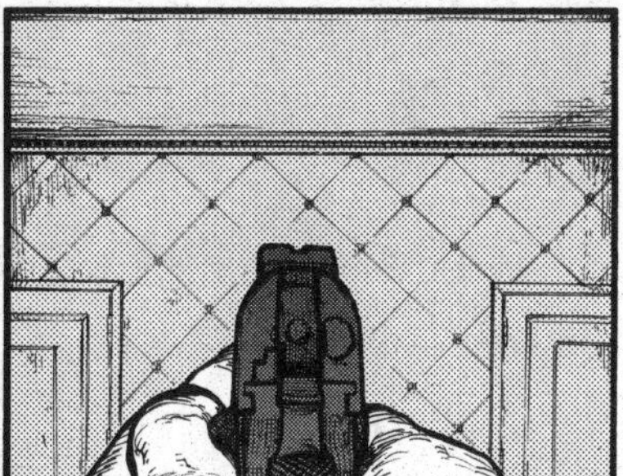

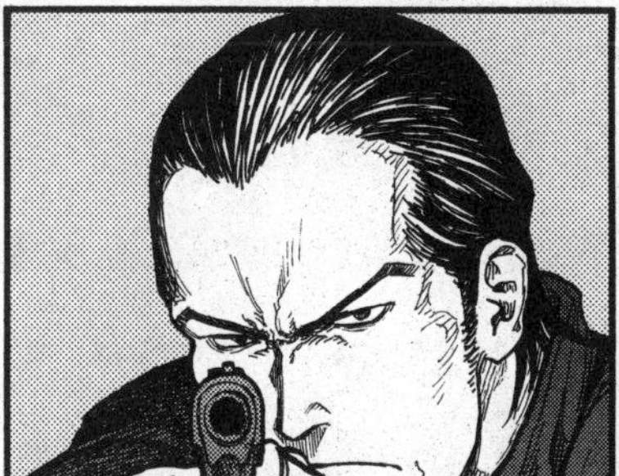

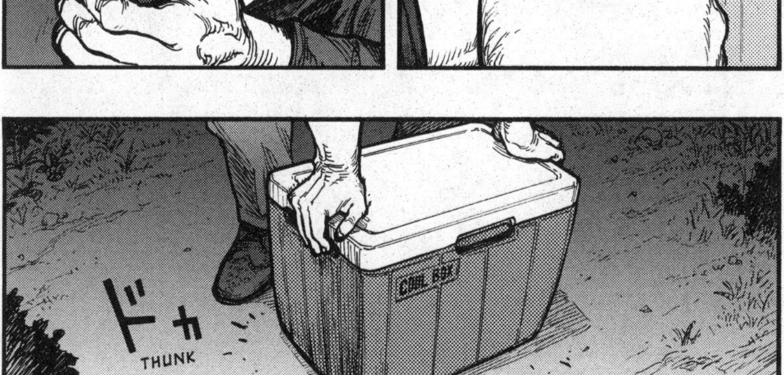
COOL BOX
ドヵ
THUNK

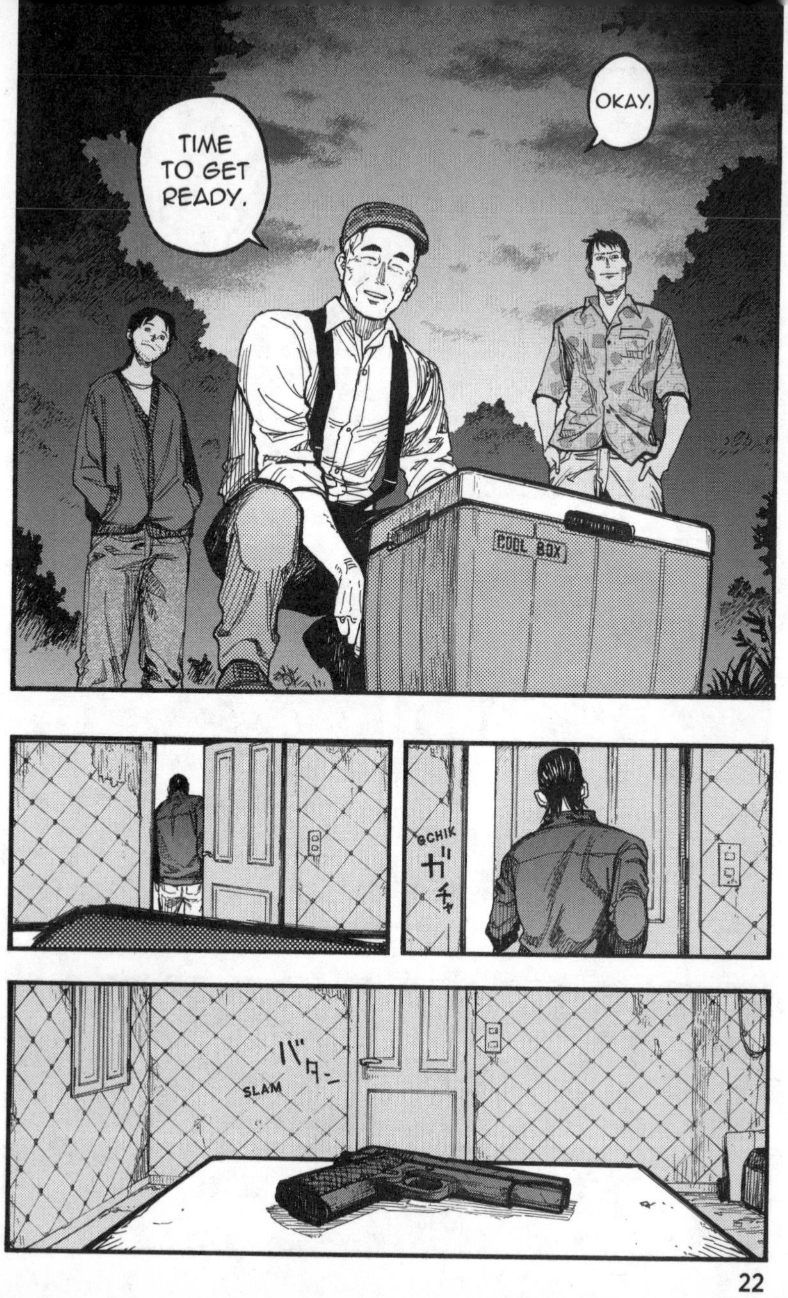
TIME TO GET READY.
OKAY.
GCHIK
ガチャ
SLAM
バタン

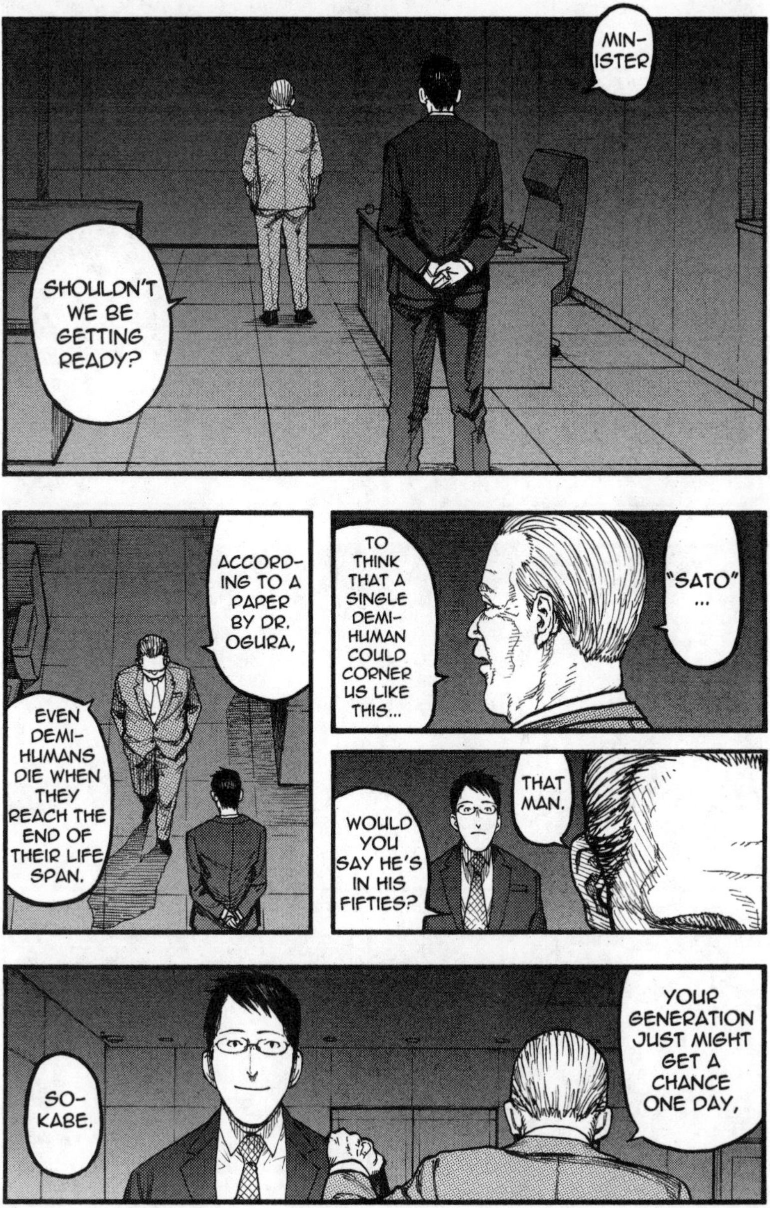
MIN-ISTER
SHOULDN'T WE BE GETTING READY?
"SATO" ...
TO THINK THAT A SINGLE DEMI-HUMAN COULD CORNER US LIKE THIS...
THAT MAN.
WOULD YOU SAY HE'S IN HIS FIFTIES?
ACCORD-ING TO A PAPER BY DR. OGURA,
EVEN DEMI-HUMANS DIE WHEN THEY REACH THE END OF THEIR LIFE SPAN.
YOUR GENERATION JUST MIGHT GET A CHANCE ONE DAY,
SO-KABE.

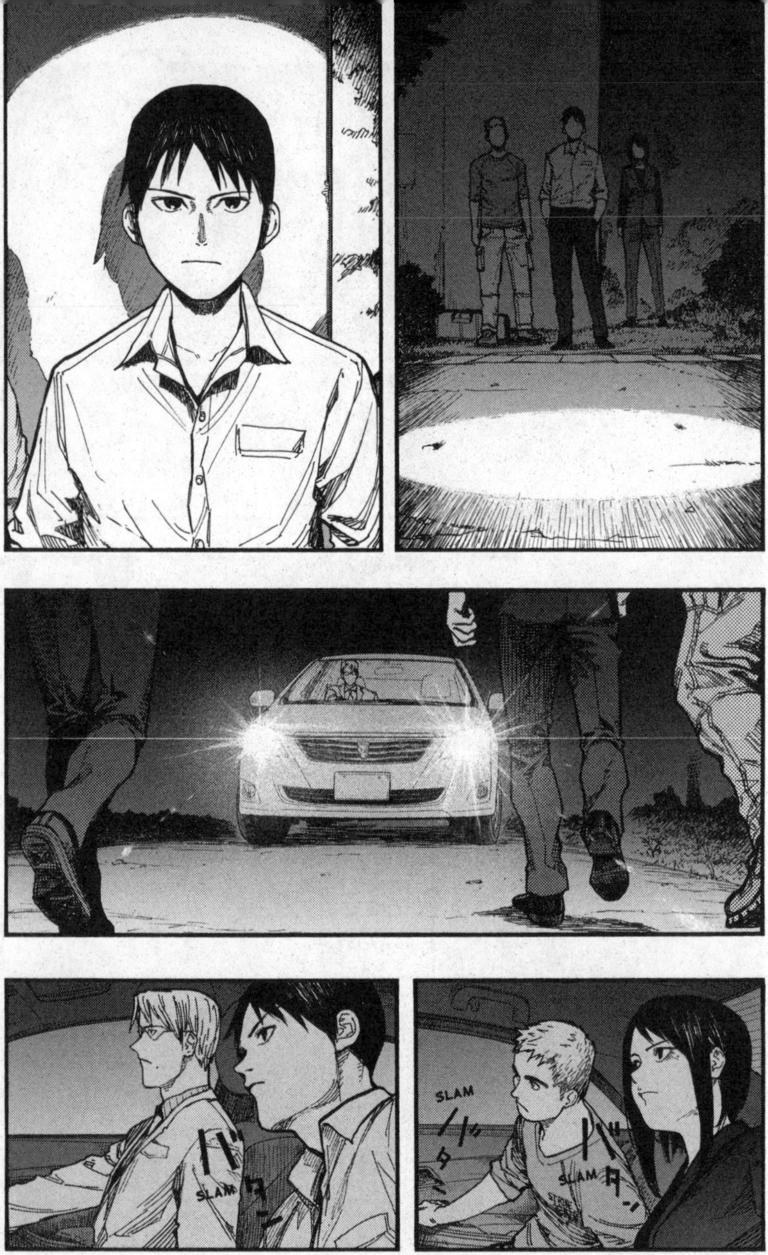
SLAM
SLAM
SLAM

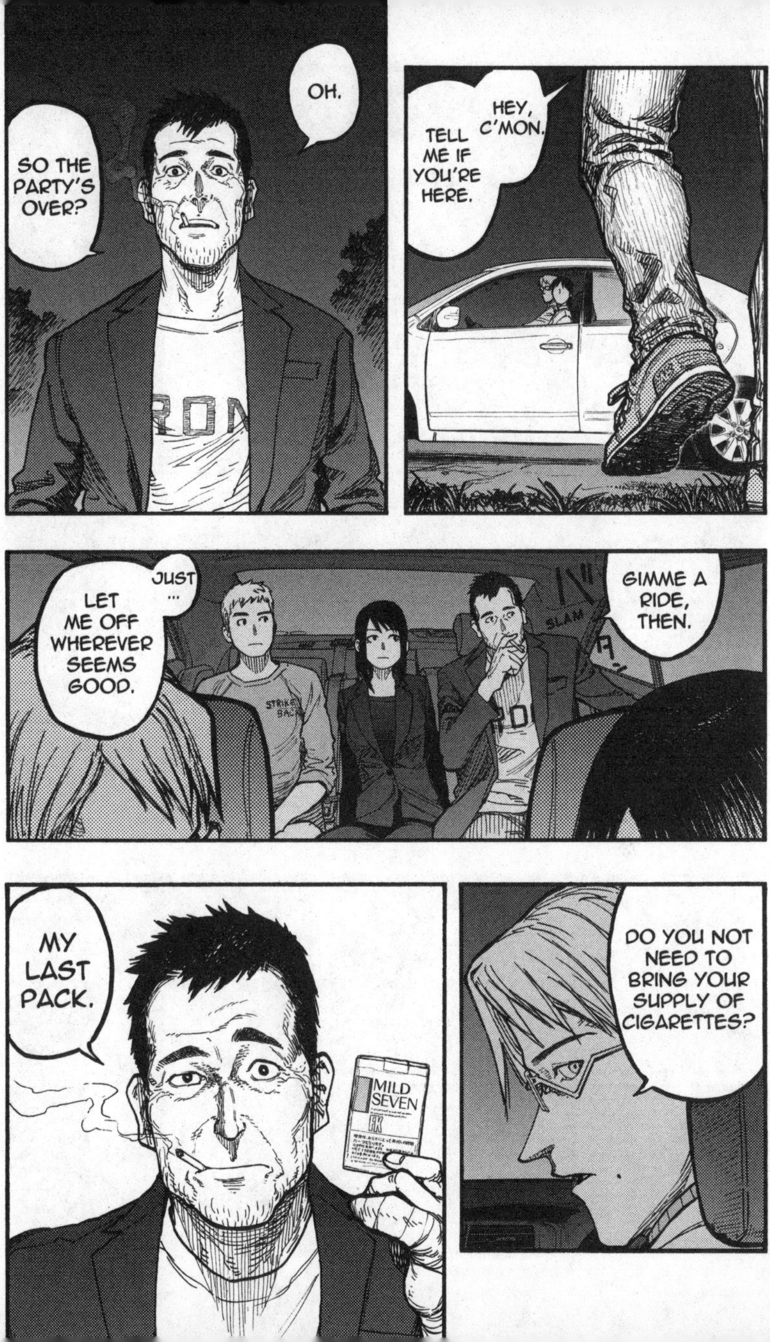
HEY, C'MON.
TELL ME IF YOU'RE HERE.
OH.
SO THE PARTY'S OVER?
GIMME A RIDE, THEN.
SLAM
JUST ...
LET ME OFF WHEREVER SEEMS GOOD.
DO YOU NOT NEED TO BRING YOUR SUPPLY OF CIGARETTES?
MY LAST PACK.
MILD SEVEN

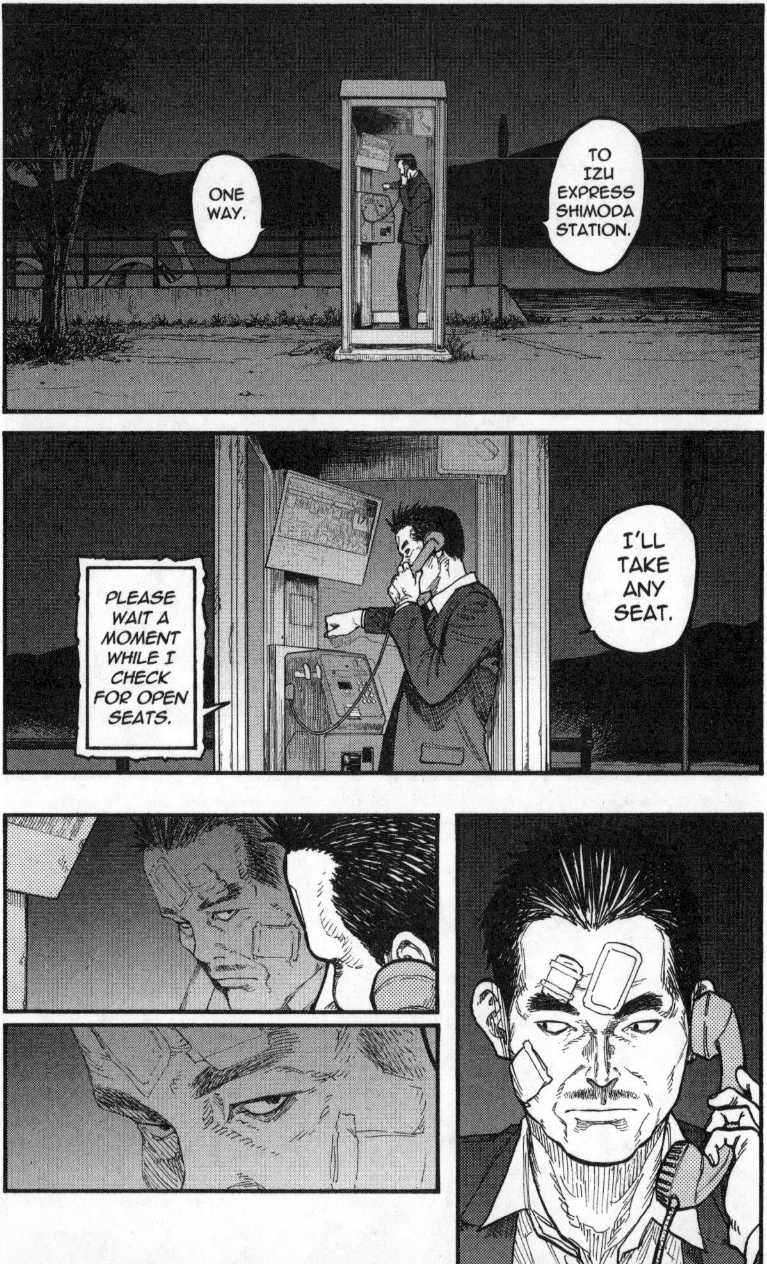
TO IZU EXPRESS SHIMODA STATION.
ONE WAY.
I'LL TAKE ANY SEAT.
PLEASE WAIT A MOMENT WHILE I CHECK FOR OPEN SEATS.

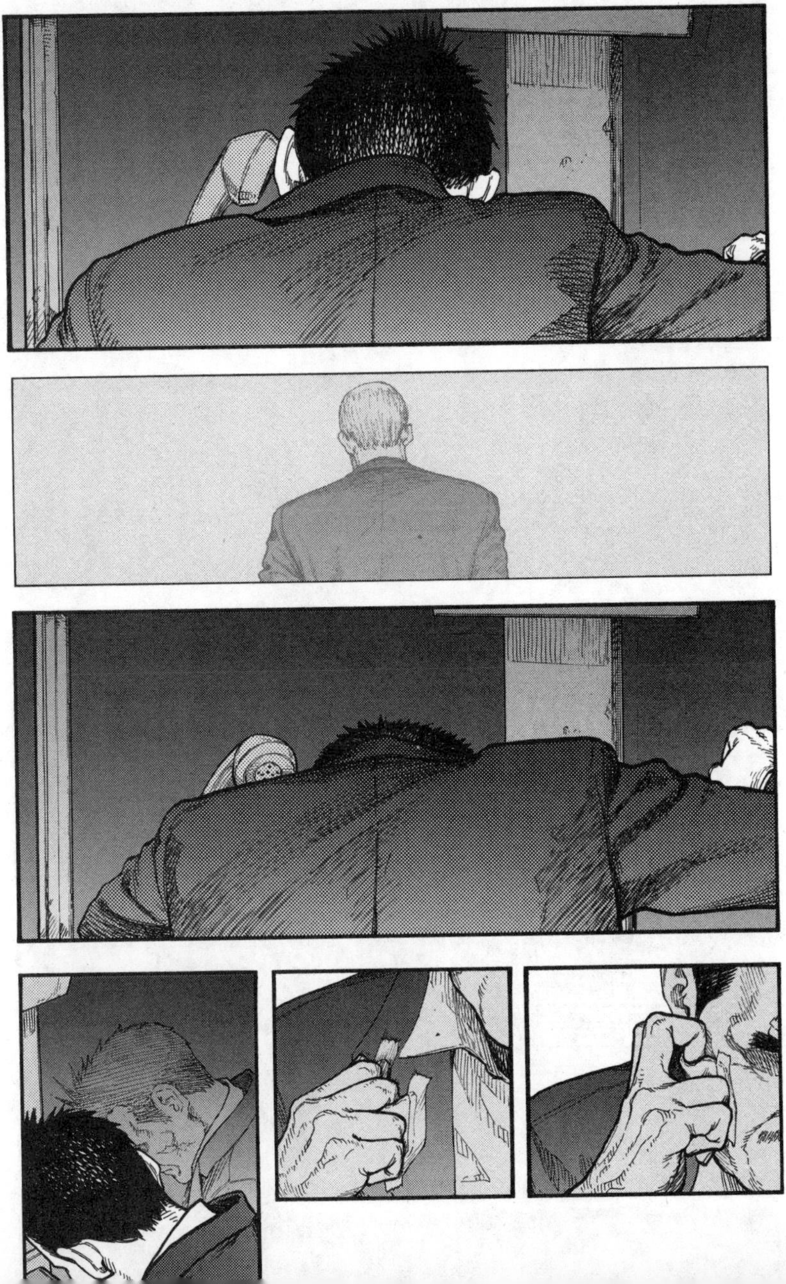

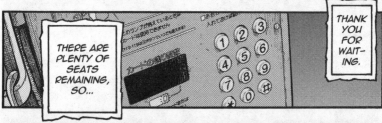

THANK YOU FOR WAIT- ING.

THERE ARE PLENTY OF SEATS REMAINING, SO...

SIR?

...

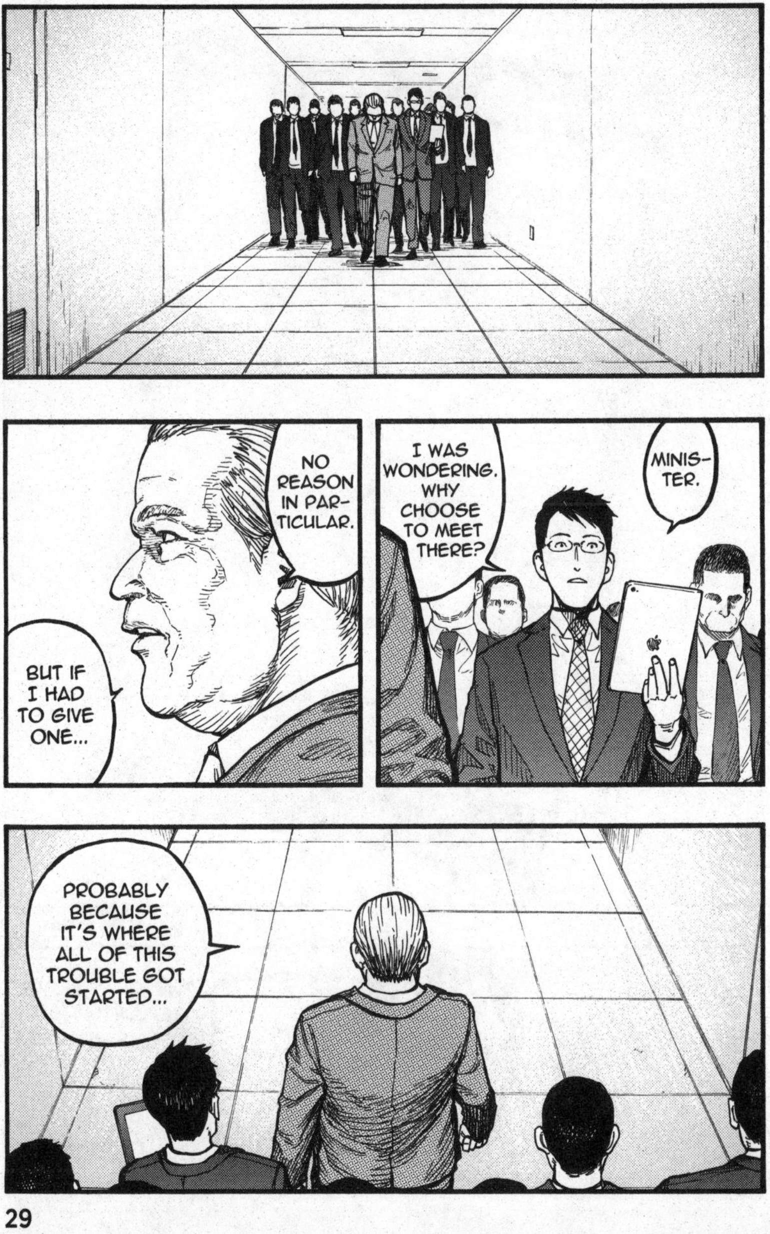
MINIS-TER.
I WAS WONDERING. WHY CHOOSE TO MEET THERE?
NO REASON IN PAR-TICULAR.
BUT IF I HAD TO GIVE ONE...
PROBABLY BECAUSE IT'S WHERE ALL OF THIS TROUBLE GOT STARTED...

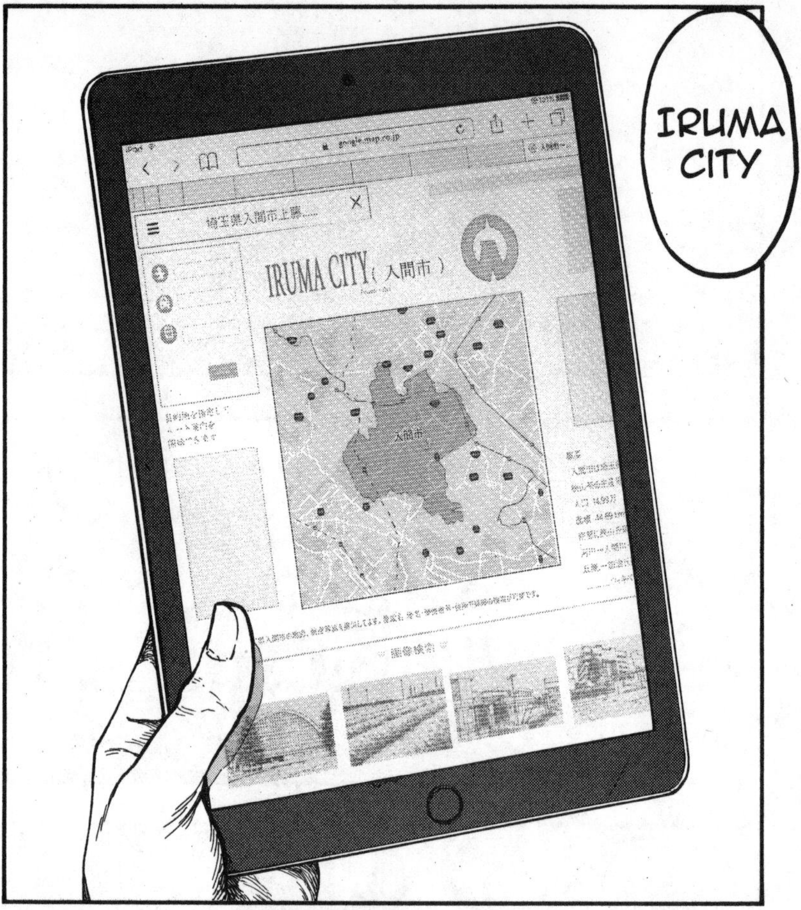
IRUMA CITY
IRUMA CITY (入間市)
入間市

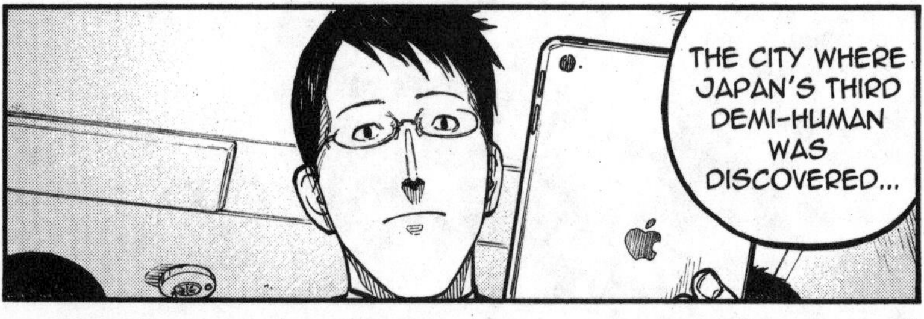
THE CITY WHERE JAPAN'S THIRD DEMI-HUMAN WAS DISCOVERED...

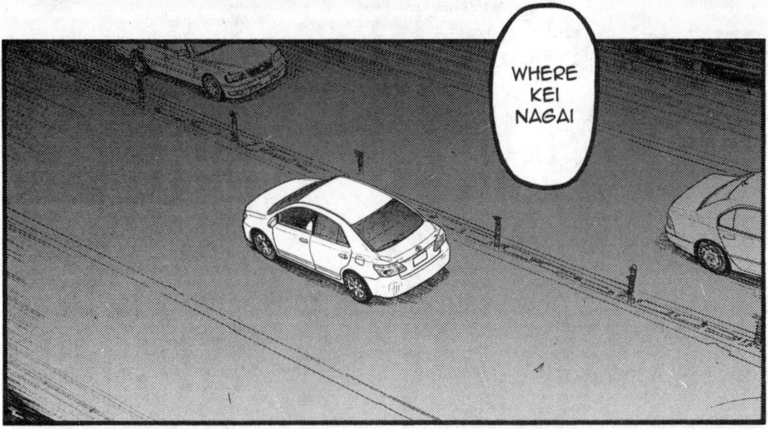
WHERE KEI NAGAI

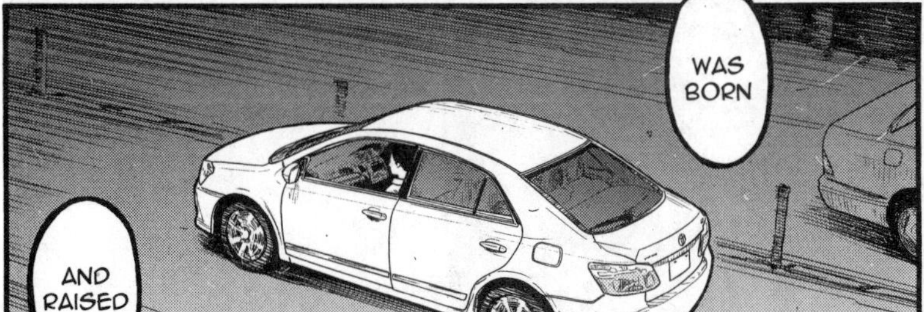
WAS BORN
AND RAISED

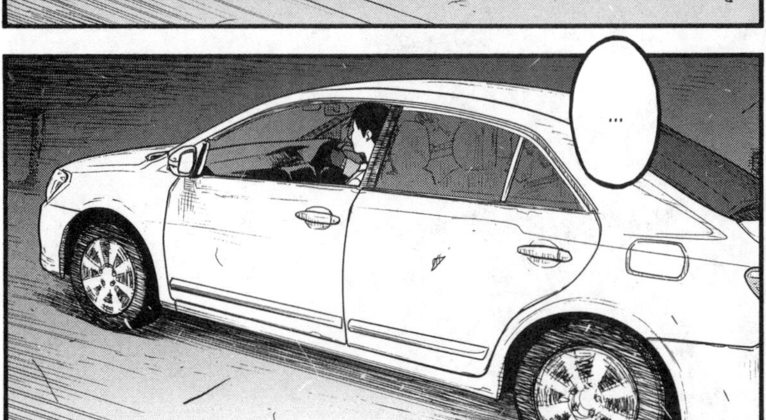
...

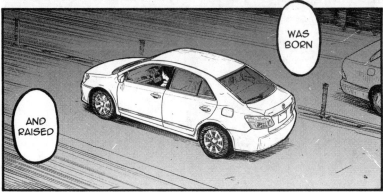

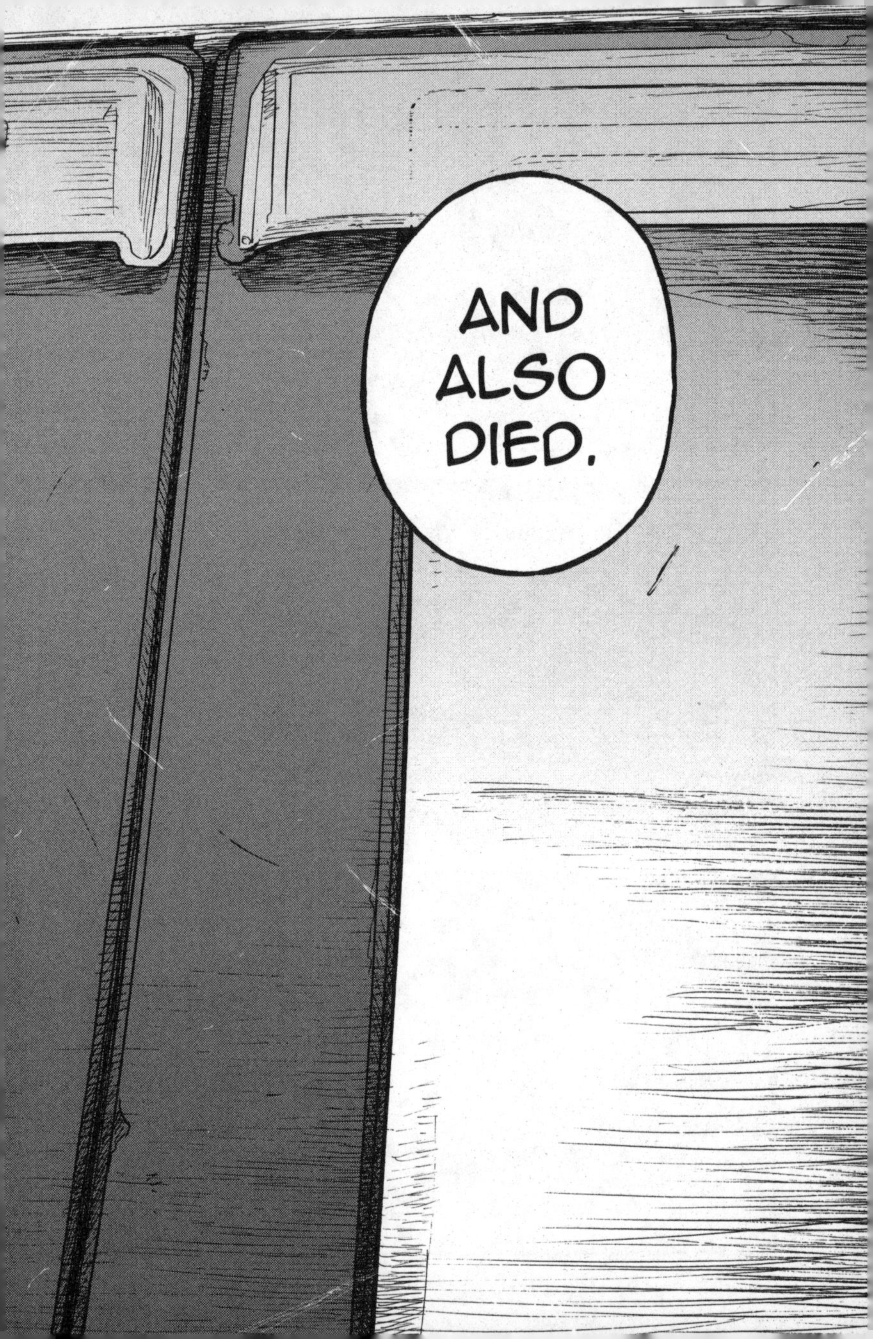
AND ALSO DIED.

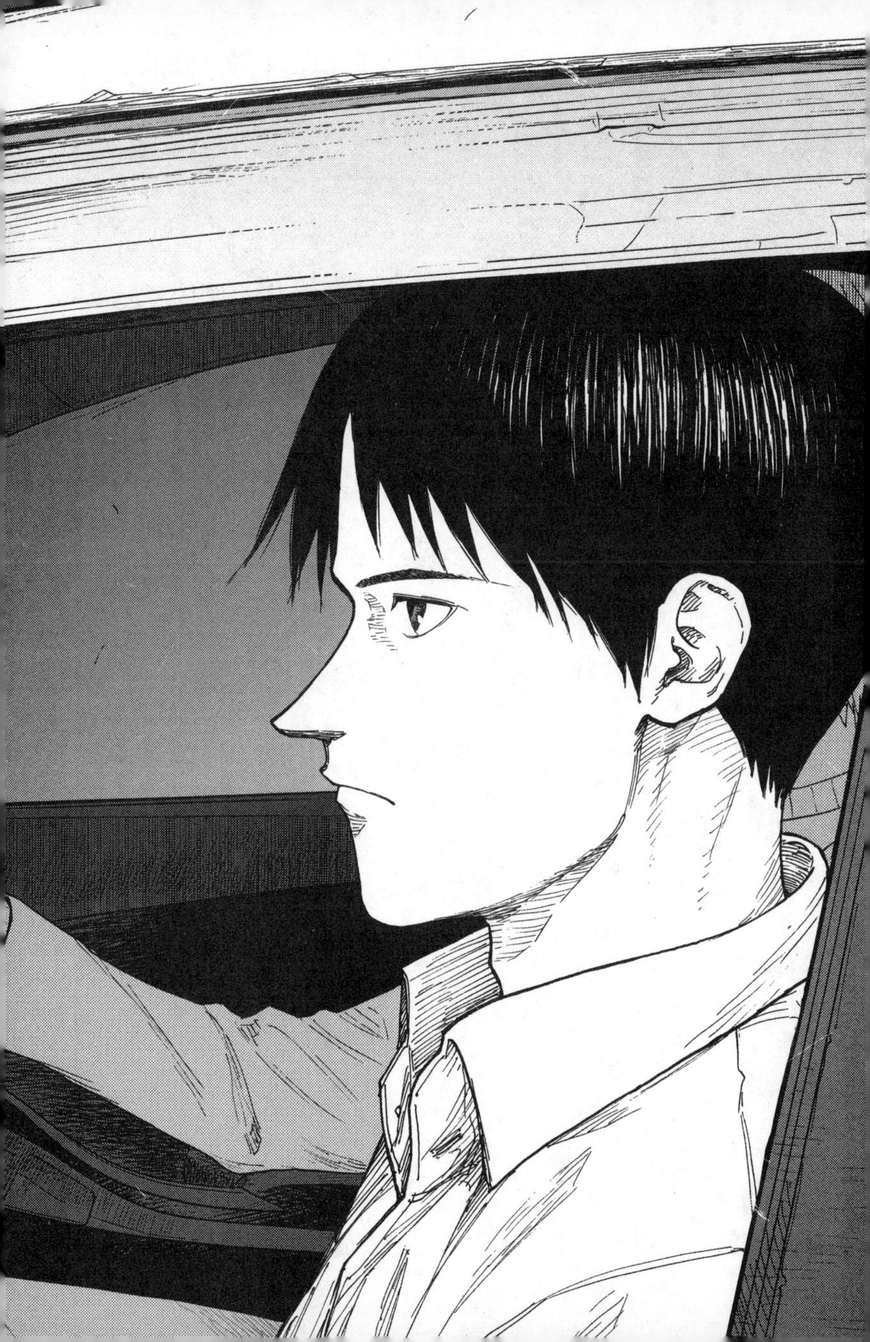

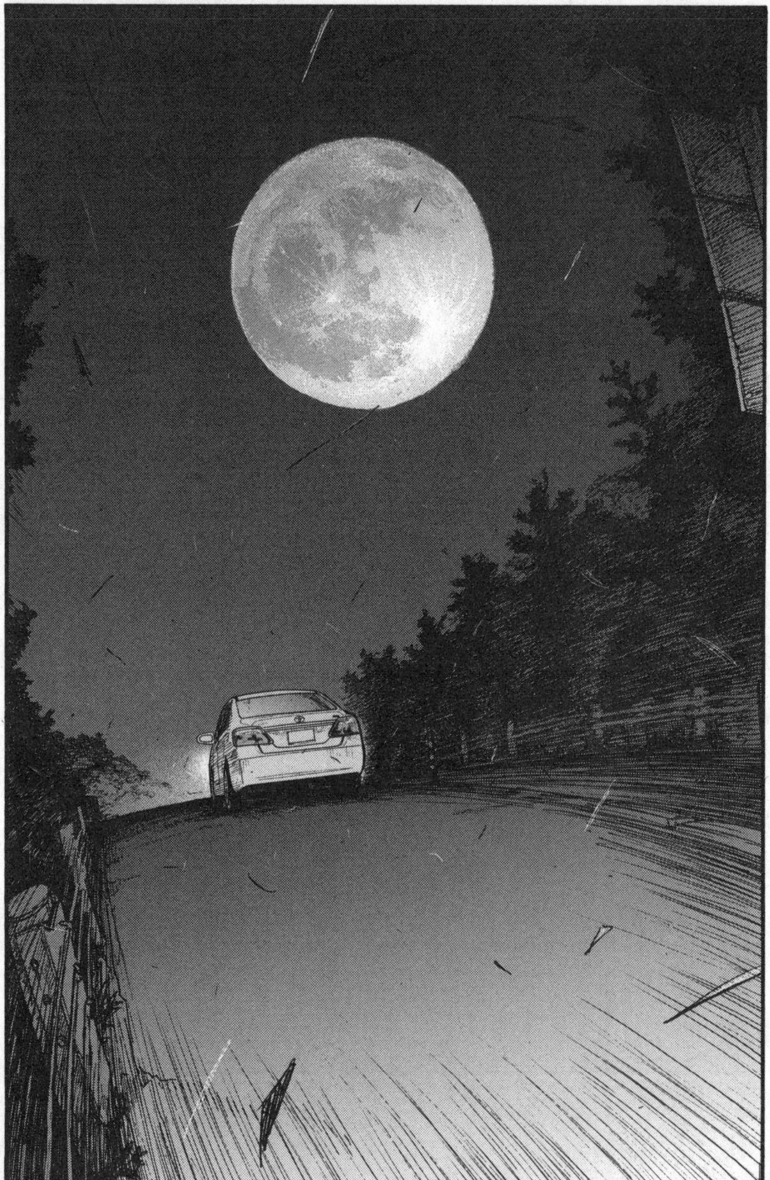

File:49 End

File 50: Promised Land

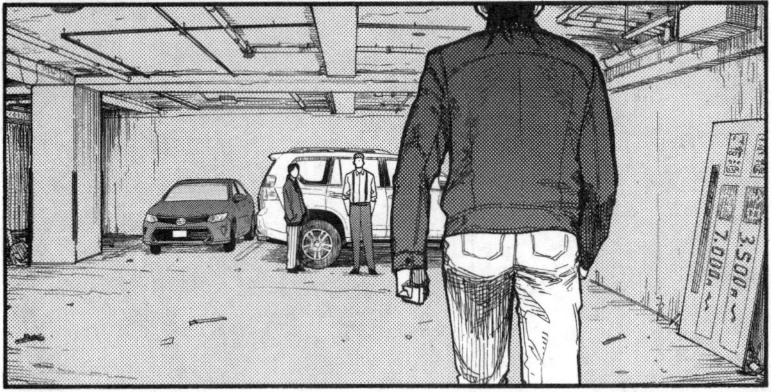

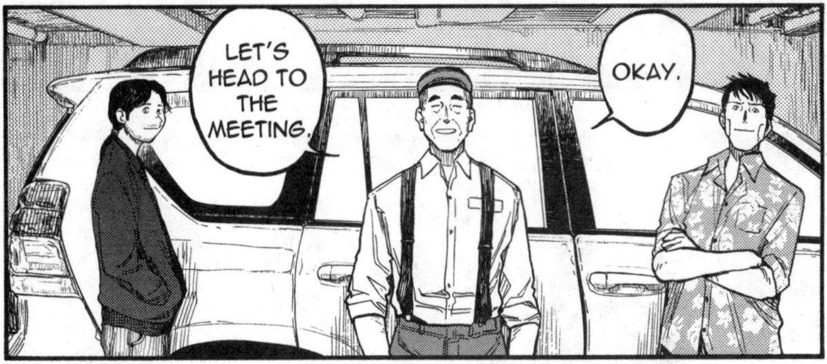
LET'S HEAD TO THE MEETING.
OKAY.

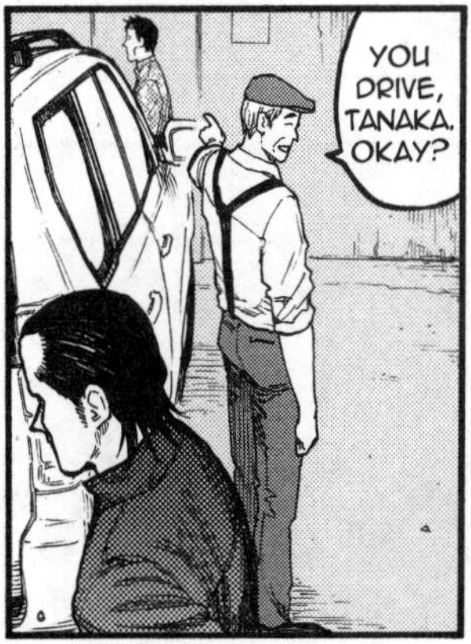
YOU DRIVE, TANAKA, OKAY?

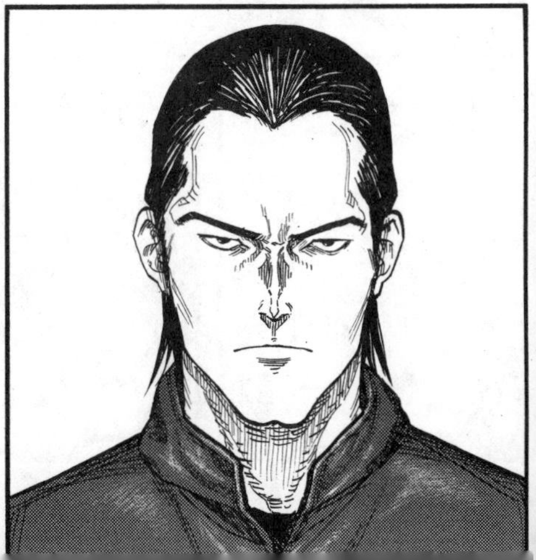

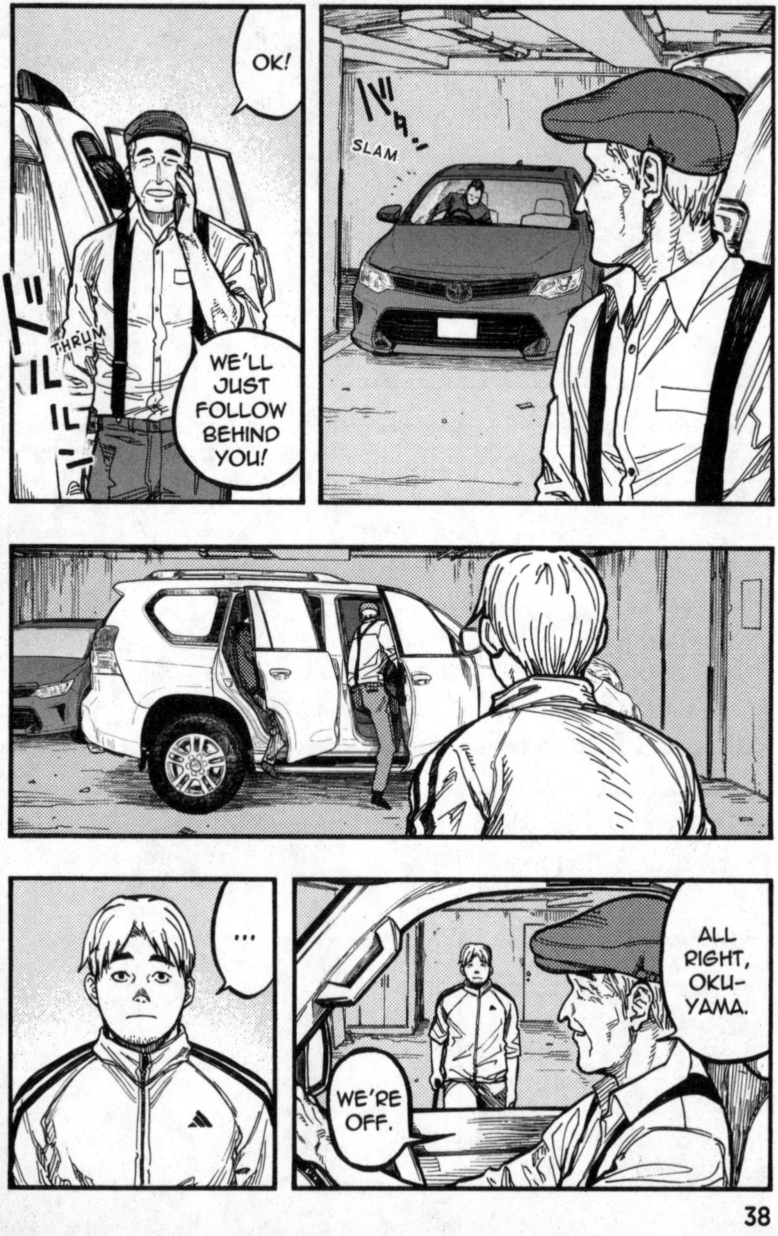
SLAM
OK!
THRUM
WE'LL JUST FOLLOW BEHIND YOU!
ALL RIGHT, OKU-YAMA.
WE'RE OFF.
...

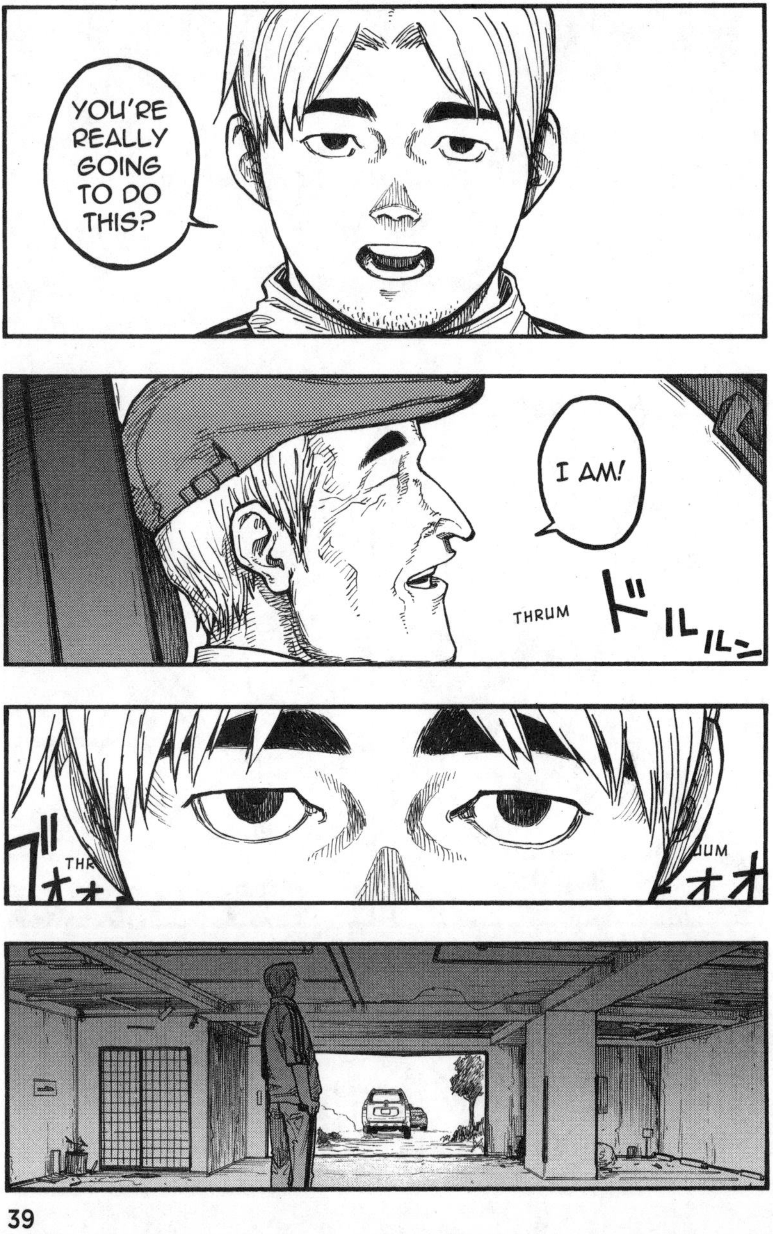
YOU'RE REALLY GOING TO DO THIS?
I AM!
THRUM
ドルルン

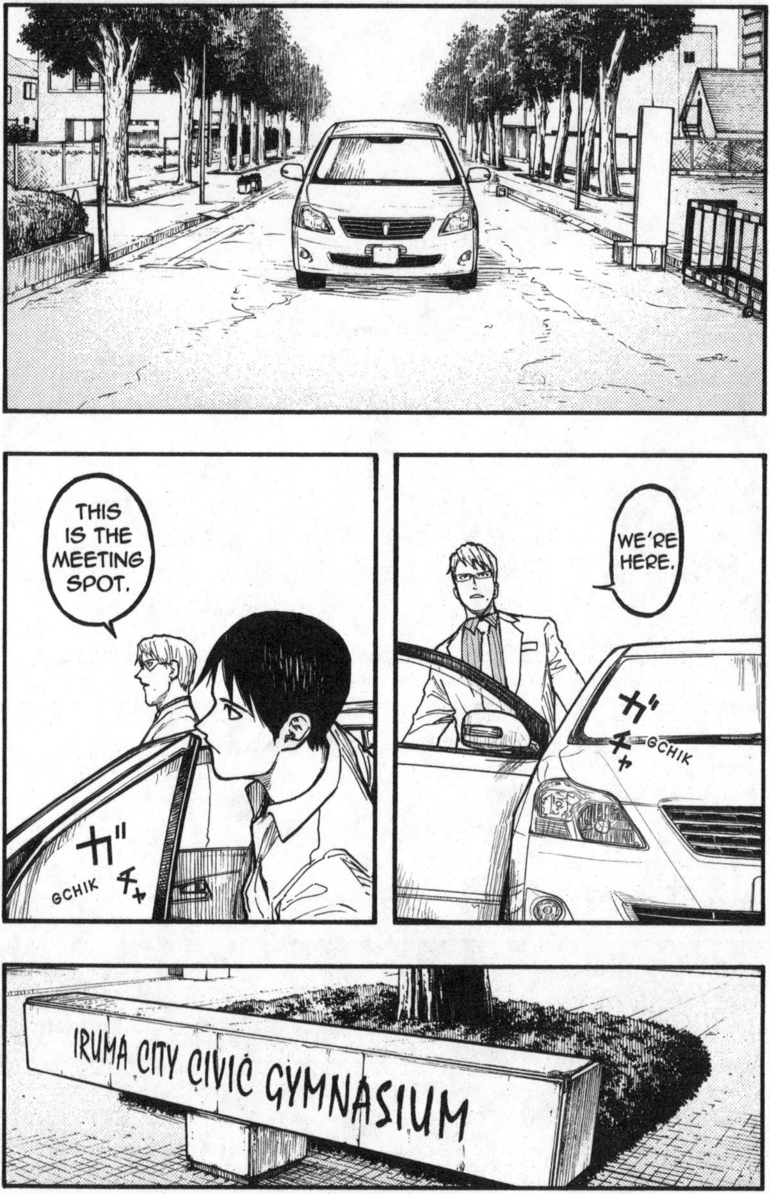
WE'RE HERE.
ガチャ
GCHIK
THIS IS THE MEETING SPOT.
ガチャ
GCHIK
IRUMA CITY CIVIC GYMNASIUM

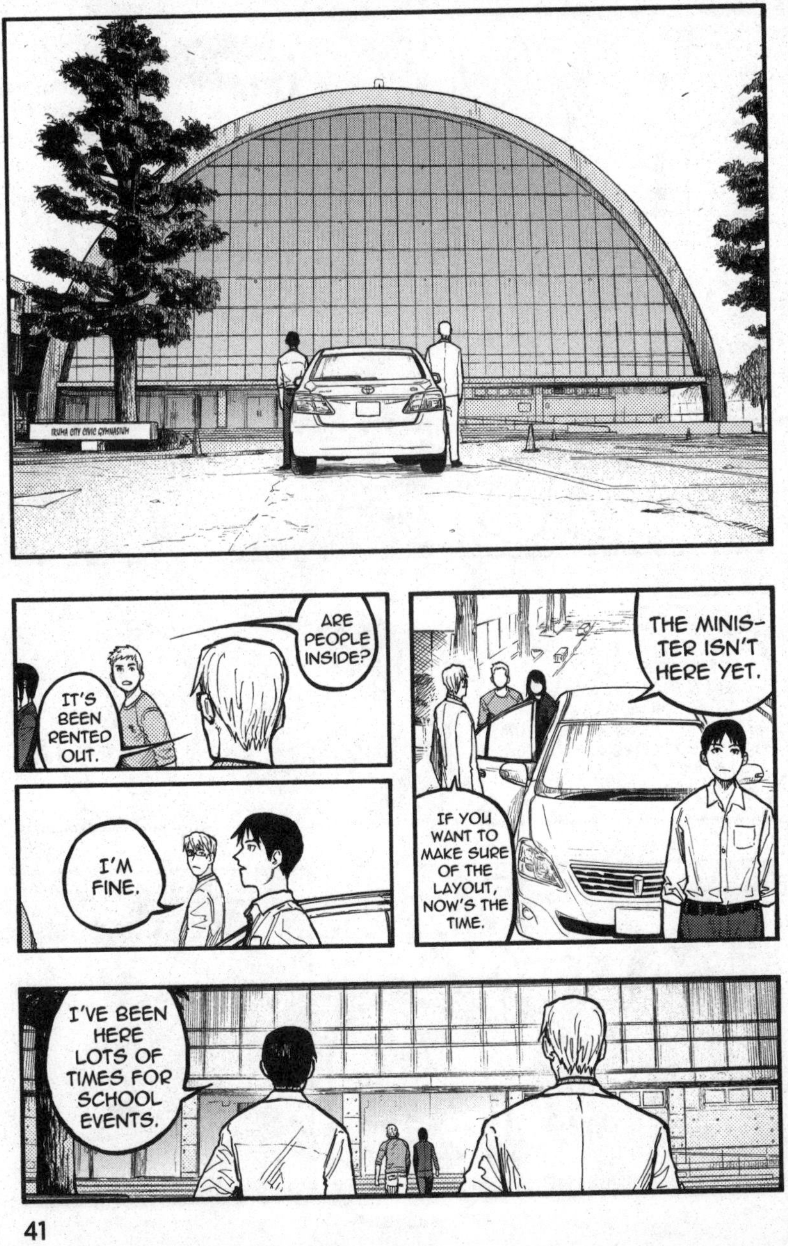
IRUMA CITY CIVIC GYMNASIUM
THE MINIS-TER ISN'T HERE YET.
IF YOU WANT TO MAKE SURE OF THE LAYOUT, NOW'S THE TIME.
ARE PEOPLE INSIDE?
IT'S BEEN RENTED OUT.
I'M FINE.
I'VE BEEN HERE LOTS OF TIMES FOR SCHOOL EVENTS.

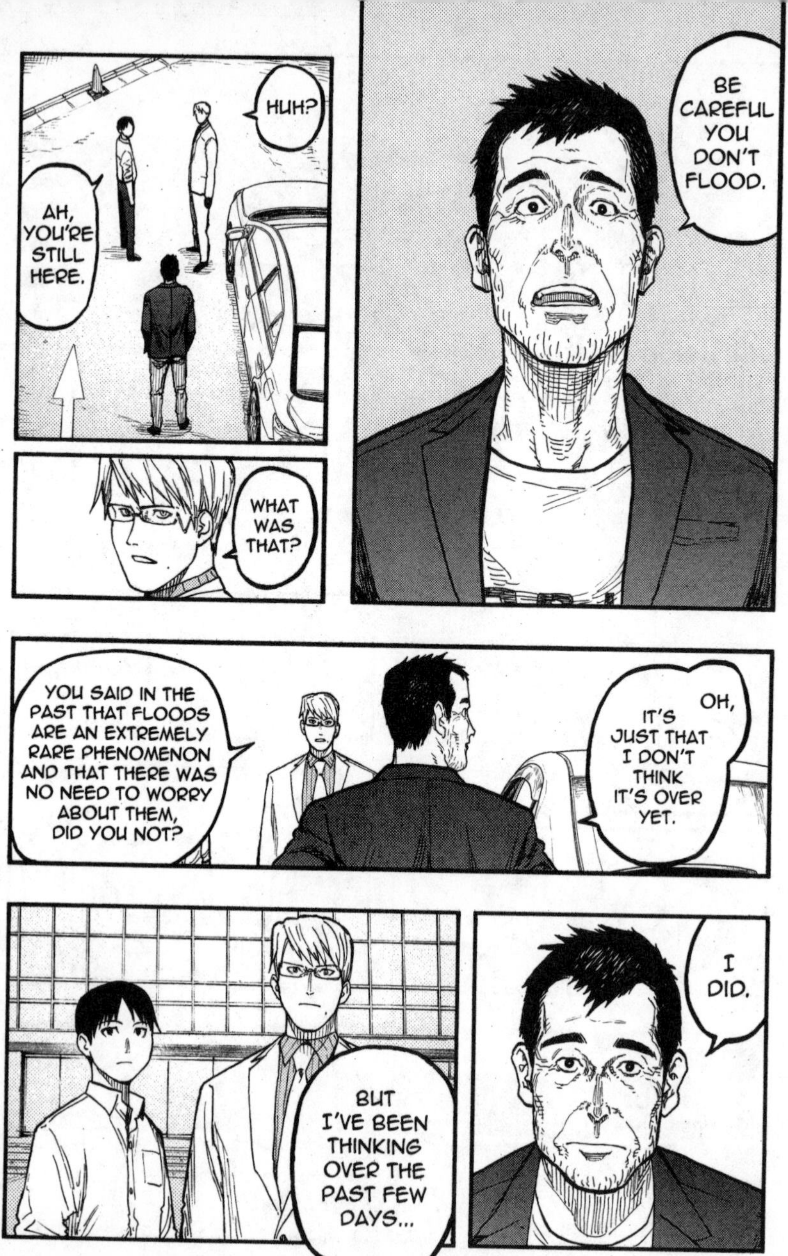
BE CAREFUL YOU DON'T FLOOD.
HUH?
AH, YOU'RE STILL HERE.
WHAT WAS THAT?
OH, IT'S JUST THAT I DON'T THINK IT'S OVER YET.
YOU SAID IN THE PAST THAT FLOODS ARE AN EXTREMELY RARE PHENOMENON AND THAT THERE WAS NO NEED TO WORRY ABOUT THEM, DID YOU NOT?
I DID.
BUT I'VE BEEN THINKING OVER THE PAST FEW DAYS...

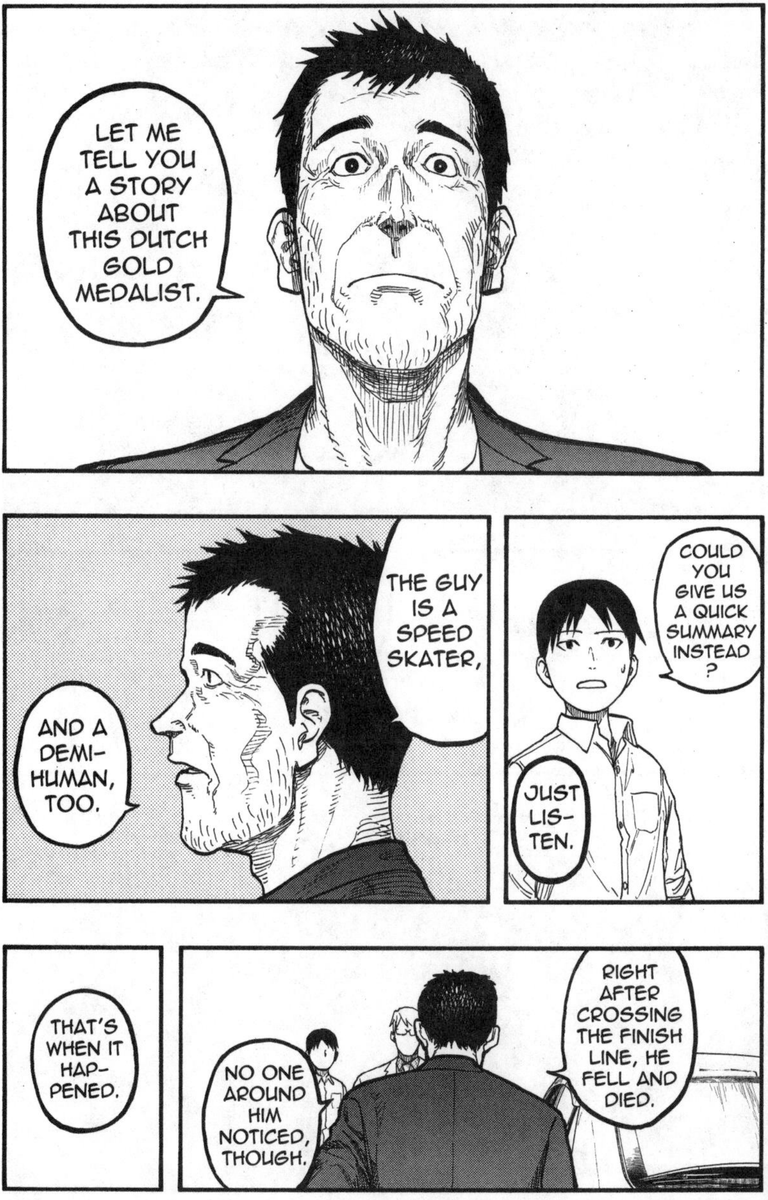
LET ME TELL YOU A STORY ABOUT THIS DUTCH GOLD MEDALIST.
COULD YOU GIVE US A QUICK SUMMARY INSTEAD?
JUST LISTEN.
THE GUY IS A SPEED SKATER,
AND A DEMI-HUMAN, TOO.
RIGHT AFTER CROSSING THE FINISH LINE, HE FELL AND DIED.
NO ONE AROUND HIM NOTICED, THOUGH.
THAT'S WHEN IT HAPPENED.

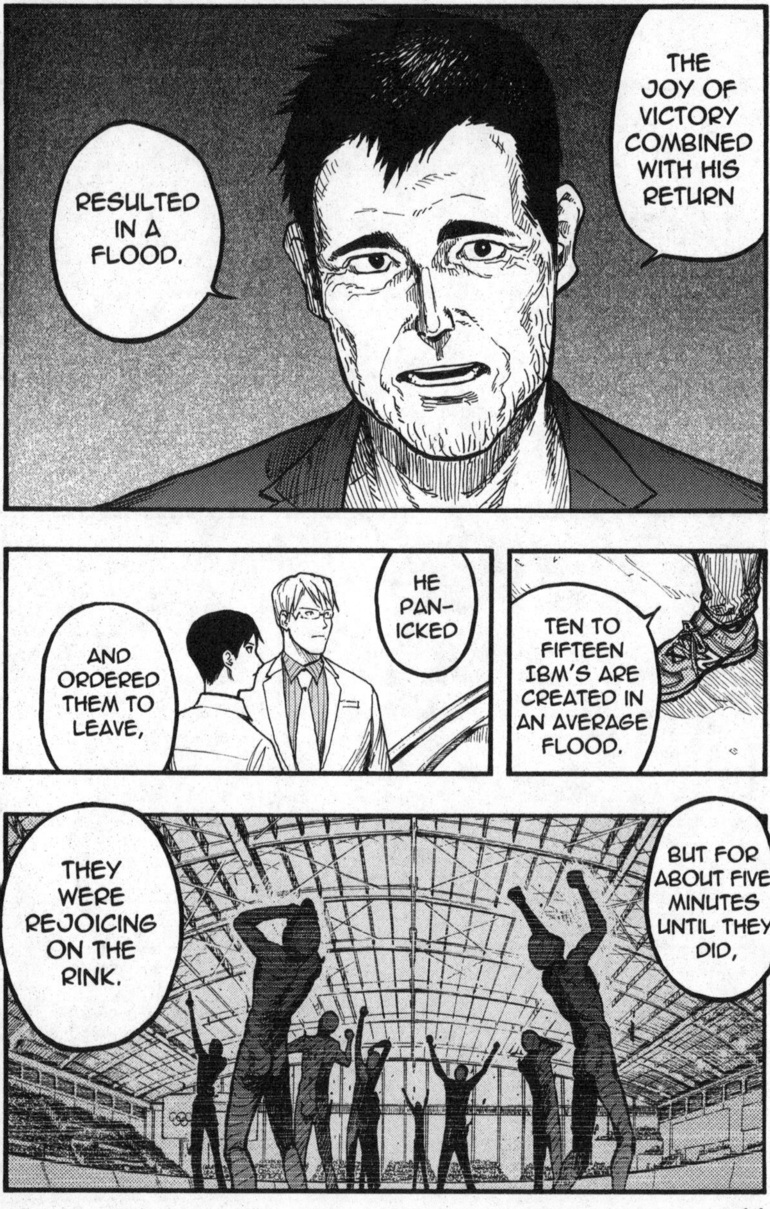
THE JOY OF VICTORY COMBINED WITH HIS RETURN
RESULTED IN A FLOOD.
TEN TO FIFTEEN IBM'S ARE CREATED IN AN AVERAGE FLOOD.
HE PAN-ICKED
AND ORDERED THEM TO LEAVE,
BUT FOR ABOUT FIVE MINUTES UNTIL THEY DID,
THEY WERE REJOICING ON THE RINK.

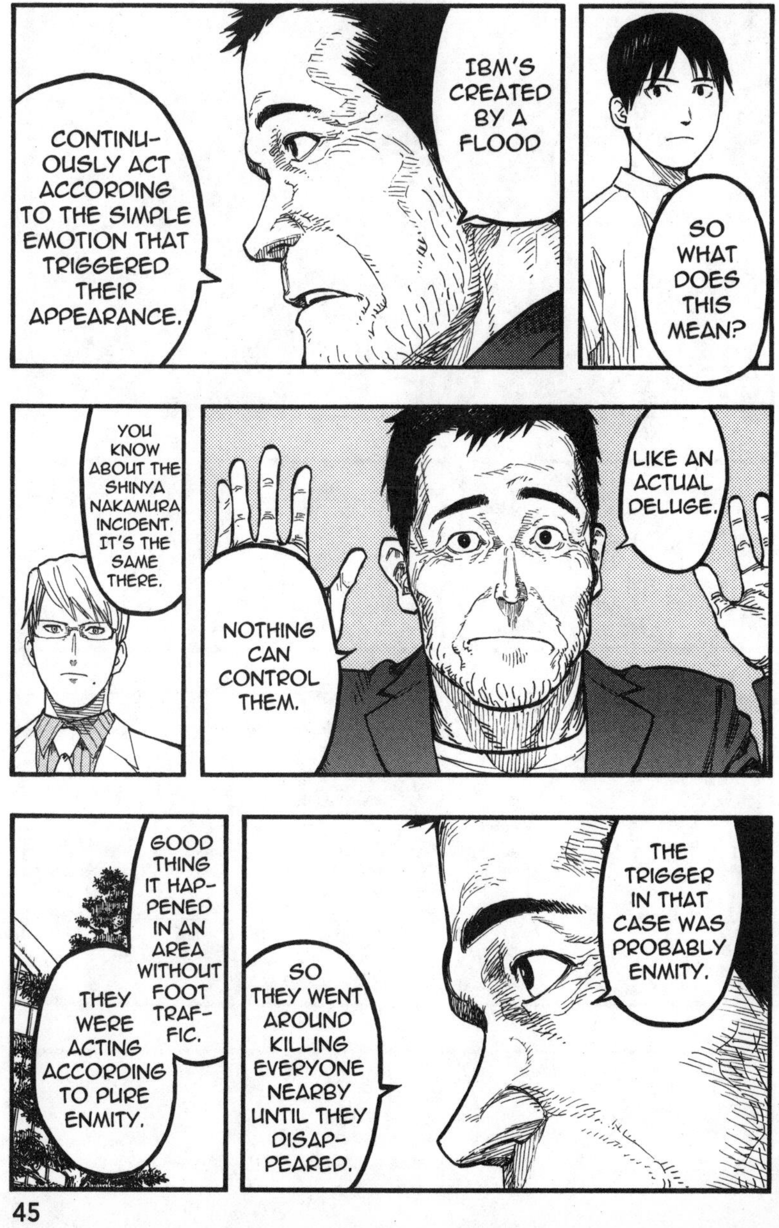
SO WHAT DOES THIS MEAN?
IBM'S CREATED BY A FLOOD
CONTINU-OUSLY ACT ACCORDING TO THE SIMPLE EMOTION THAT TRIGGERED THEIR APPEARANCE.
LIKE AN ACTUAL DELUGE.
NOTHING CAN CONTROL THEM.
YOU KNOW ABOUT THE SHINYA NAKAMURA INCIDENT. IT'S THE SAME THERE.
THE TRIGGER IN THAT CASE WAS PROBABLY ENMITY.
SO THEY WENT AROUND KILLING EVERYONE NEARBY UNTIL THEY DISAP-PEARED.
GOOD THING IT HAP-PENED IN AN AREA WITHOUT FOOT TRAF-FIC.
THEY WERE ACTING ACCORDING TO PURE ENMITY.

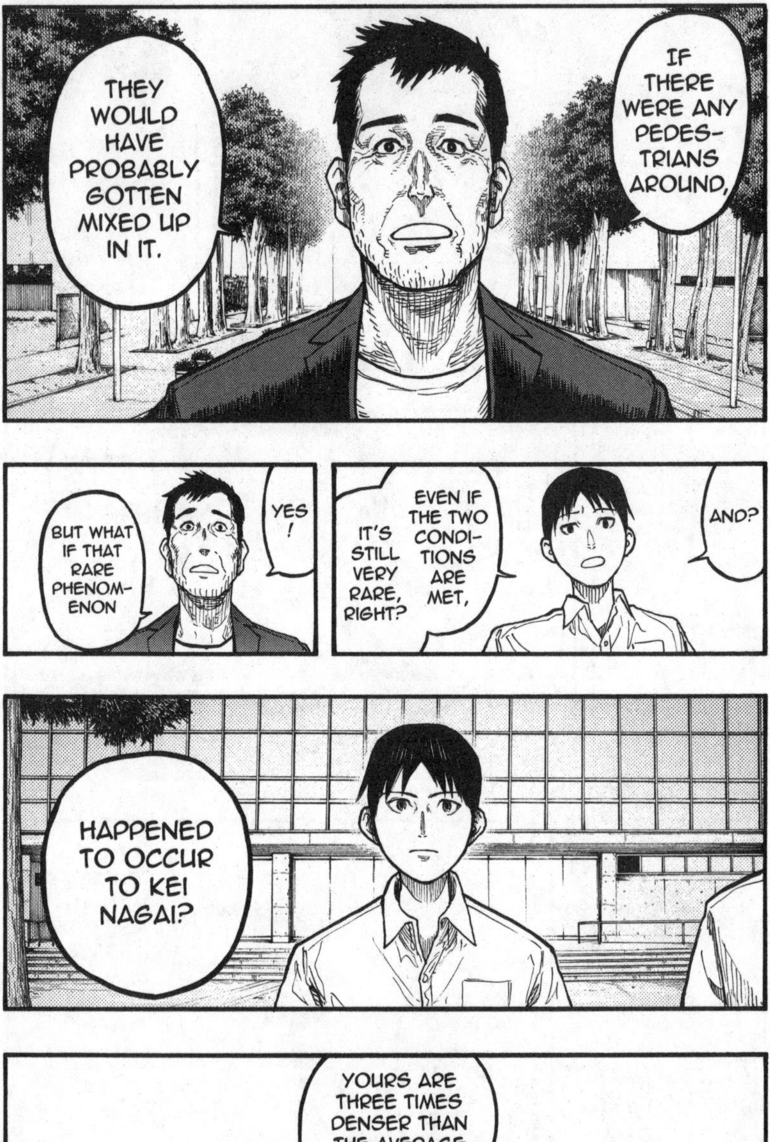
IF THERE WERE ANY PEDES-TRIANS AROUND,
THEY WOULD HAVE PROBABLY GOTTEN MIXED UP IN IT.
AND?
EVEN IF THE TWO CONDI-TIONS ARE MET,
IT'S STILL VERY RARE, RIGHT?
YES!
BUT WHAT IF THAT RARE PHENOM-ENON
HAPPENED TO OCCUR TO KEI NAGAI?
YOURS ARE THREE TIMES DENSER THAN THE AVERAGE DEMI-HUMAN'S.

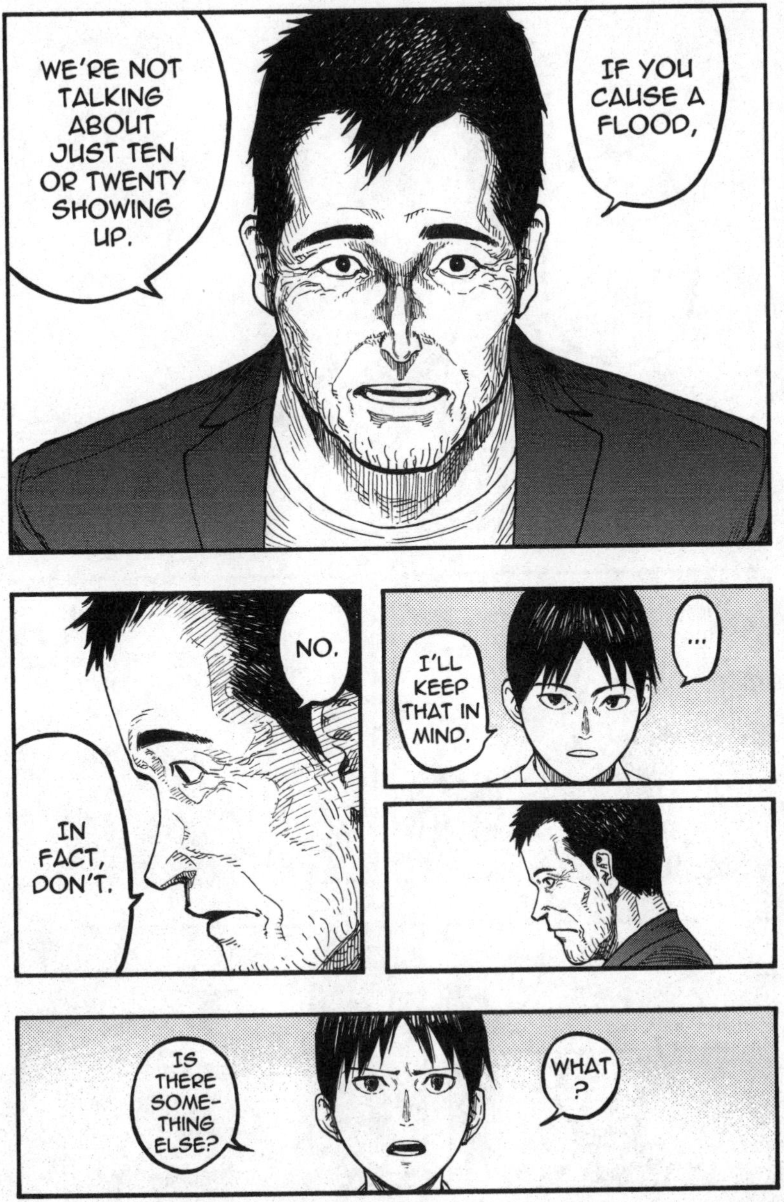
IF YOU CAUSE A FLOOD,
WE'RE NOT TALKING ABOUT JUST TEN OR TWENTY SHOWING UP.
...
I'LL KEEP THAT IN MIND.
NO.
IN FACT, DON'T.
WHAT?
IS THERE SOME-THING ELSE?

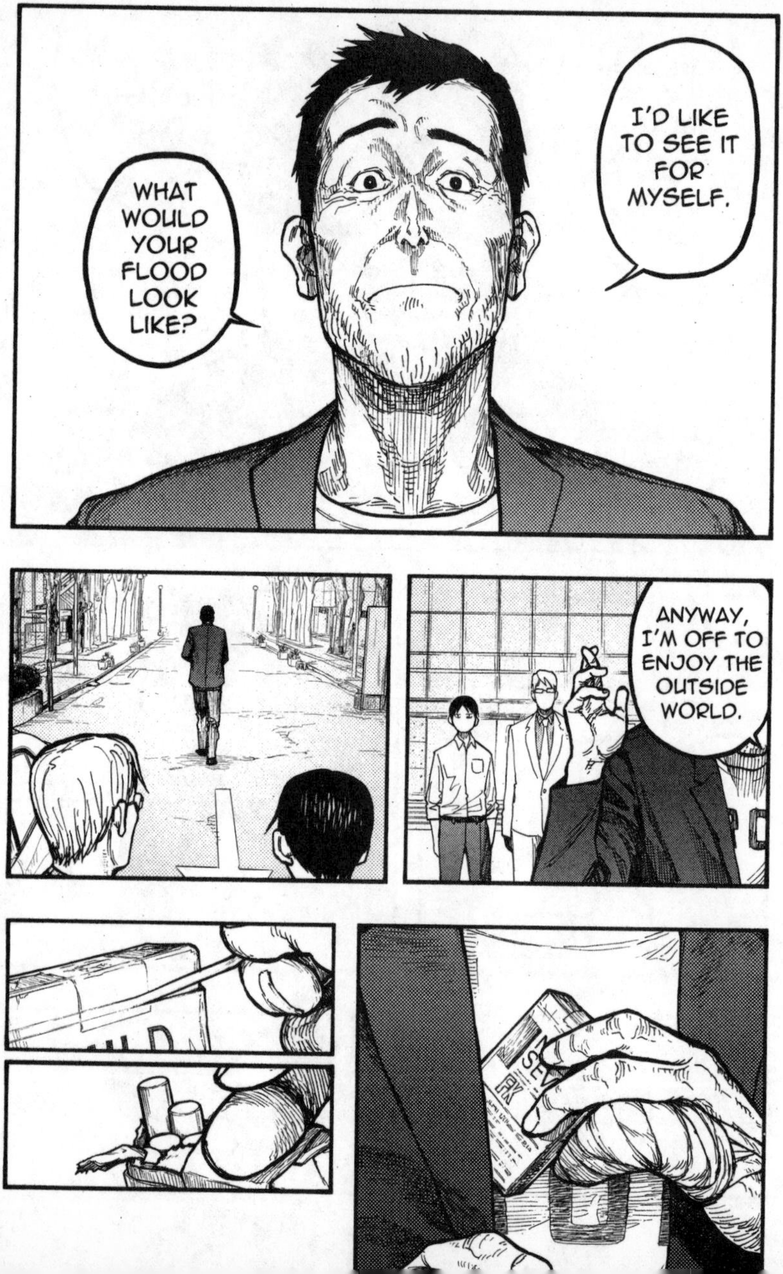
I'D LIKE TO SEE IT FOR MYSELF.
WHAT WOULD YOUR FLOOD LOOK LIKE?
ANYWAY, I'M OFF TO ENJOY THE OUTSIDE WORLD.

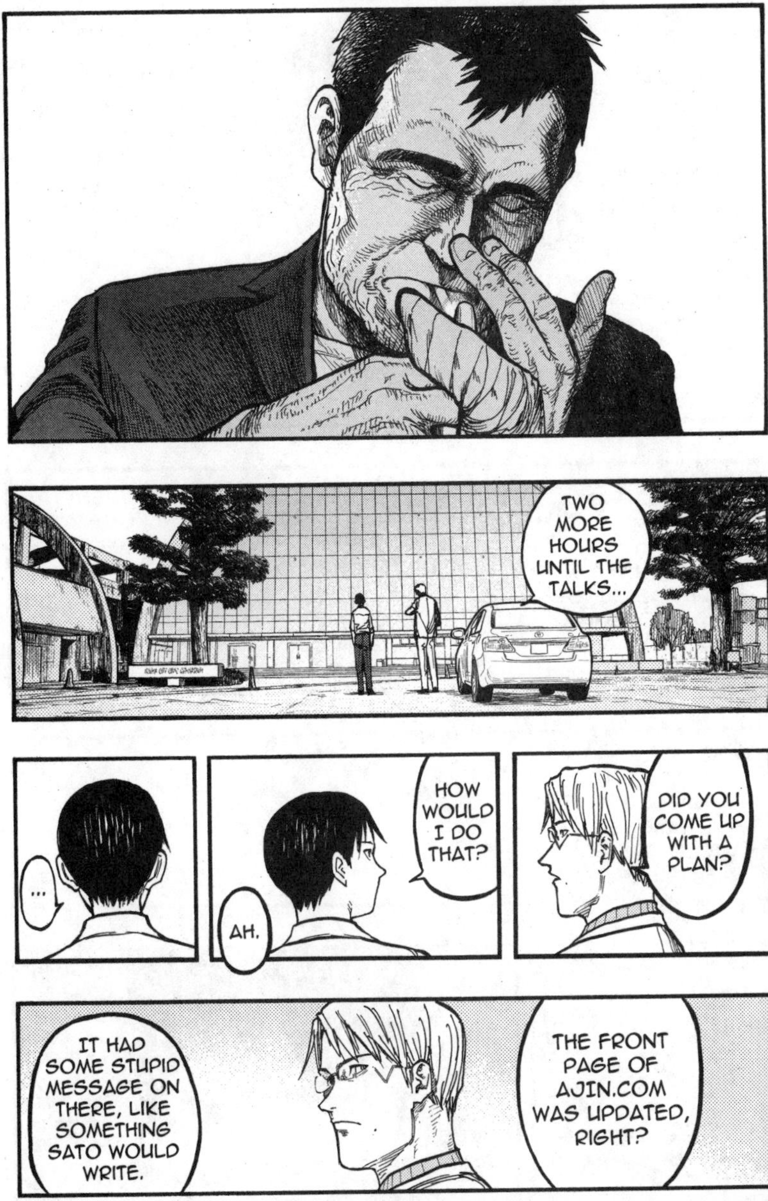
TWO MORE HOURS UNTIL THE TALKS...
DID YOU COME UP WITH A PLAN?
HOW WOULD I DO THAT?
AH.
...
THE FRONT PAGE OF AJIN.COM WAS UPDATED, RIGHT?
IT HAD SOME STUPID MESSAGE ON THERE, LIKE SOMETHING SATO WOULD WRITE.

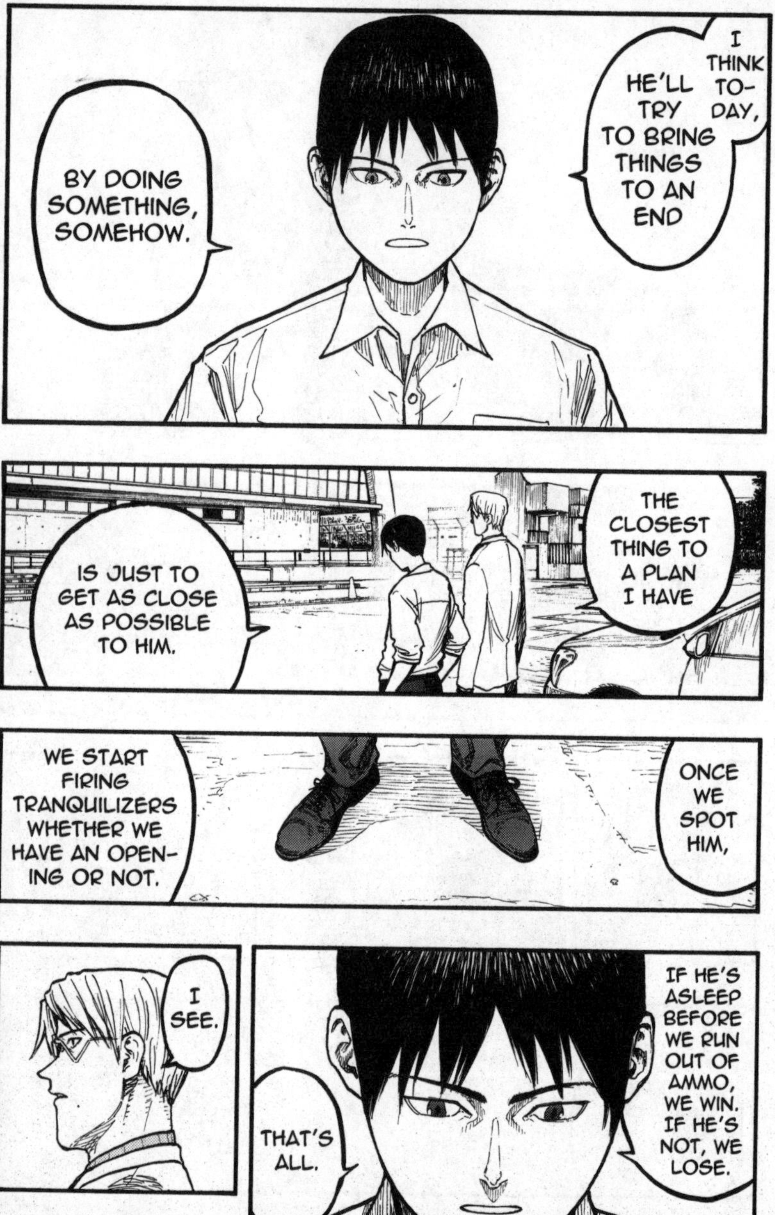
I THINK TO-DAY, HE'LL TRY TO BRING THINGS TO AN END
BY DOING SOMETHING, SOMEHOW.
THE CLOSEST THING TO A PLAN I HAVE
IS JUST TO GET AS CLOSE AS POSSIBLE TO HIM.
ONCE WE SPOT HIM,
WE START FIRING TRANQUILIZERS WHETHER WE HAVE AN OPEN-ING OR NOT.
IF HE'S ASLEEP BEFORE WE RUN OUT OF AMMO, WE WIN. IF HE'S NOT, WE LOSE.
THAT'S ALL.
I SEE.

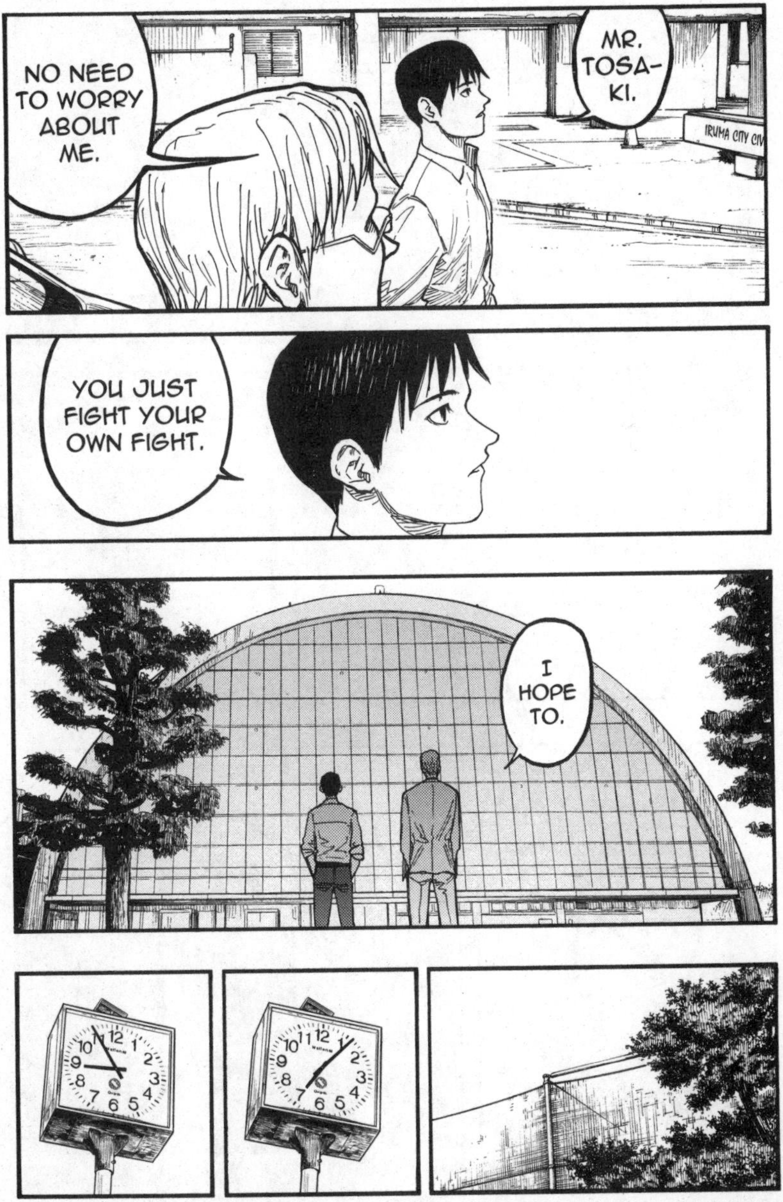
MR. TOSA-KI.
NO NEED TO WORRY ABOUT ME.
YOU JUST FIGHT YOUR OWN FIGHT.
I HOPE TO.

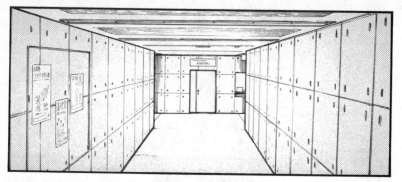

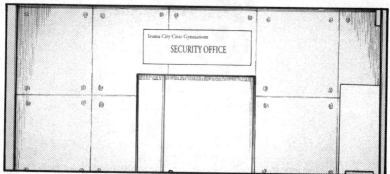

Iruma City Civic Gymnasium

SECURITY OFFICE

OH.

GCHIK

ガ4チ

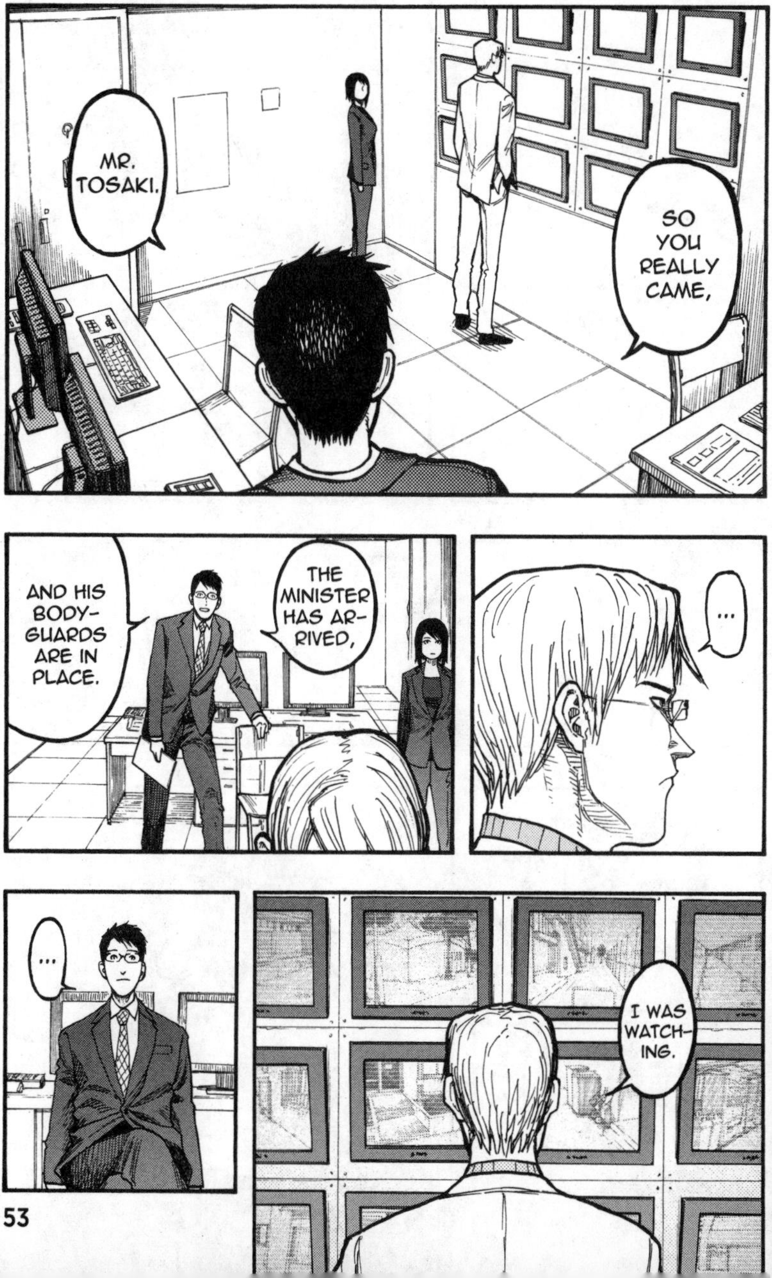
SO YOU REALLY CAME,
MR. TOSAKI.
...
THE MINISTER HAS AR-RIVED,
AND HIS BODY-GUARDS ARE IN PLACE.
I WAS WATCH-ING.
...

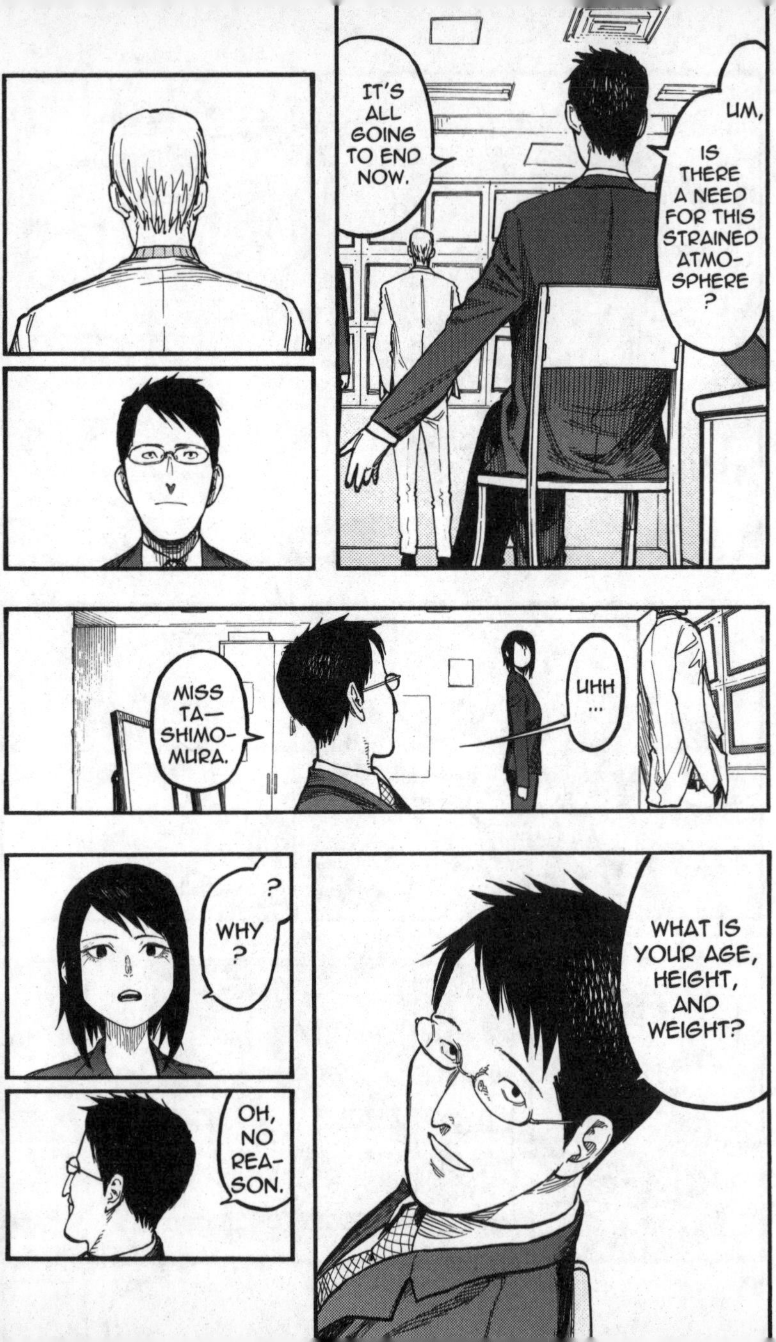
UM, IS THERE A NEED FOR THIS STRAINED ATMOSPHERE?
IT'S ALL GOING TO END NOW.
UHH ...
MISS TA—SHIMOMURA.
WHAT IS YOUR AGE, HEIGHT, AND WEIGHT?
? WHY?
OH, NO REASON.

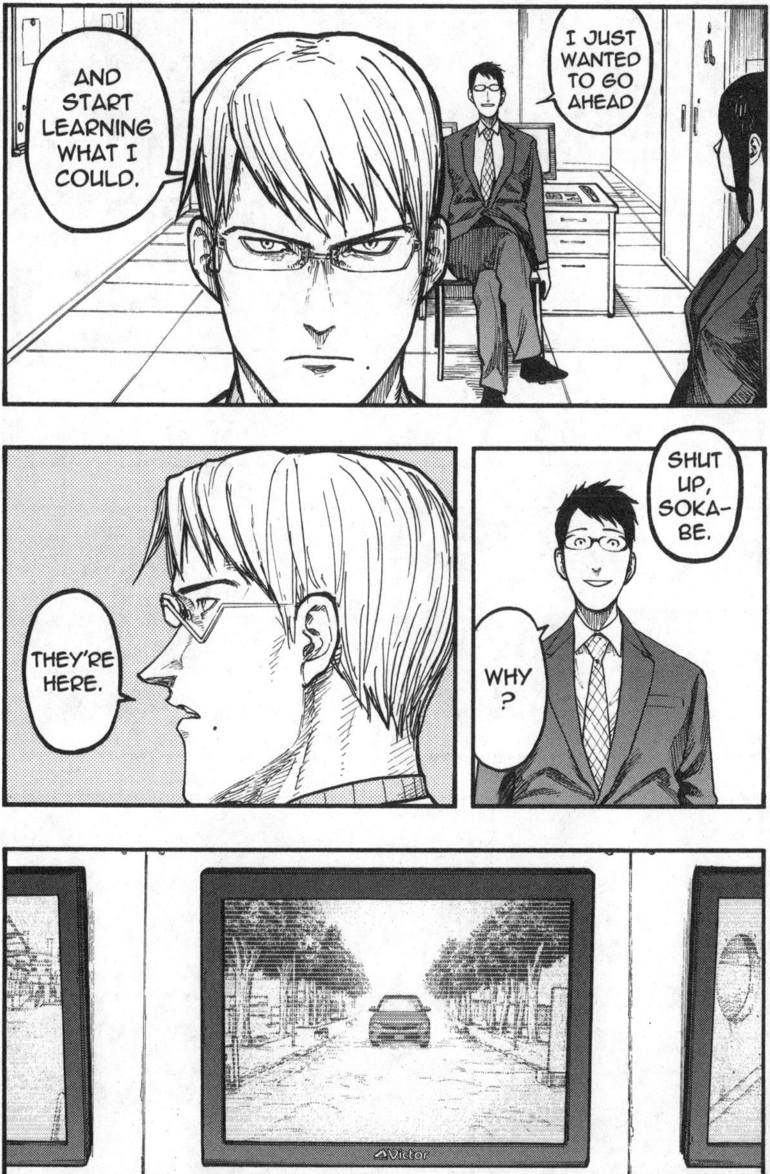
I JUST WANTED TO GO AHEAD
AND START LEARNING WHAT I COULD.
SHUT UP, SOKA-BE.
WHY?
THEY'RE HERE.
Victor

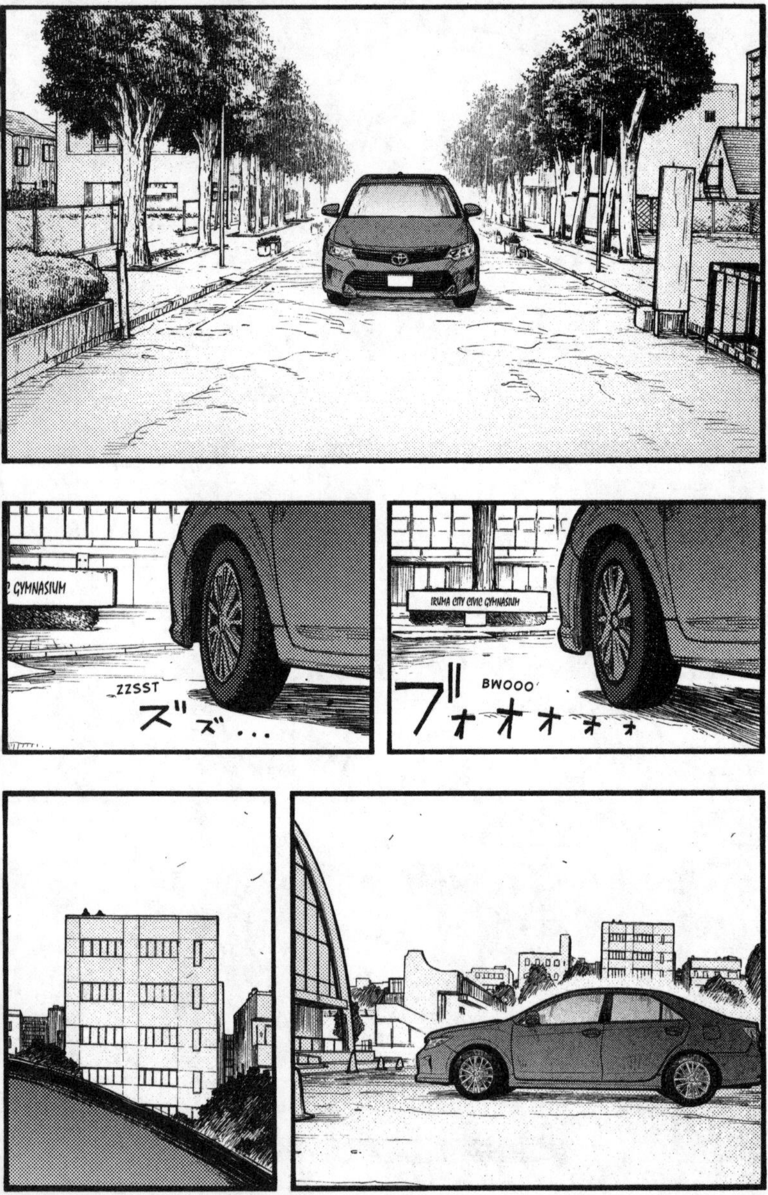
IRUMA CITY CIVIC GYMNASIUM
BWOOO
ブォオオォォ
GYMNASIUM
ZZSST
ズズ...

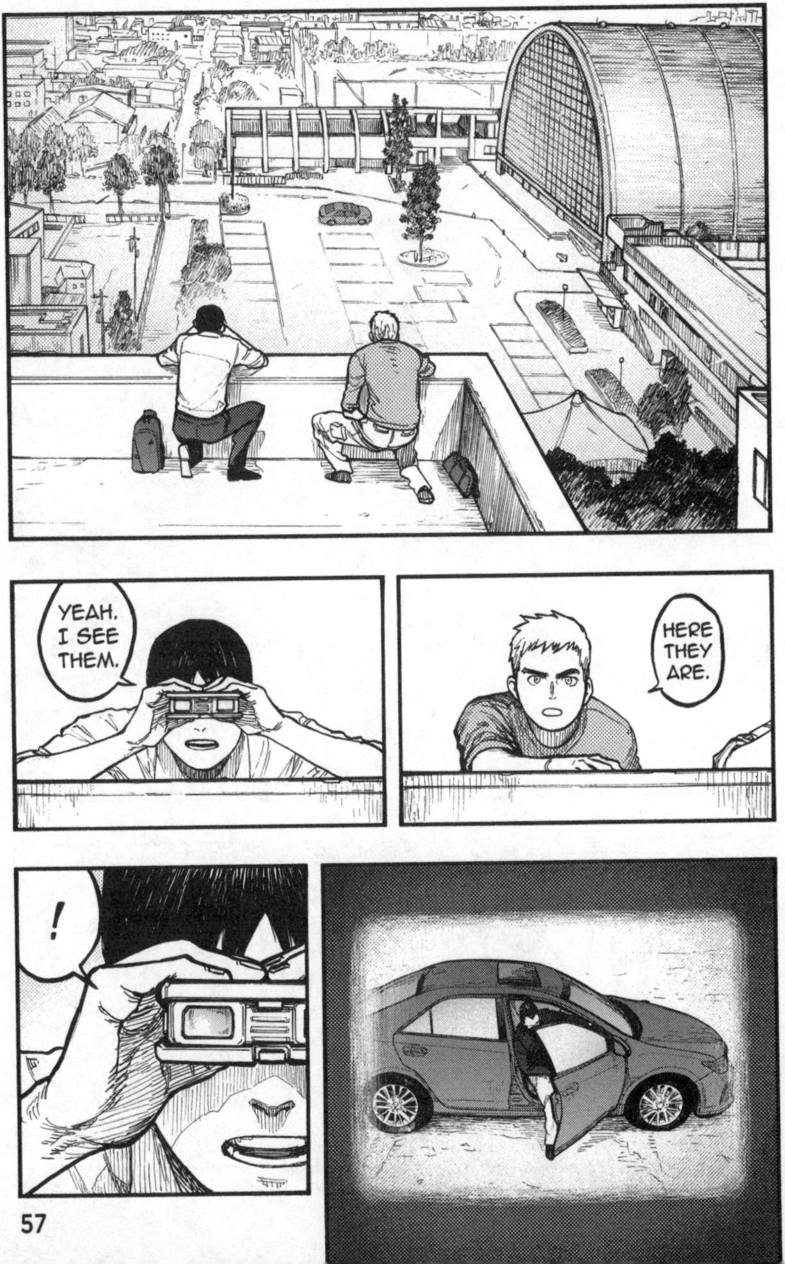
HERE THEY ARE.
YEAH. I SEE THEM.
!

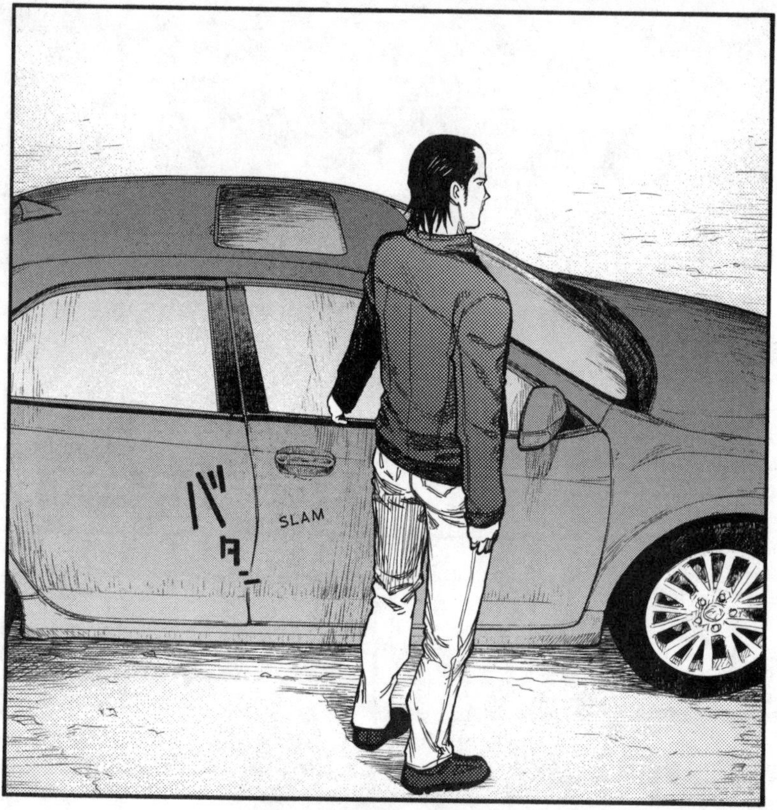
バタ
SLAM

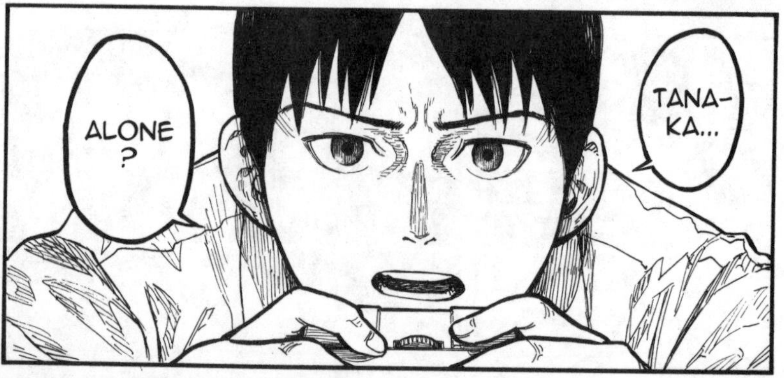
TANA-
KA...
ALONE
?

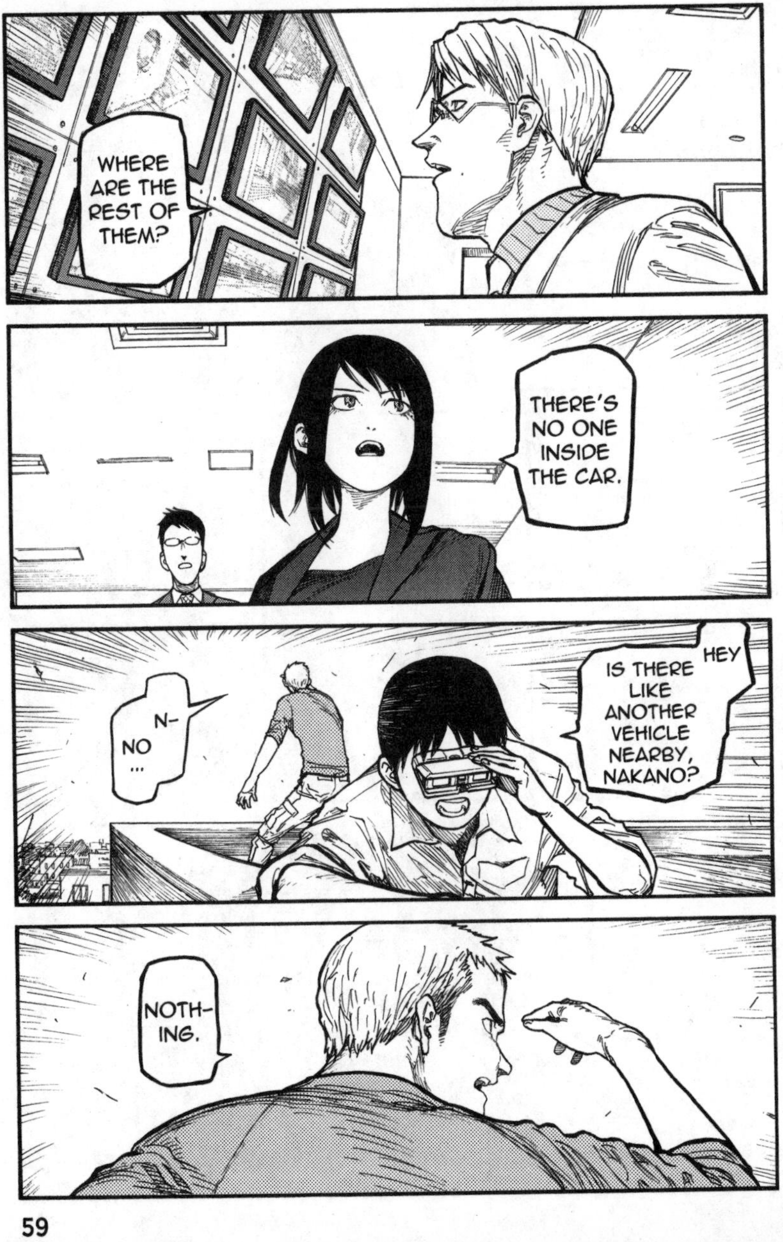
WHERE ARE THE REST OF THEM?
THERE'S NO ONE INSIDE THE CAR.
HEY IS THERE LIKE ANOTHER VEHICLE NEARBY, NAKANO?
N- NO ...
NOTH-ING.

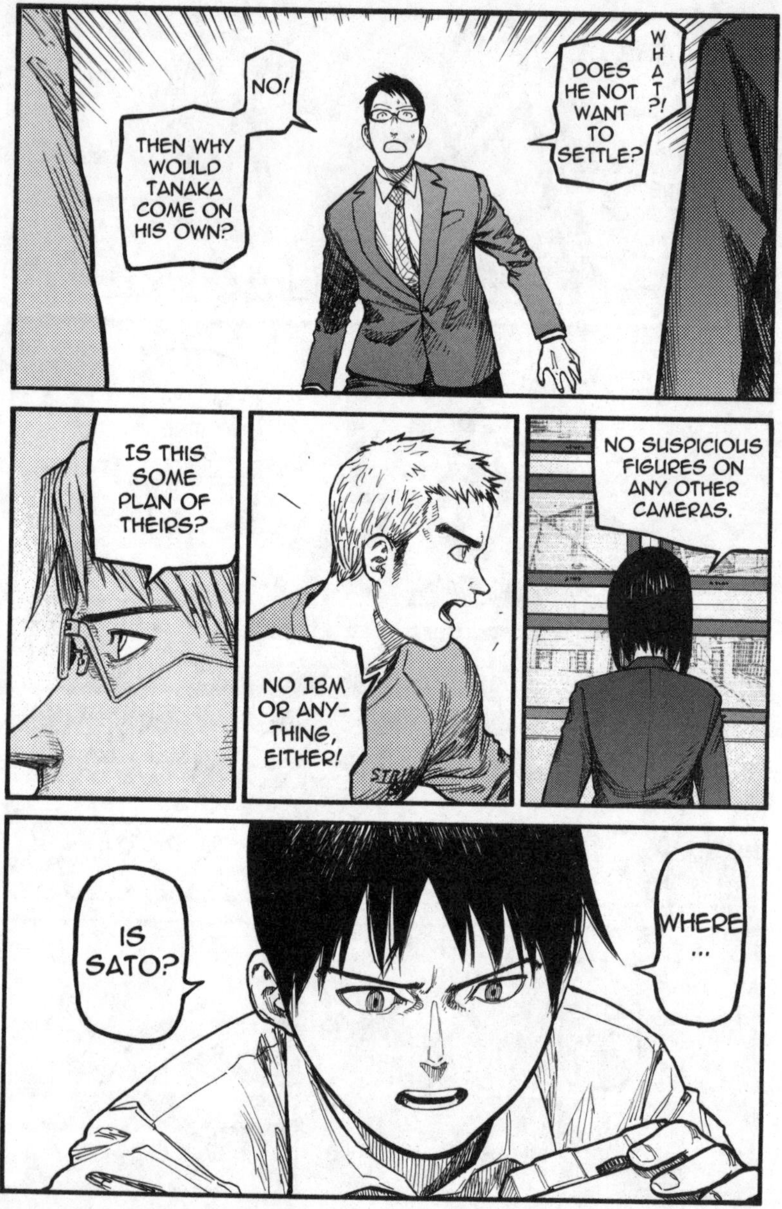
WHAT?!
DOES HE NOT WANT TO SETTLE?
NO!
THEN WHY WOULD TANAKA COME ON HIS OWN?
NO SUSPICIOUS FIGURES ON ANY OTHER CAMERAS.
NO IBM OR ANY-THING, EITHER!
IS THIS SOME PLAN OF THEIRS?
WHERE ...
IS SATO?

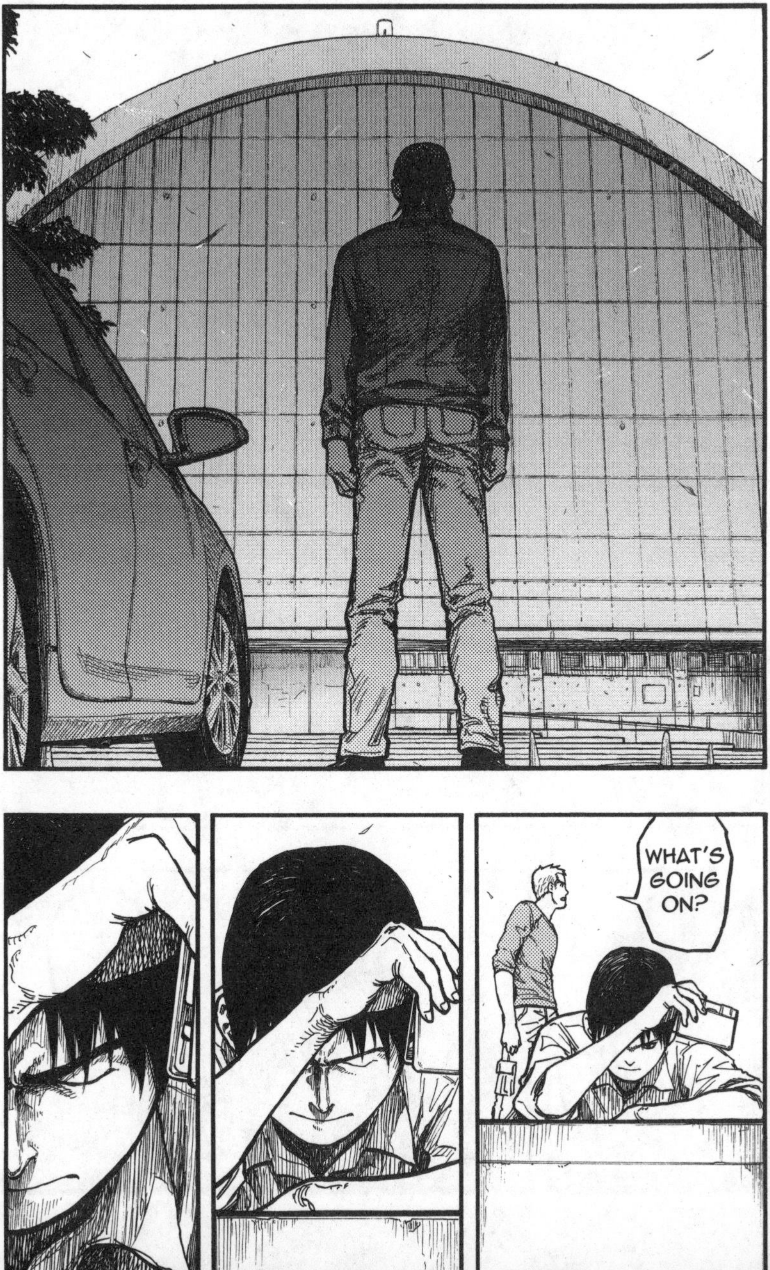
WHAT'S GOING ON?

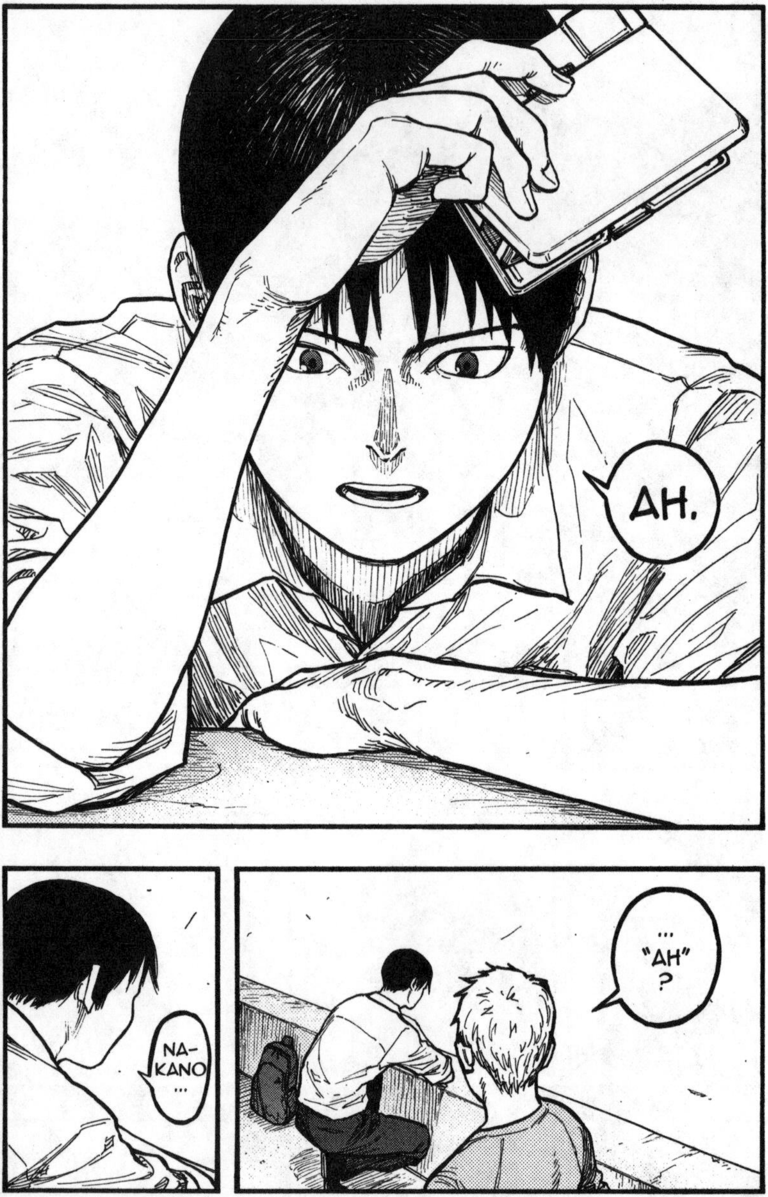
AH.
... "AH" ?
NA-KANO ...

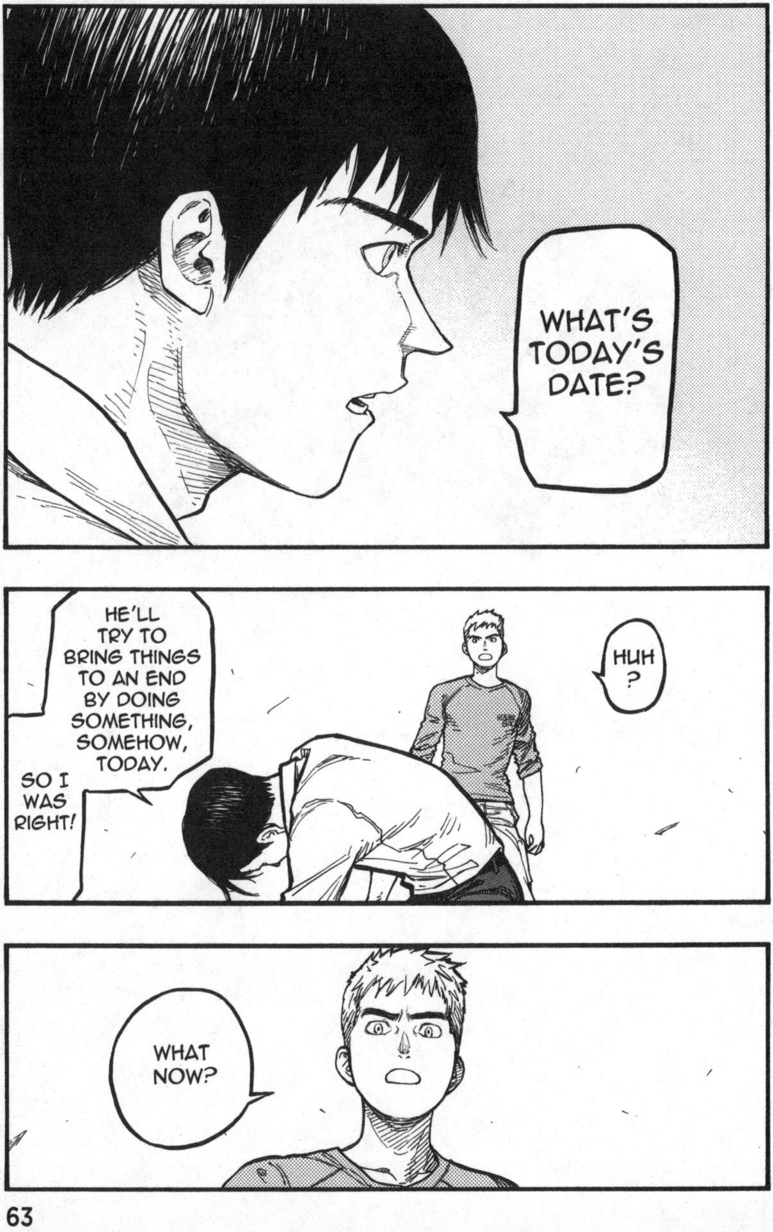
WHAT'S TODAY'S DATE?
HUH?
HE'LL TRY TO BRING THINGS TO AN END BY DOING SOMETHING, SOMEHOW, TODAY.
SO I WAS RIGHT!
WHAT NOW?

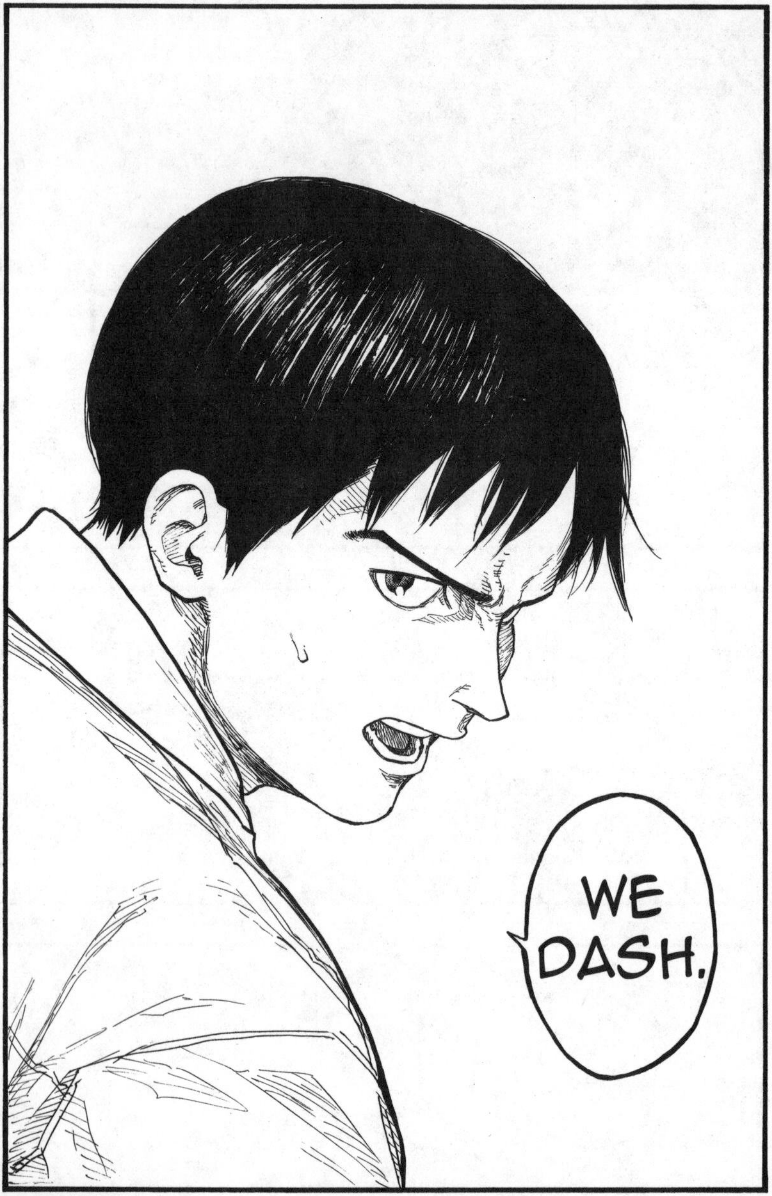
WE DASH.

File:50 End

002

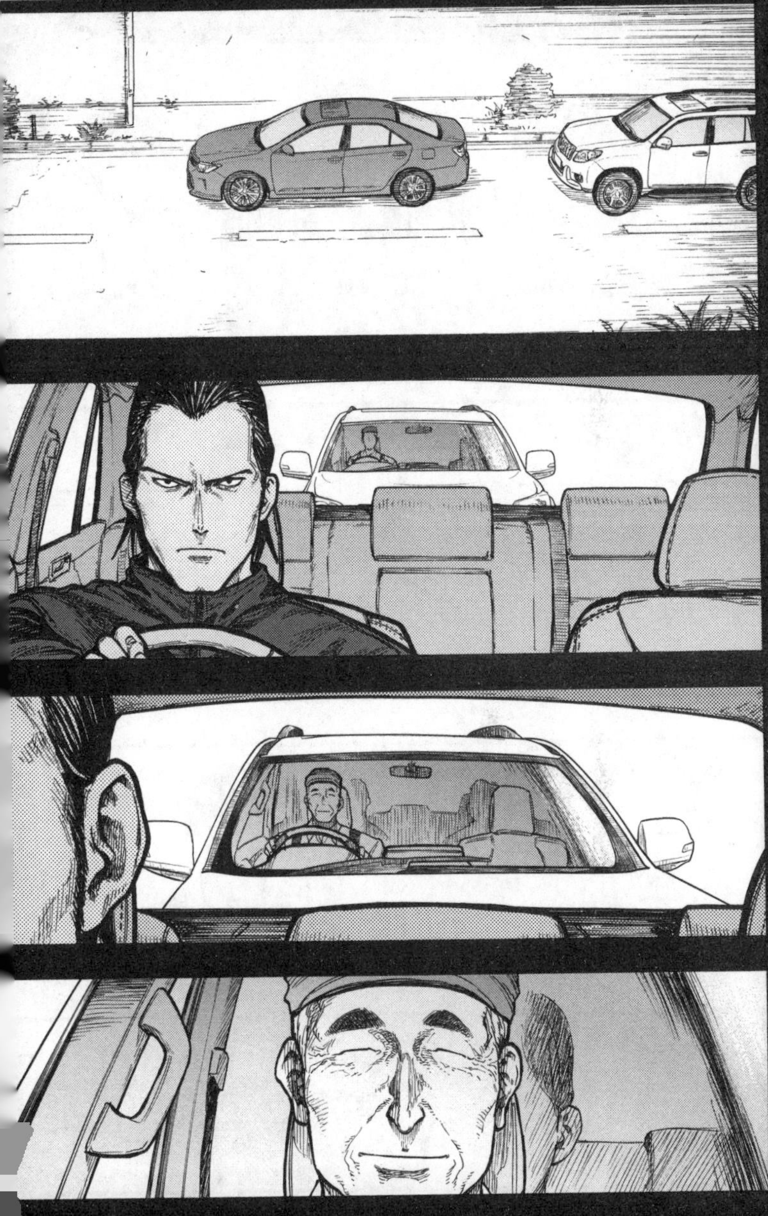

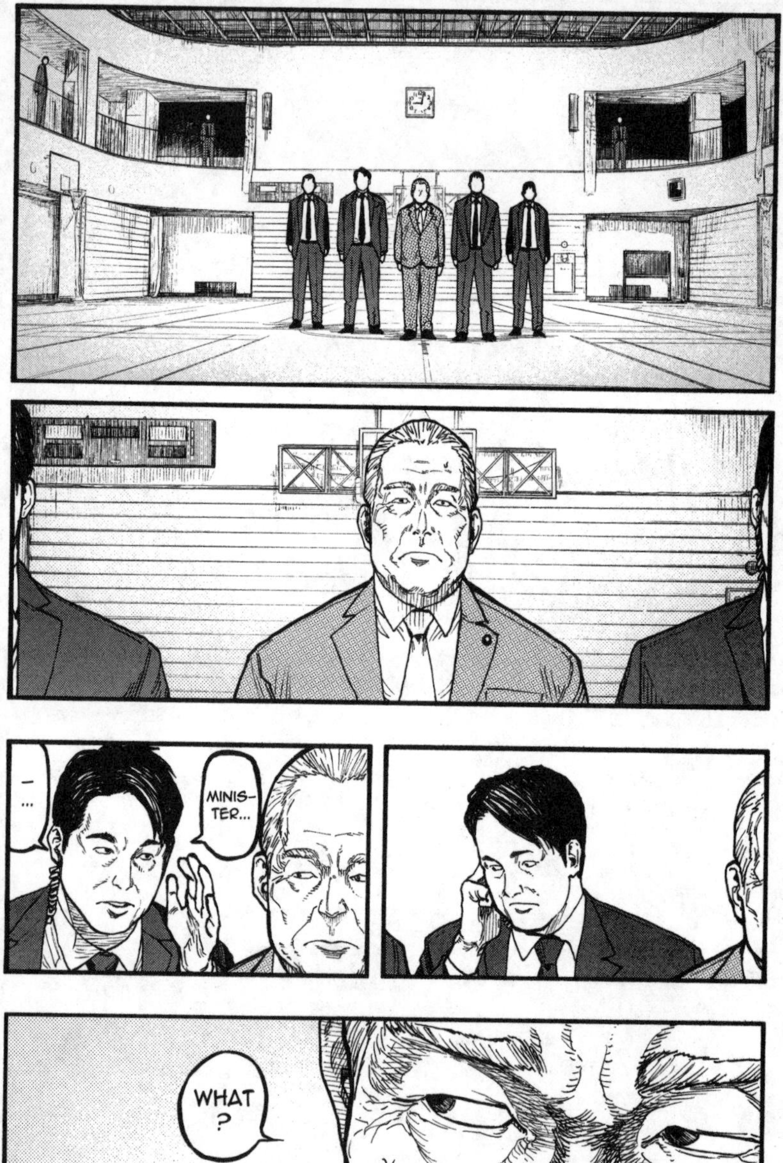
MINIS-
TER...
—...
WHAT
?

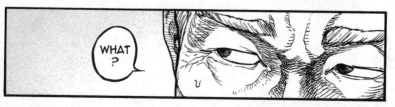

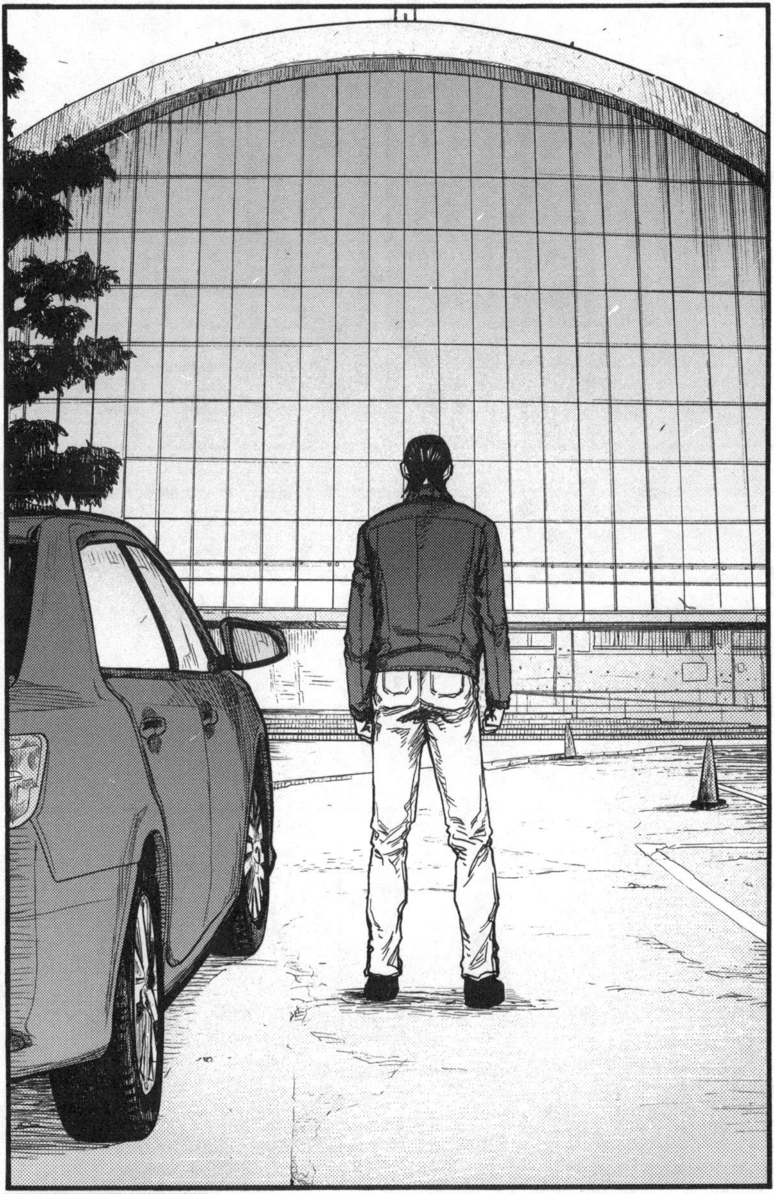

File 51: Fury

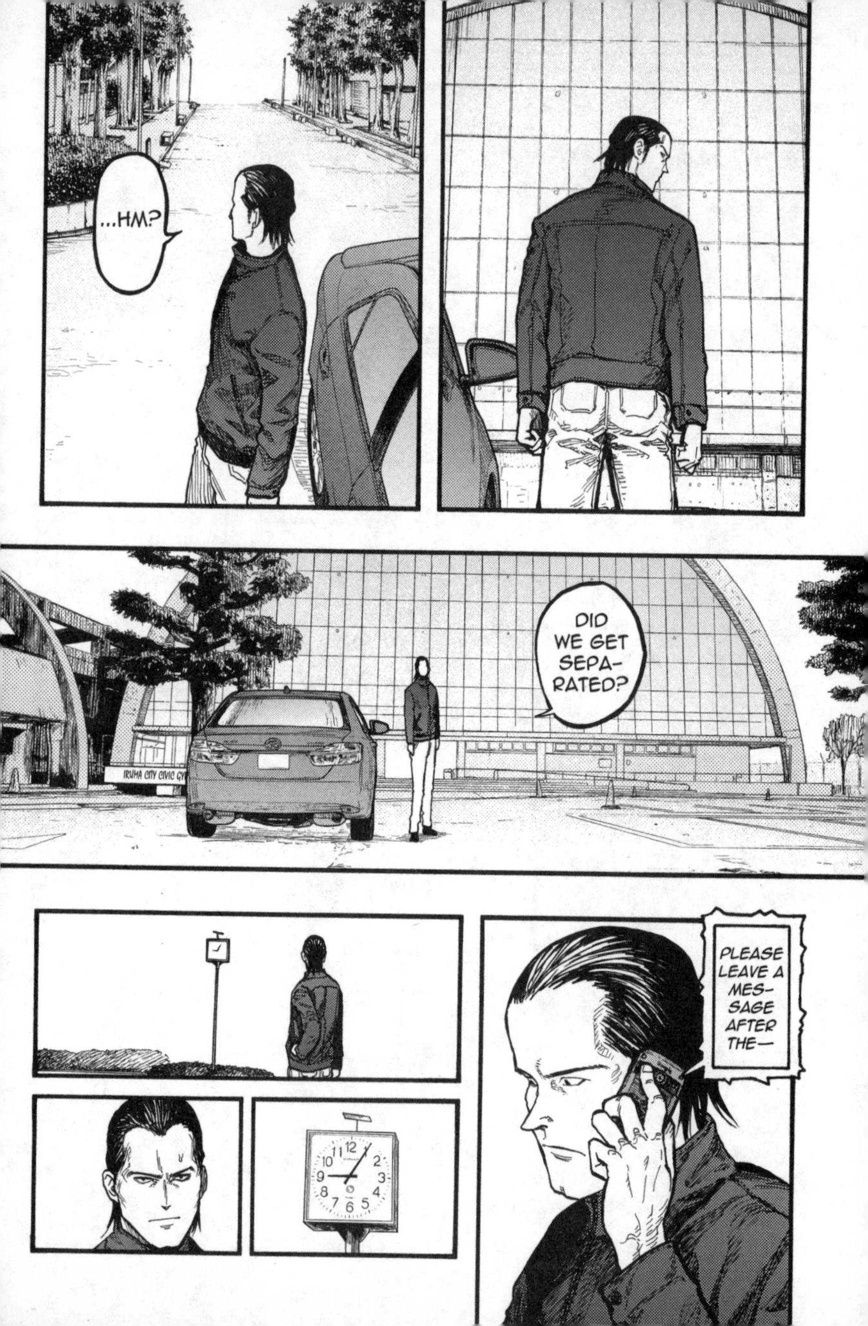
...HM?
DID WE GET SEPA-RATED?
IRUMA CITY CIVIC GY
PLEASE LEAVE A MES-SAGE AFTER THE—

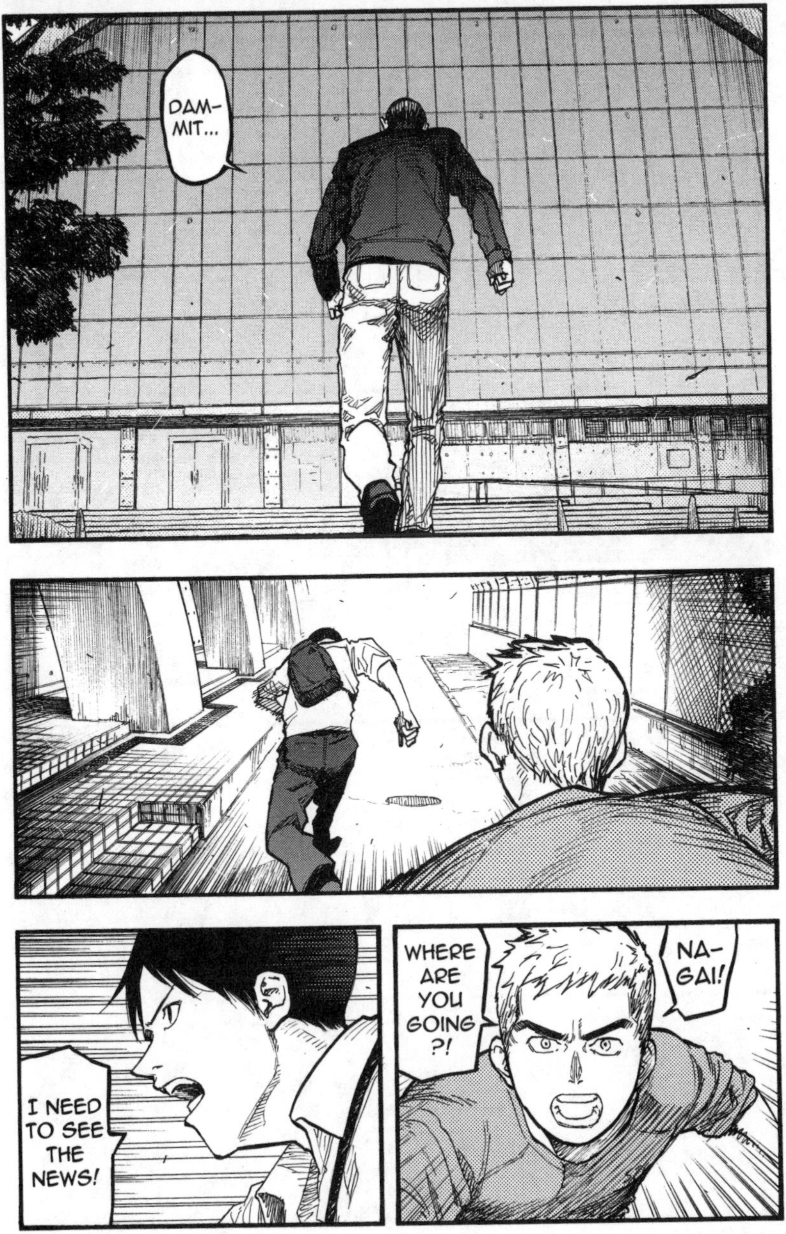
DAM-MIT...
NA-GAI!
WHERE ARE YOU GOING ?!
I NEED TO SEE THE NEWS!

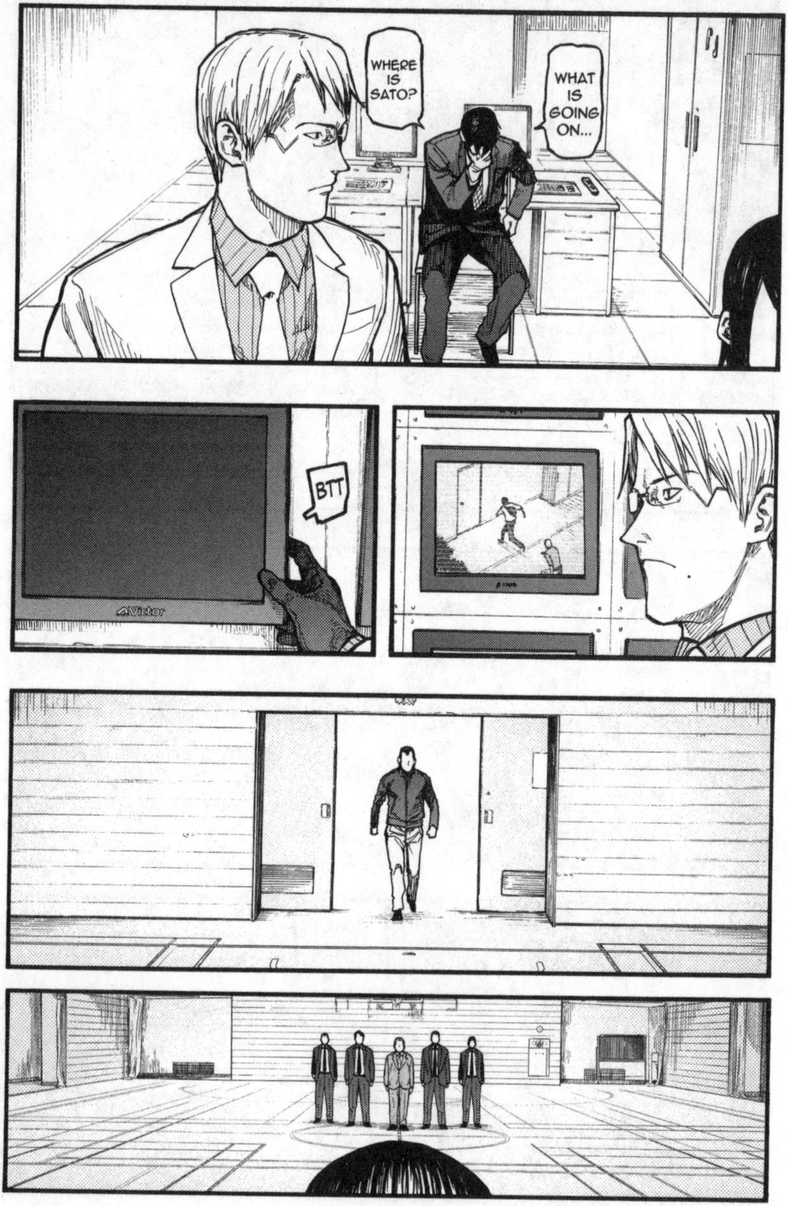
WHAT IS GOING ON...
WHERE IS SATO?
BTT

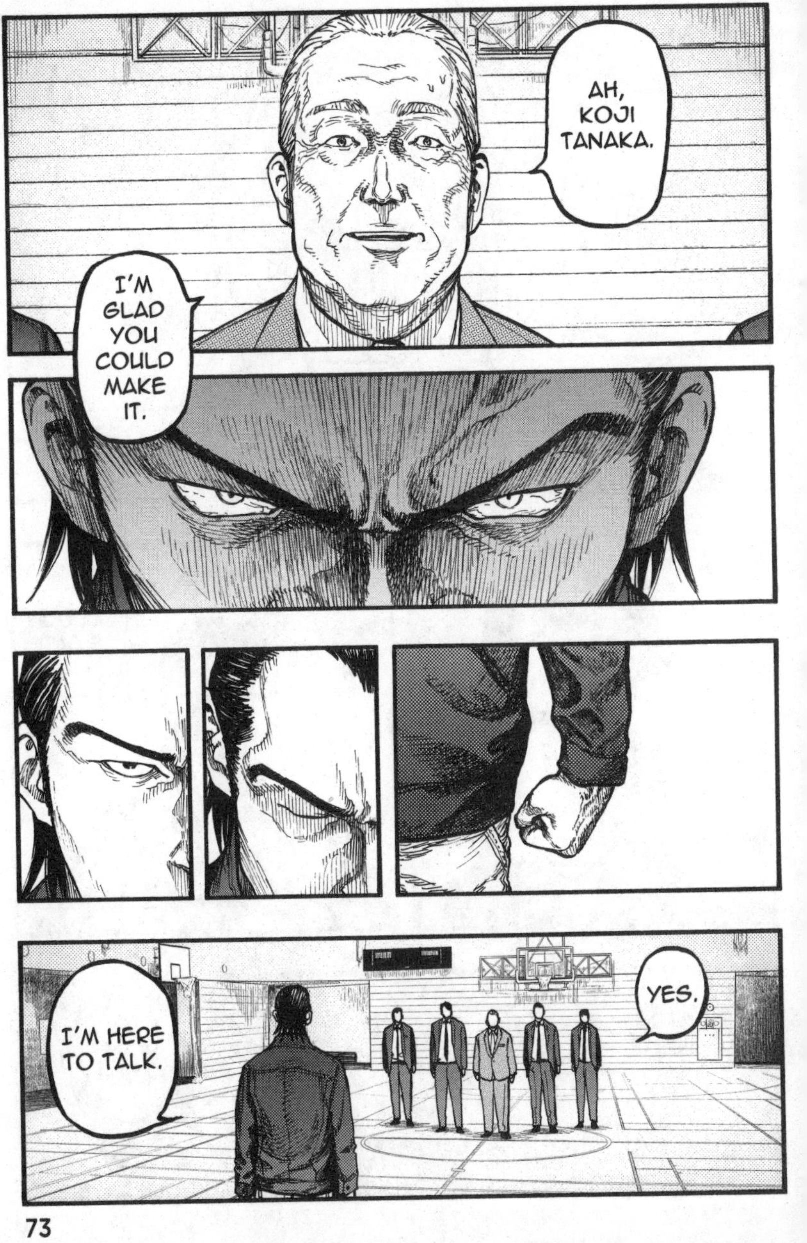
AH, KOJI TANAKA.
I'M GLAD YOU COULD MAKE IT.
YES.
I'M HERE TO TALK.

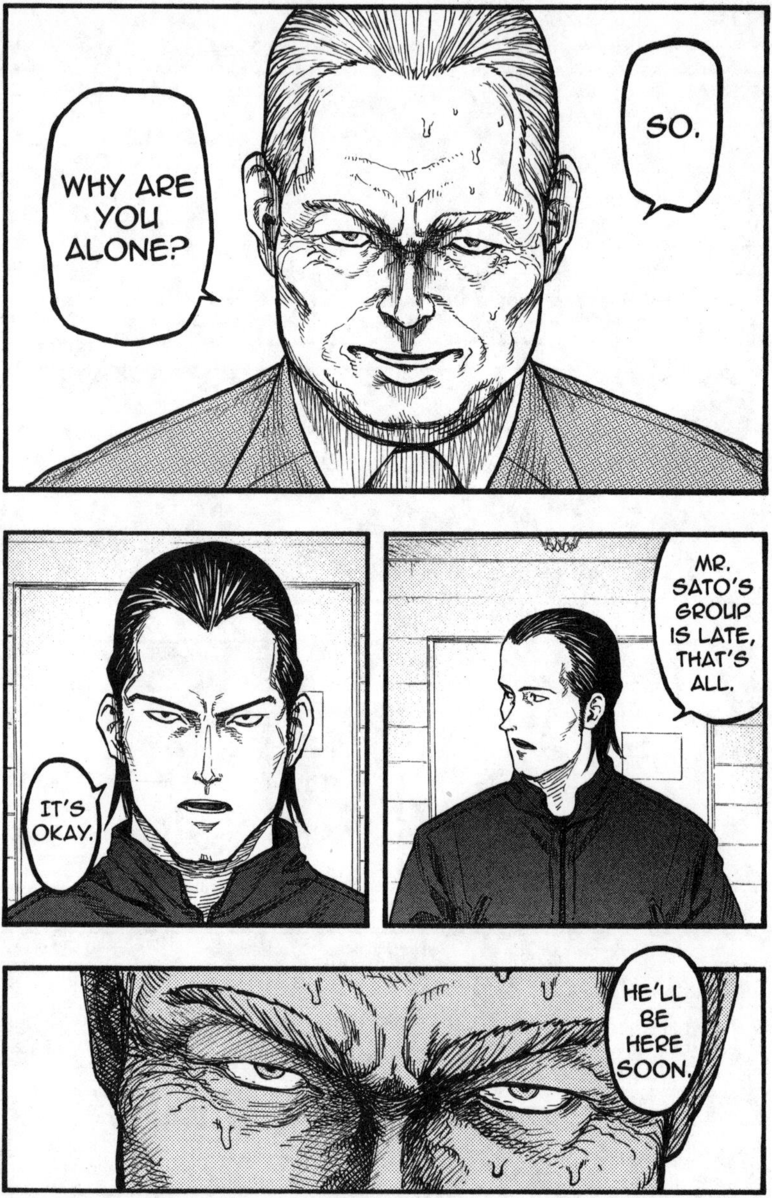
SO.
WHY ARE YOU ALONE?
MR. SATO'S GROUP IS LATE, THAT'S ALL.
IT'S OKAY.
HE'LL BE HERE SOON.

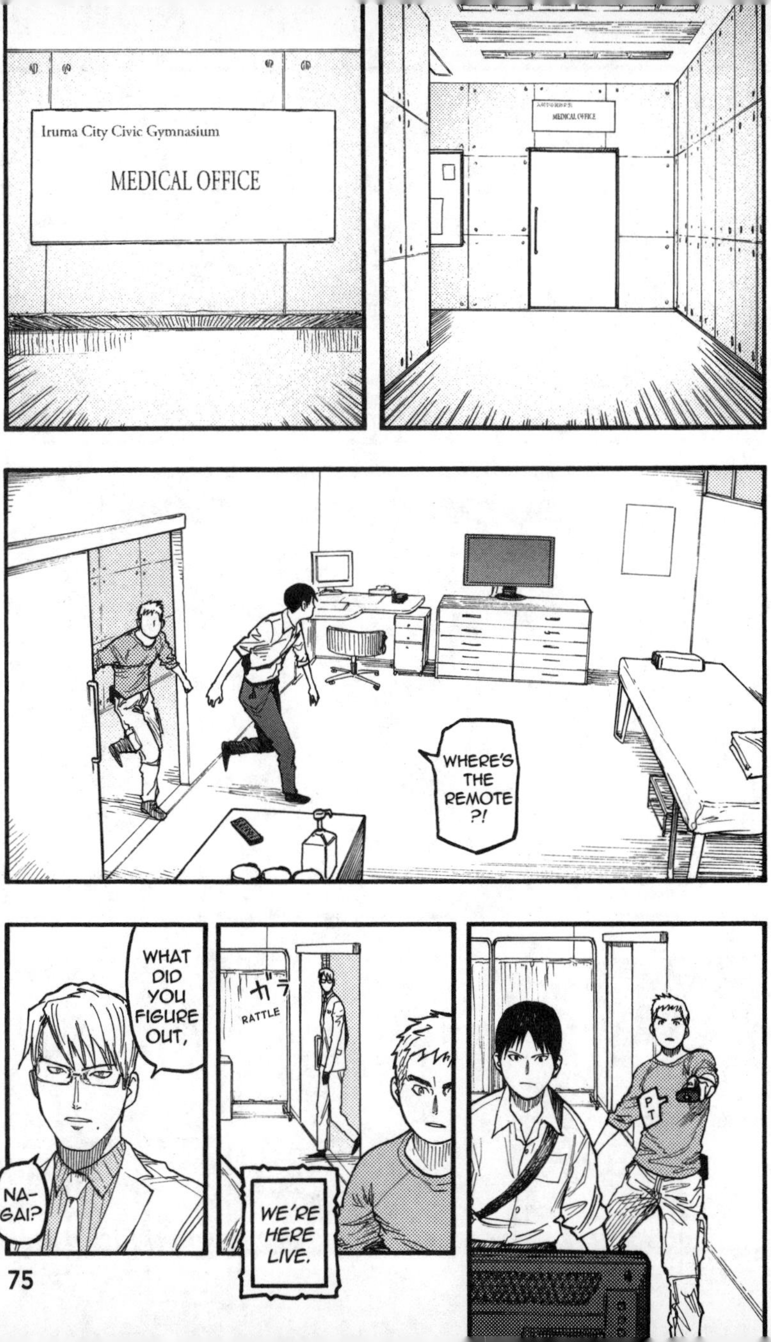
MEDICAL OFFICE
Iruma City Civic Gymnasium
MEDICAL OFFICE
WHERE'S THE REMOTE?!
ガラ
RATTLE
WE'RE HERE LIVE.
WHAT DID YOU FIGURE OUT,
NA-GAI?

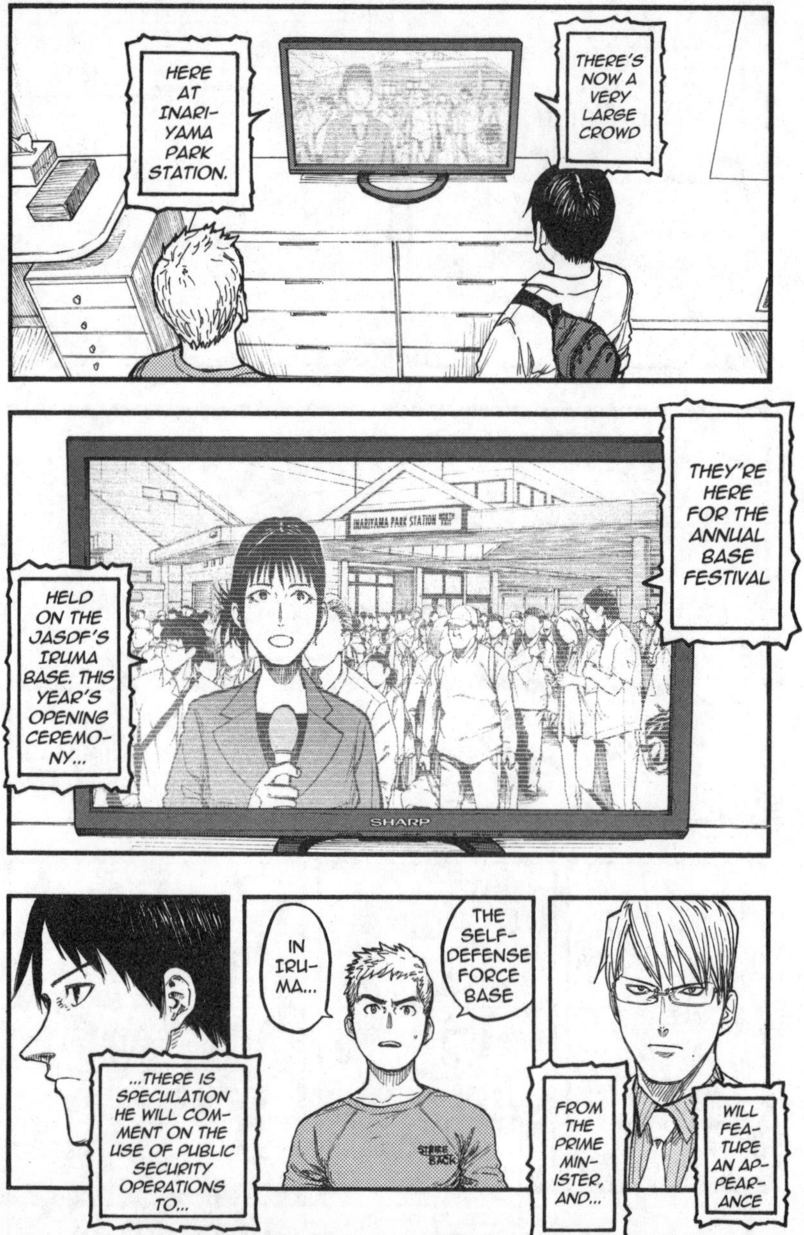
THERE'S NOW A VERY LARGE CROWD
HERE AT INARI-YAMA PARK STATION.
THEY'RE HERE FOR THE ANNUAL BASE FESTIVAL
INARIYAMA PARK STATION
HELD ON THE JASDF'S IRUMA BASE. THIS YEAR'S OPENING CEREMO-NY...
SHARP
WILL FEA-TURE AN AP-PEAR-ANCE
FROM THE PRIME MIN-ISTER, AND...
THE SELF-DEFENSE FORCE BASE
IN IRU-MA...
STRIKE BACK
...THERE IS SPECULATION HE WILL COM-MENT ON THE USE OF PUBLIC SECURITY OPERATIONS TO...

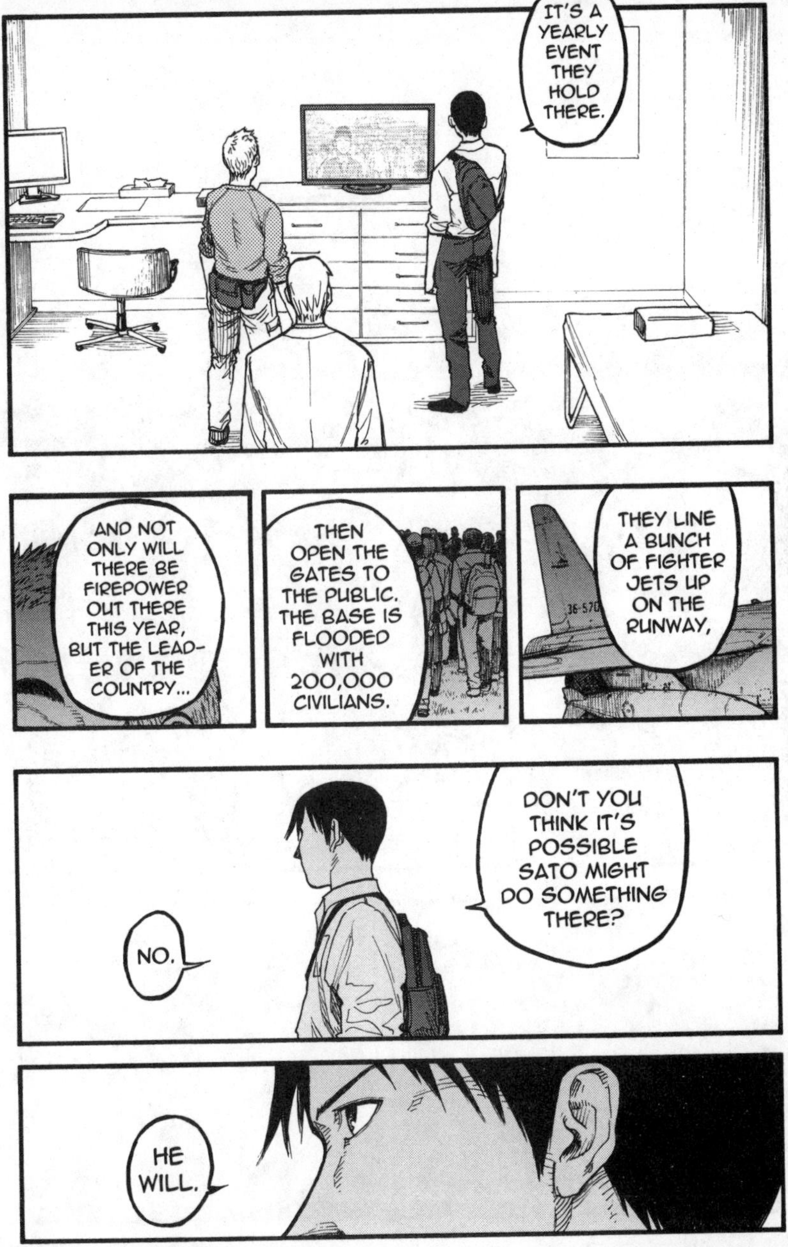
IT'S A YEARLY EVENT THEY HOLD THERE.
THEY LINE A BUNCH OF FIGHTER JETS UP ON THE RUNWAY,
THEN OPEN THE GATES TO THE PUBLIC. THE BASE IS FLOODED WITH 200,000 CIVILIANS.
AND NOT ONLY WILL THERE BE FIREPOWER OUT THERE THIS YEAR, BUT THE LEADER OF THE COUNTRY...
DON'T YOU THINK IT'S POSSIBLE SATO MIGHT DO SOMETHING THERE?
NO.
HE WILL.

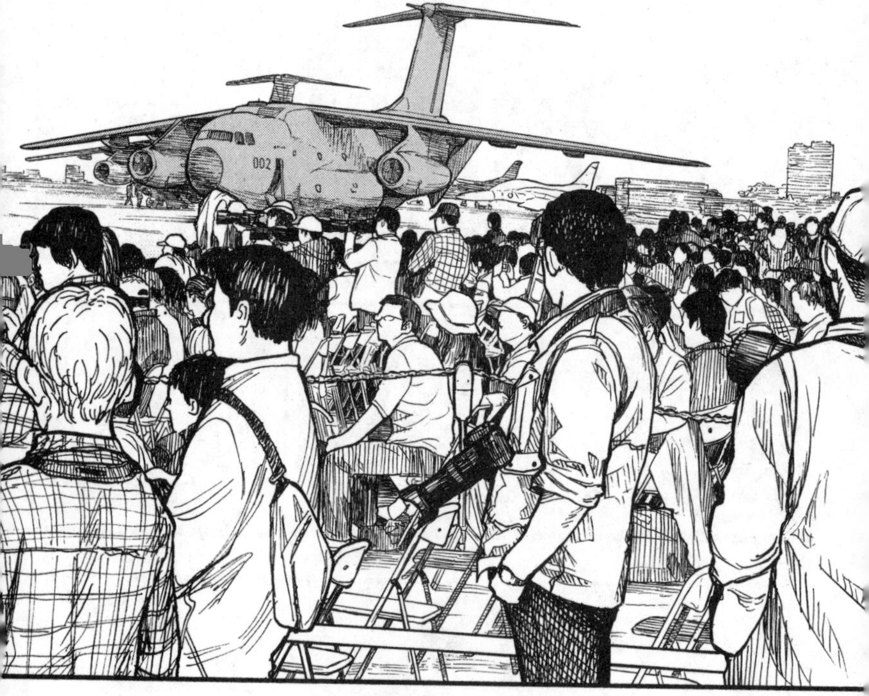
002
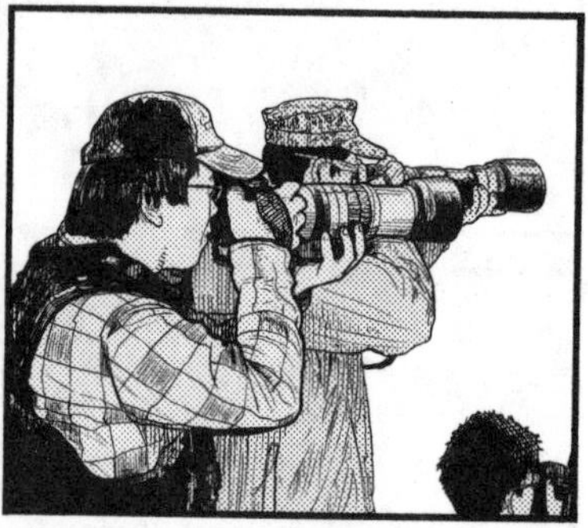
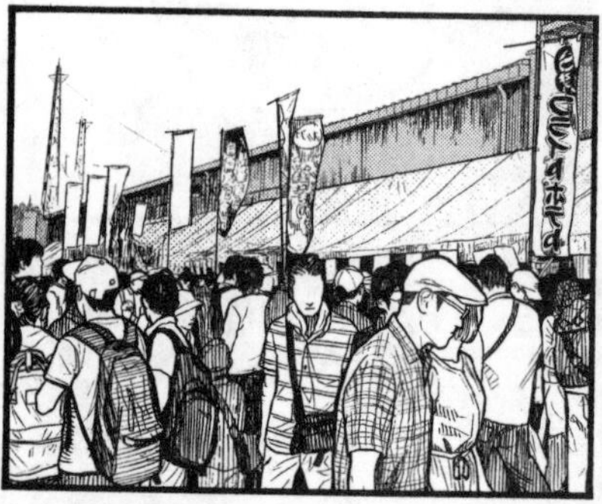

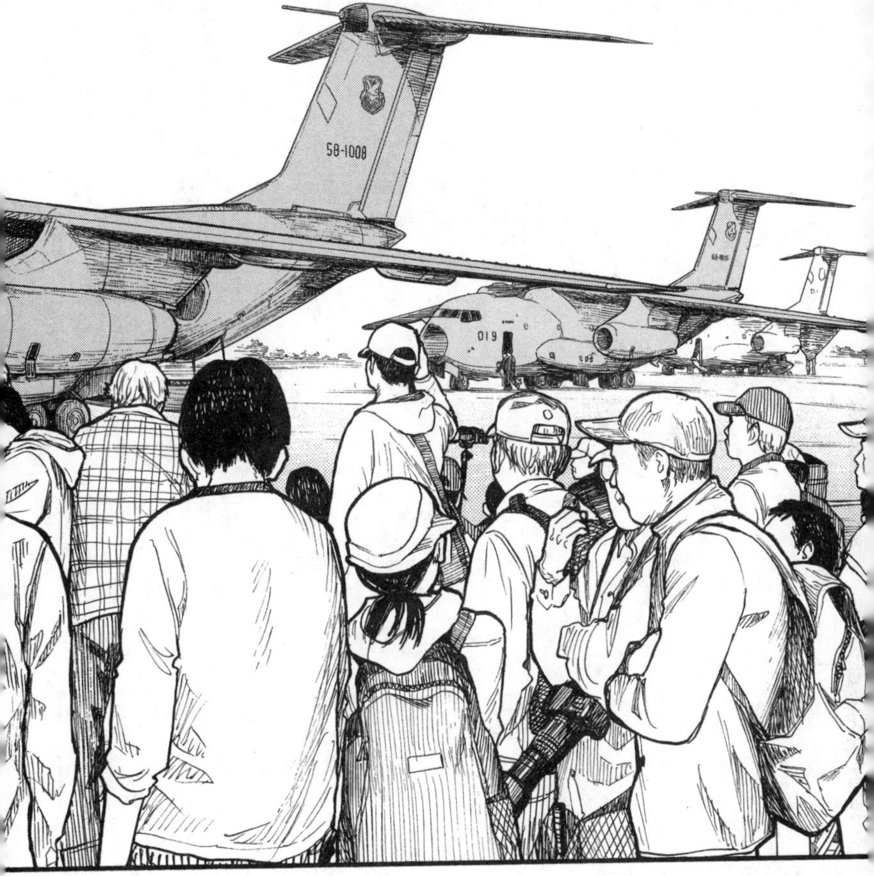
58-1008
019
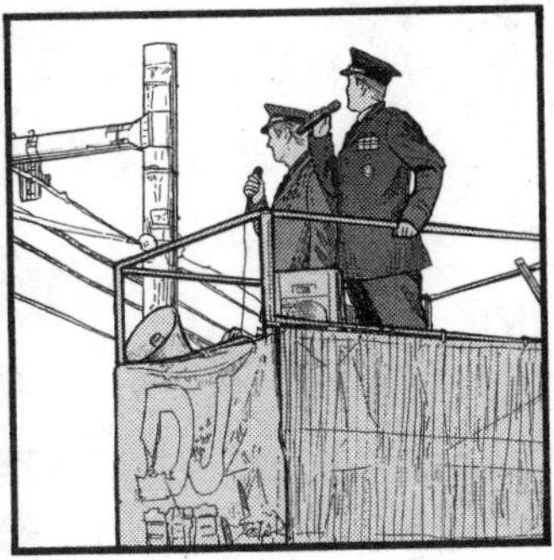
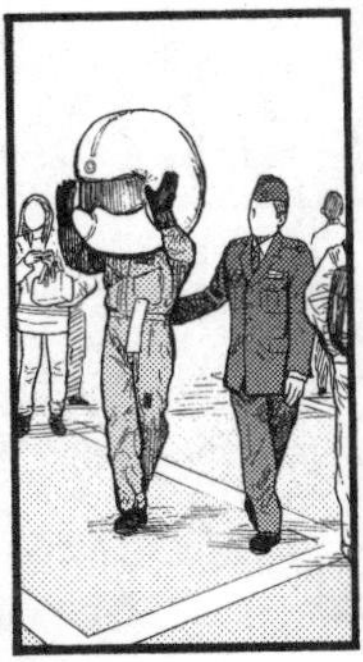
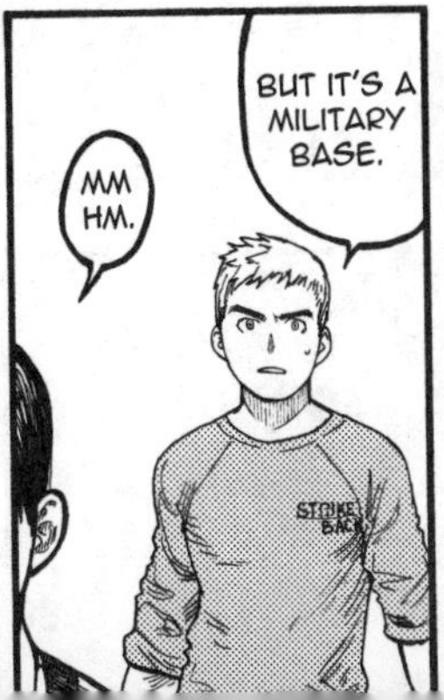
BUT IT'S A MILITARY BASE.
MM HM.

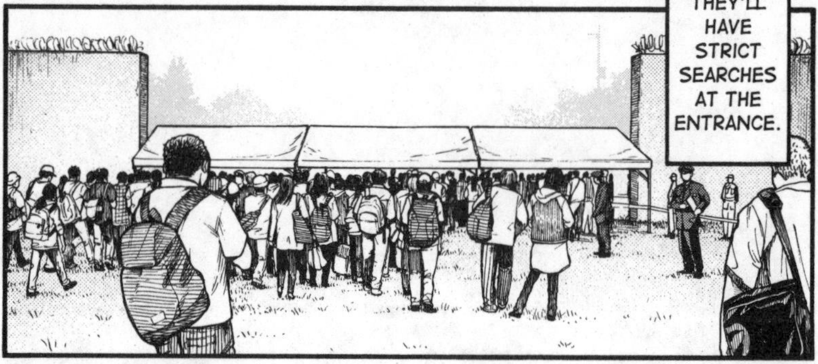
THEY'LL HAVE STRICT SEARCHES AT THE ENTRANCE.

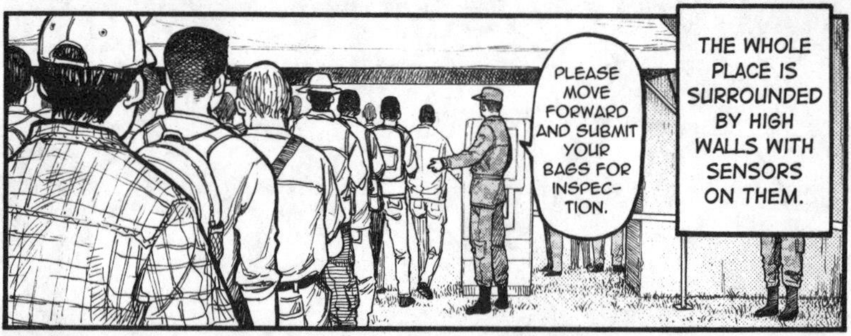
THE WHOLE PLACE IS SURROUNDED BY HIGH WALLS WITH SENSORS ON THEM.
PLEASE MOVE FORWARD AND SUBMIT YOUR BAGS FOR INSPEC-TION.

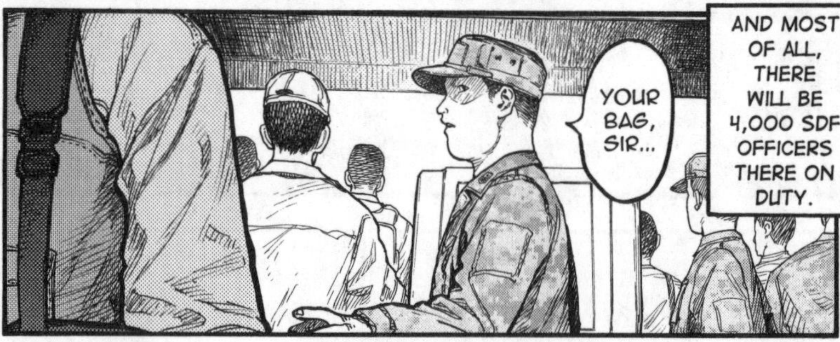
AND MOST OF ALL, THERE WILL BE 4,000 SDF OFFICERS THERE ON DUTY.
YOUR BAG, SIR...

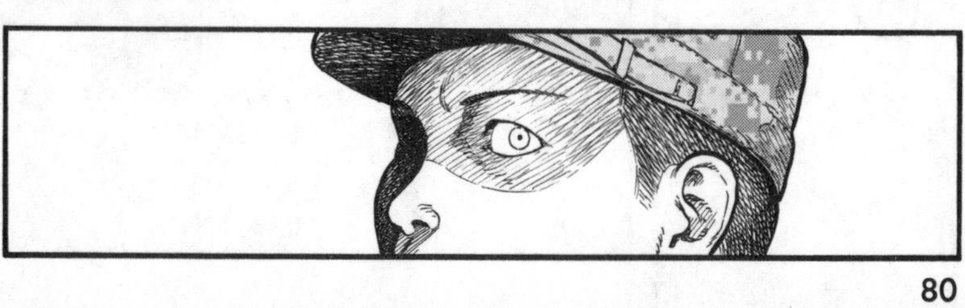

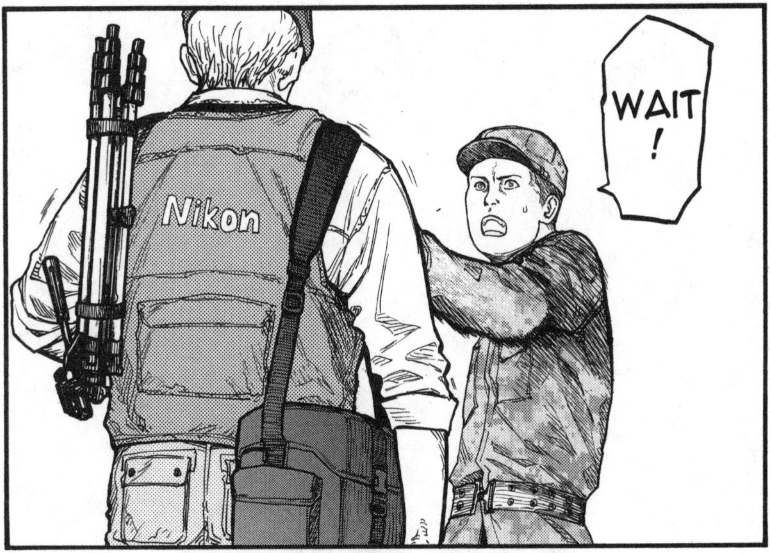
WAIT
!
Nikon

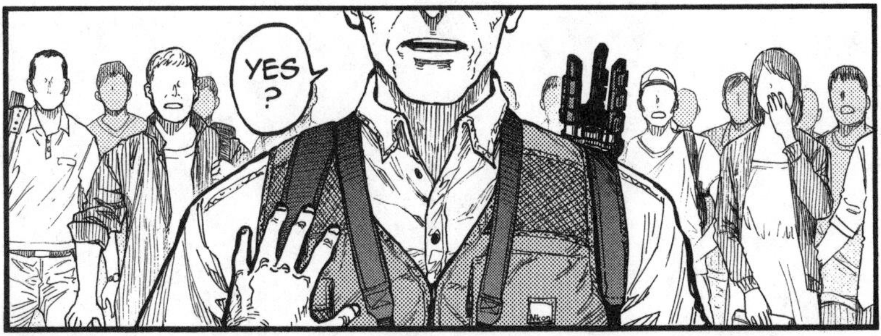
YES
?

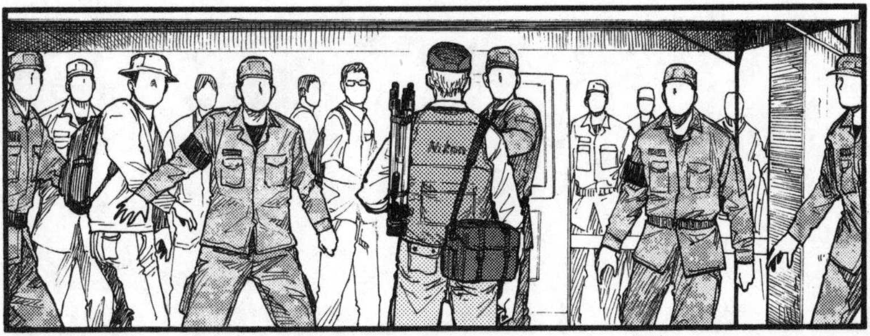
Nikon

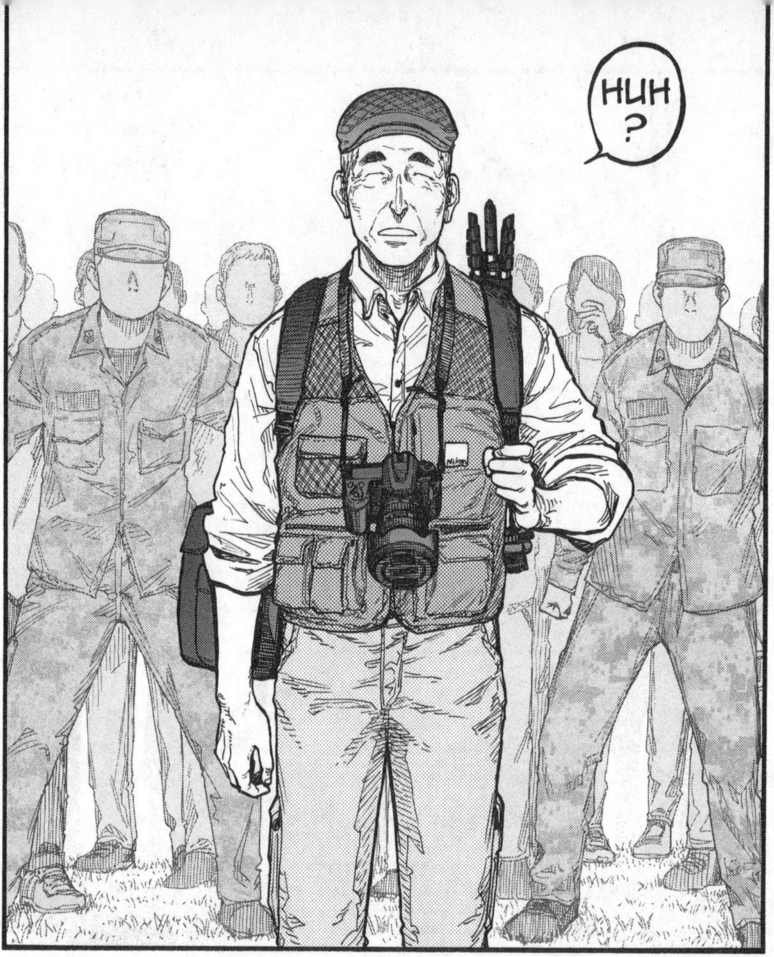
HUH?
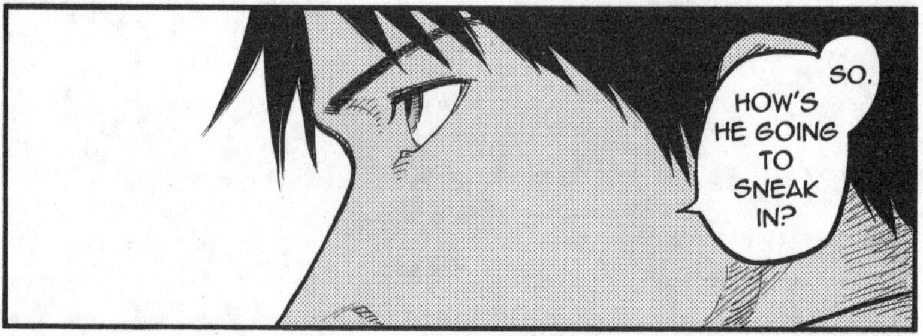
SO. HOW'S HE GOING TO SNEAK IN?

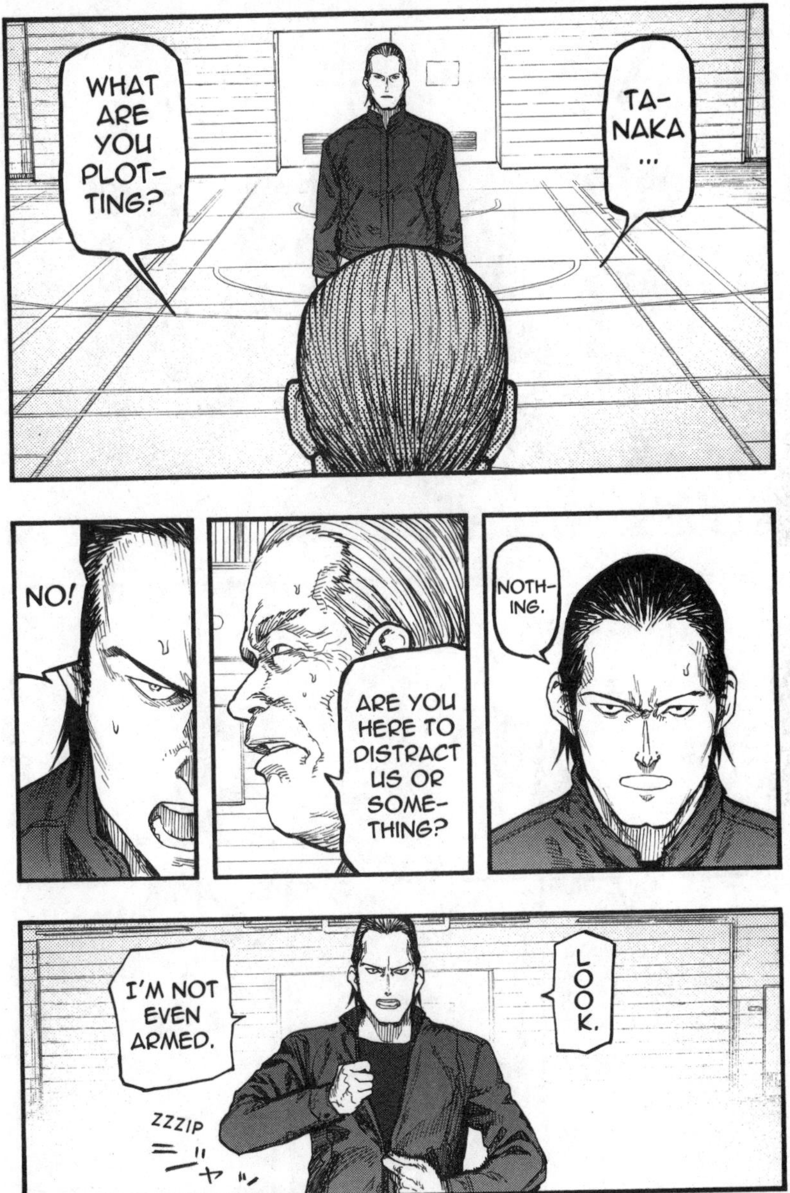
TA-NAKA...
WHAT ARE YOU PLOT-TING?
NOTH-ING.
ARE YOU HERE TO DISTRACT US OR SOME-THING?
NO!
LOOK.
I'M NOT EVEN ARMED.
ZZZIP

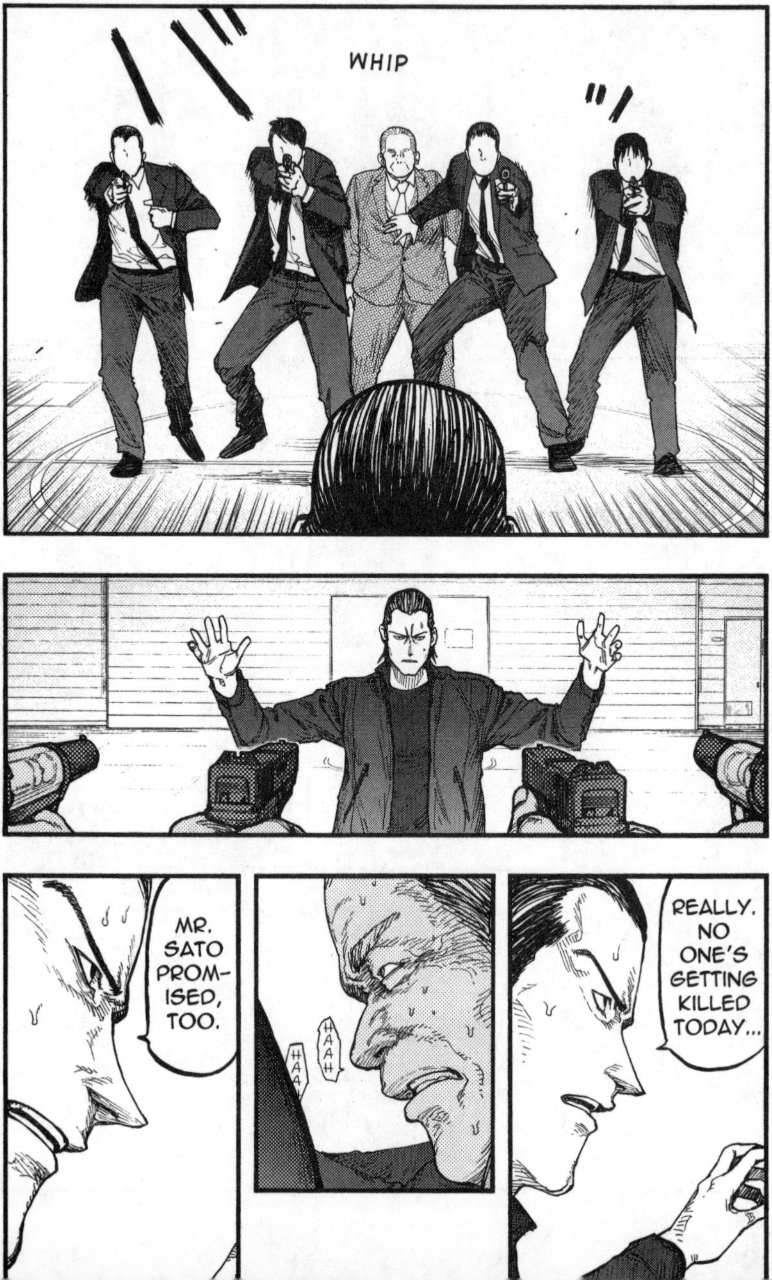
WHIP
REALLY. NO ONE'S GETTING KILLED TODAY...
HAAH
MR. SATO PROM-ISED, TOO.

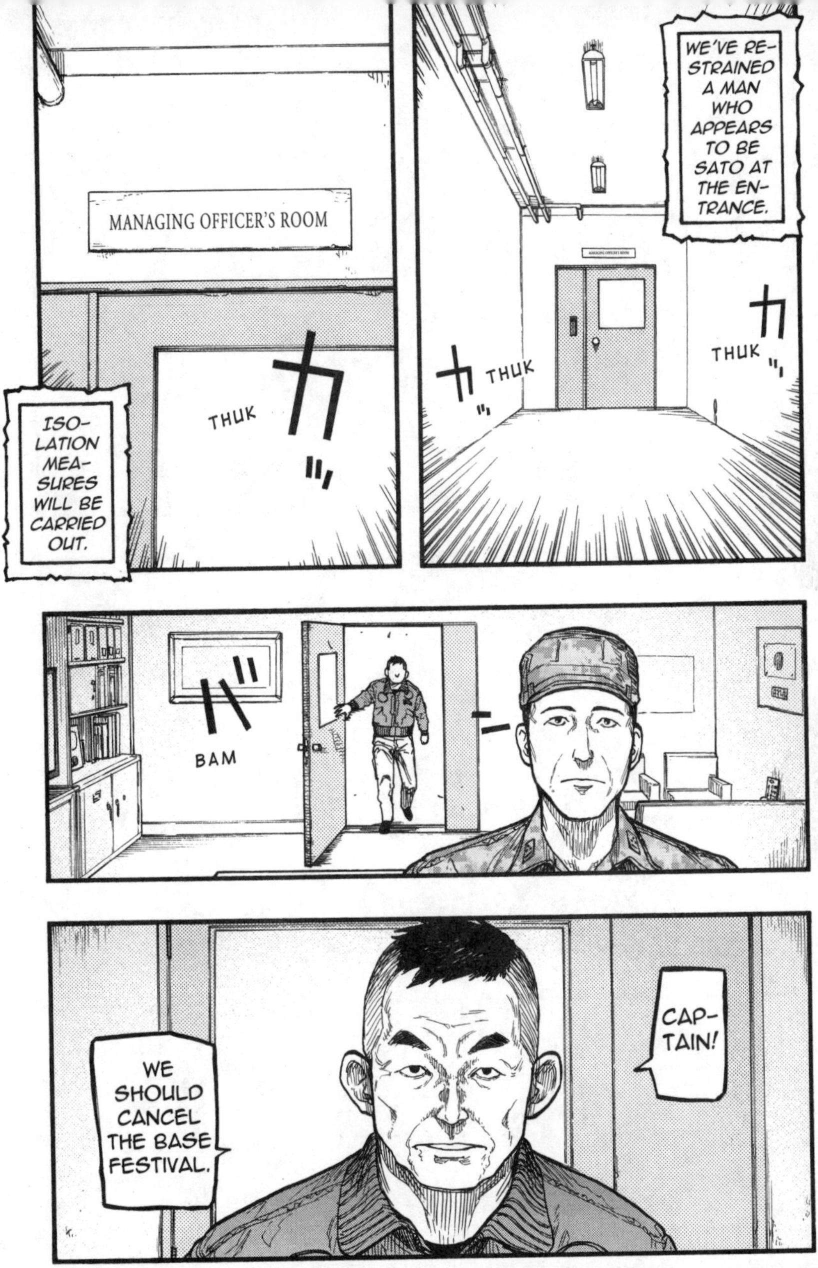
WE'VE RE-STRAINED A MAN WHO APPEARS TO BE SATO AT THE EN-TRANCE.
MANAGING OFFICER'S ROOM
THUK
THUK
MANAGING OFFICER'S ROOM
THUK
ISO-LATION MEA-SURES WILL BE CARRIED OUT.
BAM
CAP-TAIN!
WE SHOULD CANCEL THE BASE FESTIVAL.

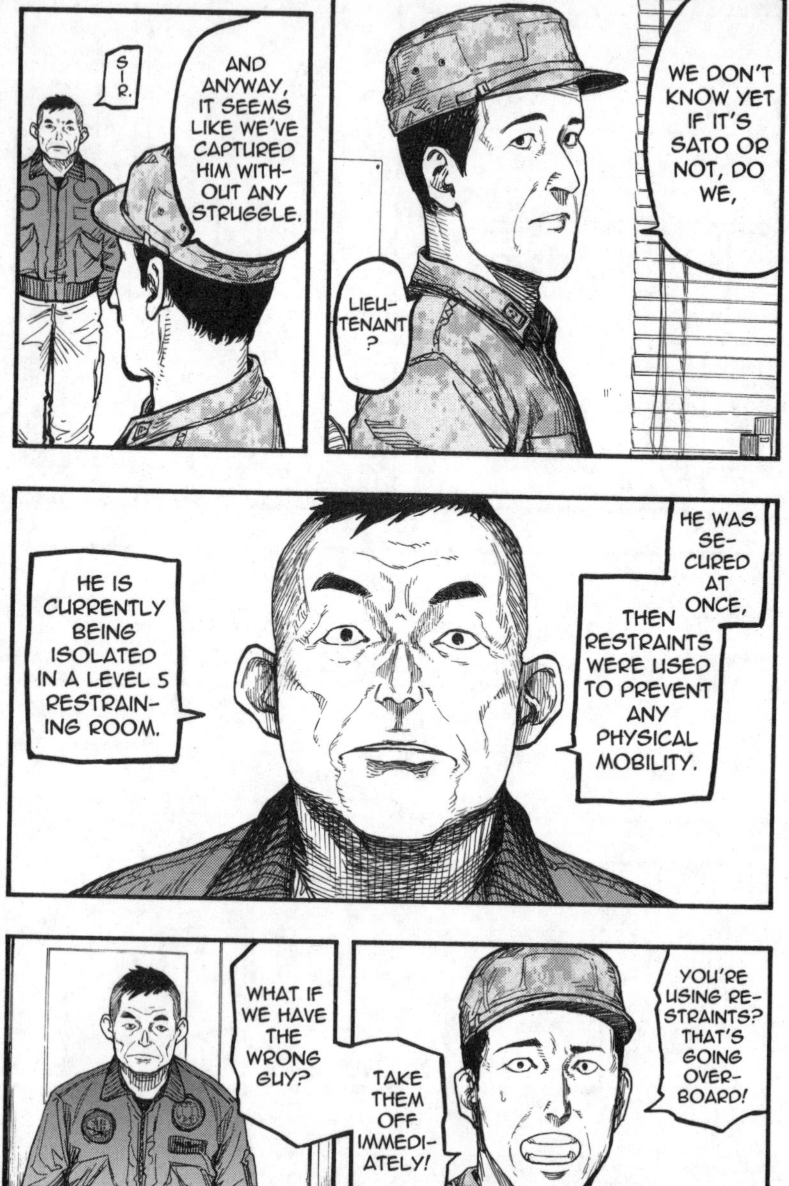
WE DON'T KNOW YET IF IT'S SATO OR NOT, DO WE,
LIEU-TENANT?
AND ANYWAY, IT SEEMS LIKE WE'VE CAPTURED HIM WITH-OUT ANY STRUGGLE.
SIR.
HE WAS SE-CURED AT ONCE,
THEN RESTRAINTS WERE USED TO PREVENT ANY PHYSICAL MOBILITY.
HE IS CURRENTLY BEING ISOLATED IN A LEVEL 5 RESTRAIN-ING ROOM.
YOU'RE USING RE-STRAINTS? THAT'S GOING OVER-BOARD!
TAKE THEM OFF IMMEDI-ATELY!
WHAT IF WE HAVE THE WRONG GUY?

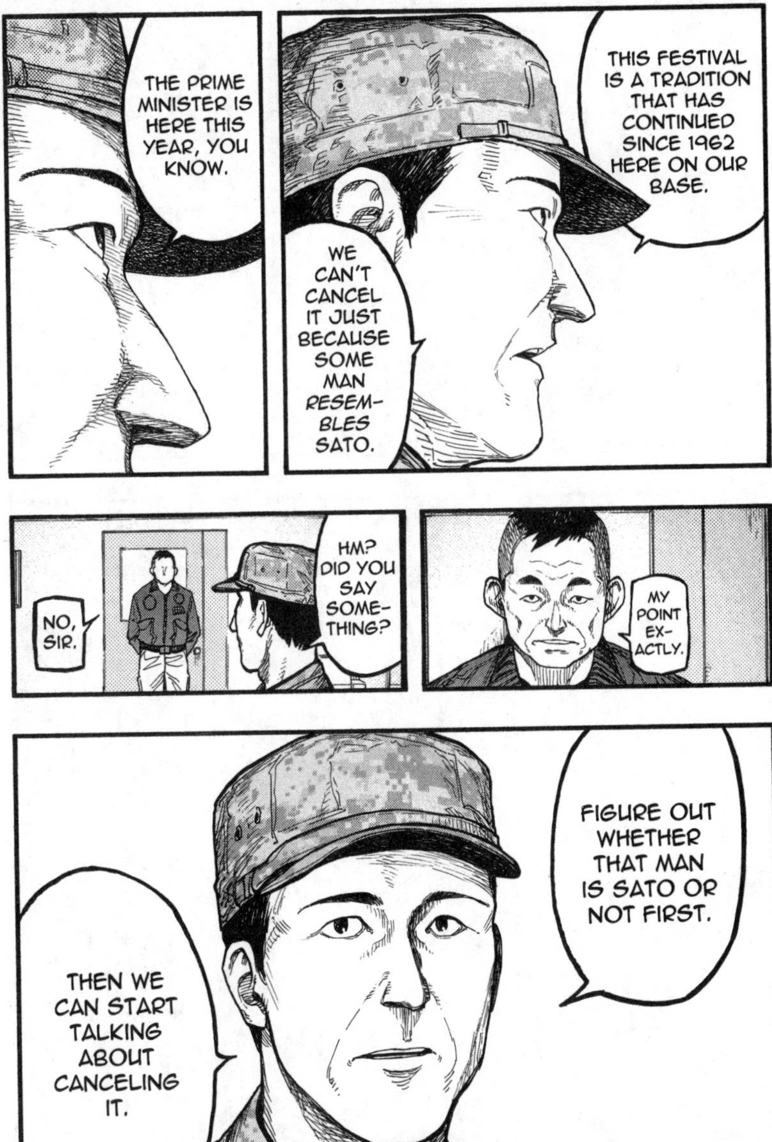
THIS FESTIVAL IS A TRADITION THAT HAS CONTINUED SINCE 1962 HERE ON OUR BASE.
WE CAN'T CANCEL IT JUST BECAUSE SOME MAN RESEMBLES SATO.
THE PRIME MINISTER IS HERE THIS YEAR, YOU KNOW.
MY POINT EXACTLY.
HM? DID YOU SAY SOMETHING?
NO, SIR.
FIGURE OUT WHETHER THAT MAN IS SATO OR NOT FIRST.
THEN WE CAN START TALKING ABOUT CANCELING IT.

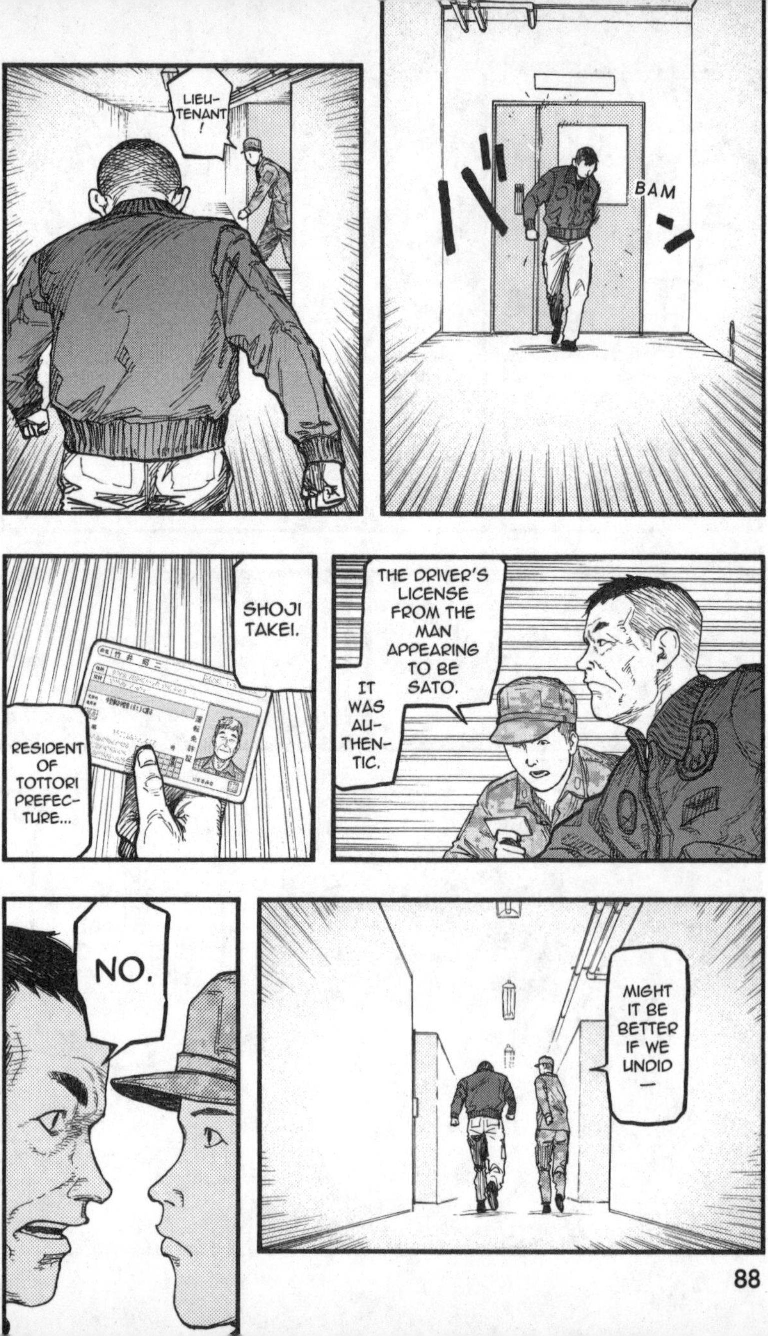

BAM
LIEU-TENANT!
THE DRIVER'S LICENSE FROM THE MAN APPEARING TO BE SATO.
IT WAS AU-THEN-TIC.
SHOJI TAKEI.
RESIDENT OF TOTTORI PREFEC-TURE...
MIGHT IT BE BETTER IF WE UNDID —
NO.

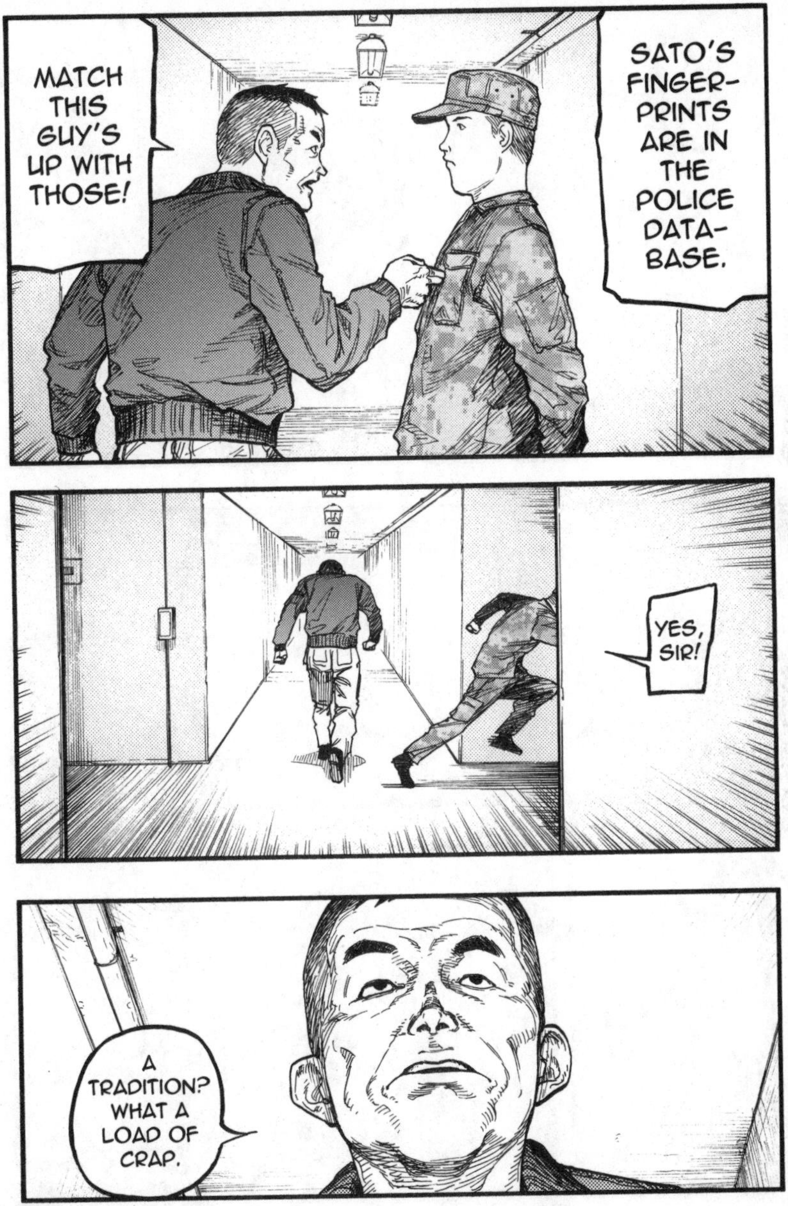
SATO'S FINGER-PRINTS ARE IN THE POLICE DATA-BASE.
MATCH THIS GUY'S UP WITH THOSE!
YES, SIR!
A TRADITION? WHAT A LOAD OF CRAP.

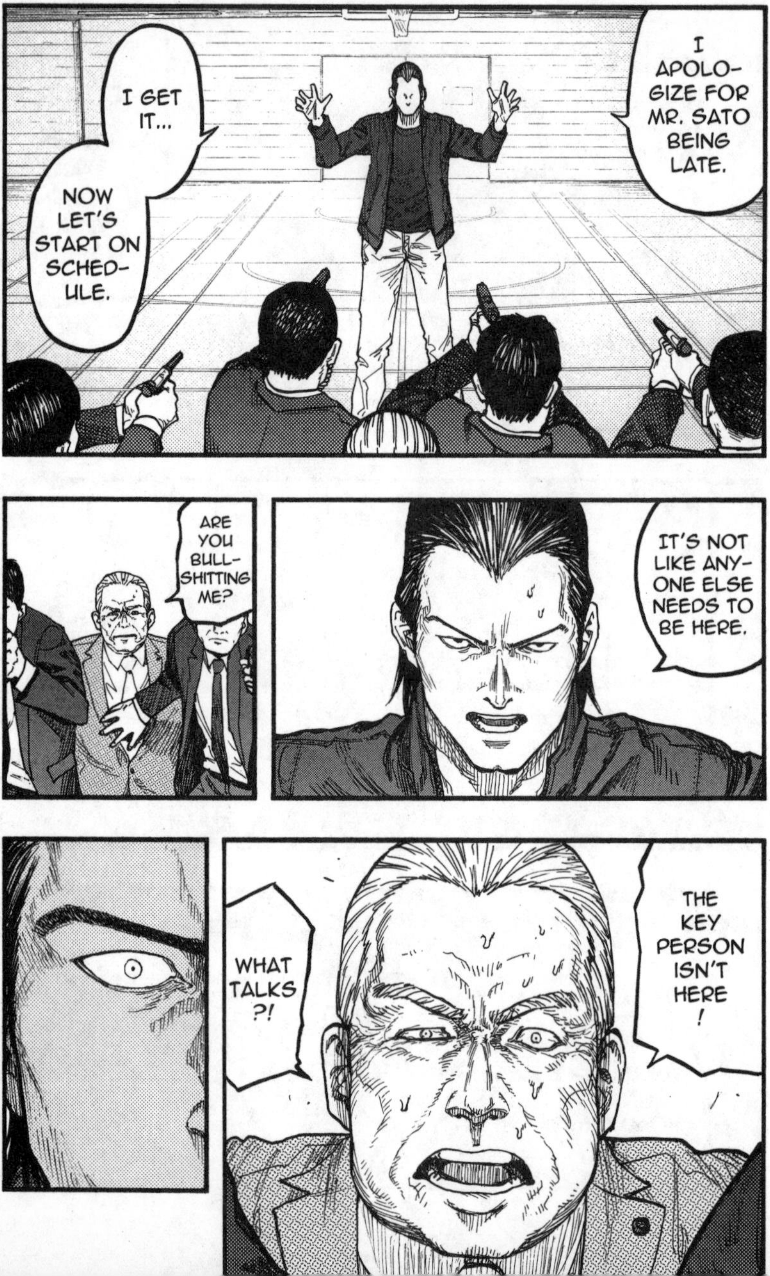
I APOLOGIZE FOR MR. SATO BEING LATE.
I GET IT...
NOW LET'S START ON SCHEDULE.
IT'S NOT LIKE ANYONE ELSE NEEDS TO BE HERE.
ARE YOU BULLSHITTING ME?
THE KEY PERSON ISN'T HERE!
WHAT TALKS?!

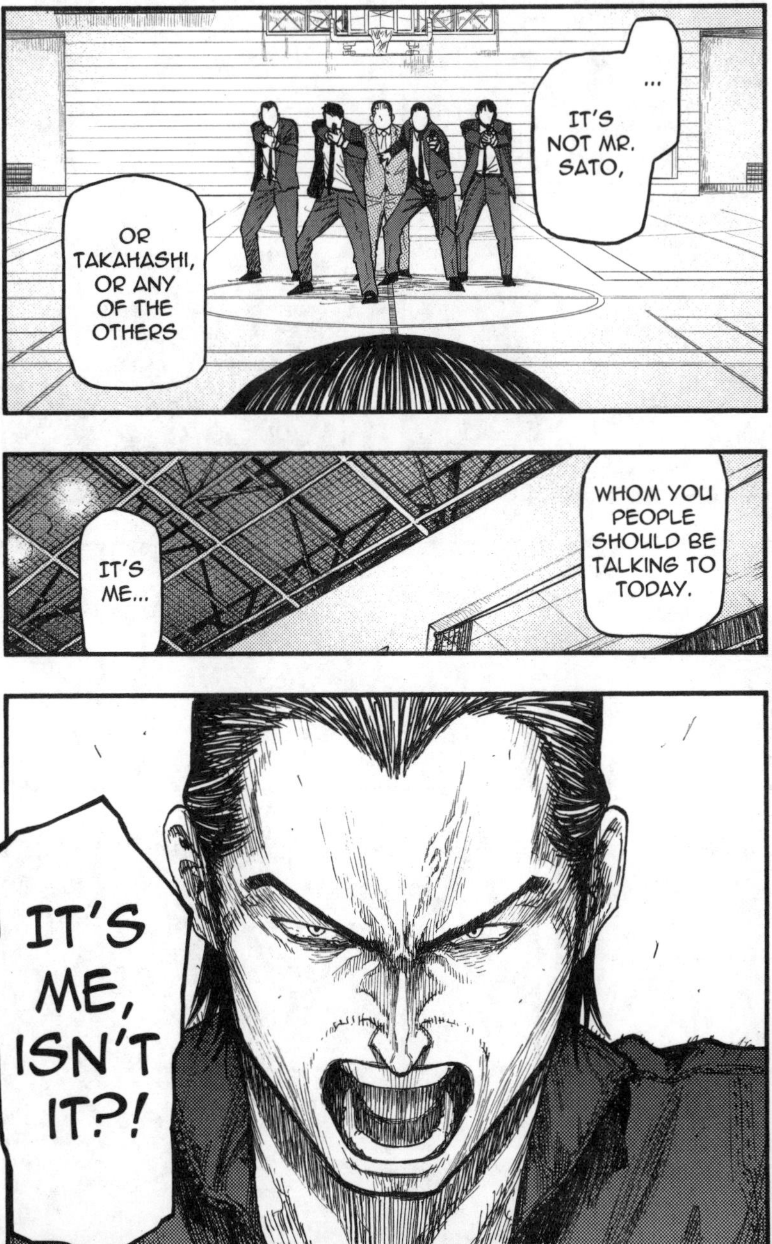
...
IT'S NOT MR. SATO,
OR TAKAHASHI, OR ANY OF THE OTHERS
WHOM YOU PEOPLE SHOULD BE TALKING TO TODAY.
IT'S ME...
IT'S ME, ISN'T IT?!

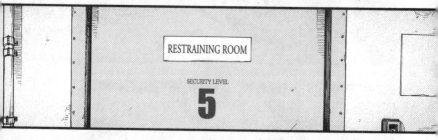

RESTRAINING ROOM

SECURITY LEVEL

5

VRRRM

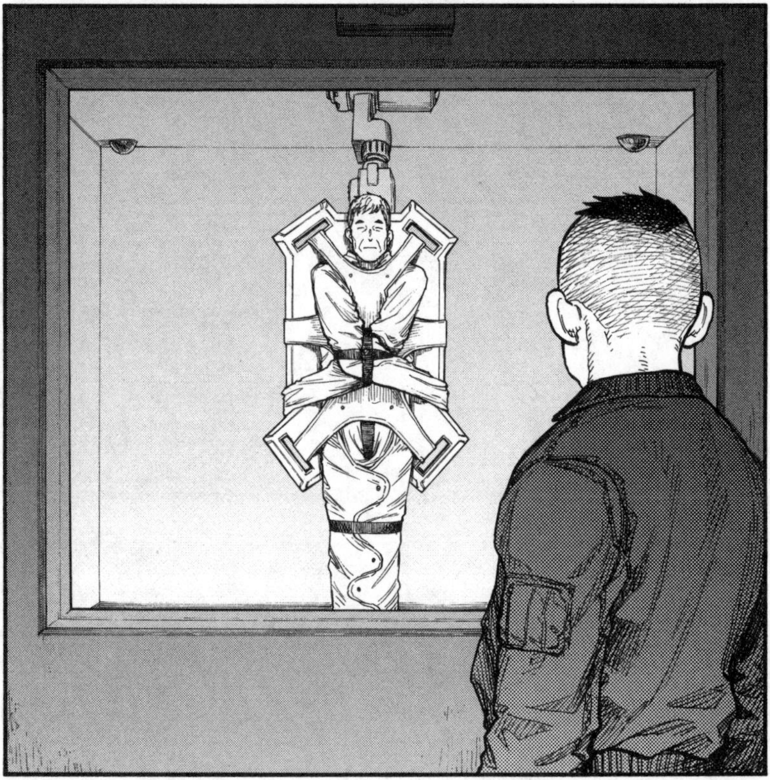
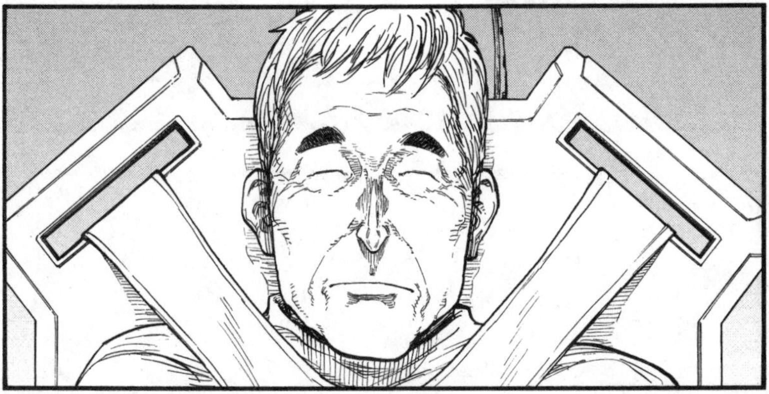

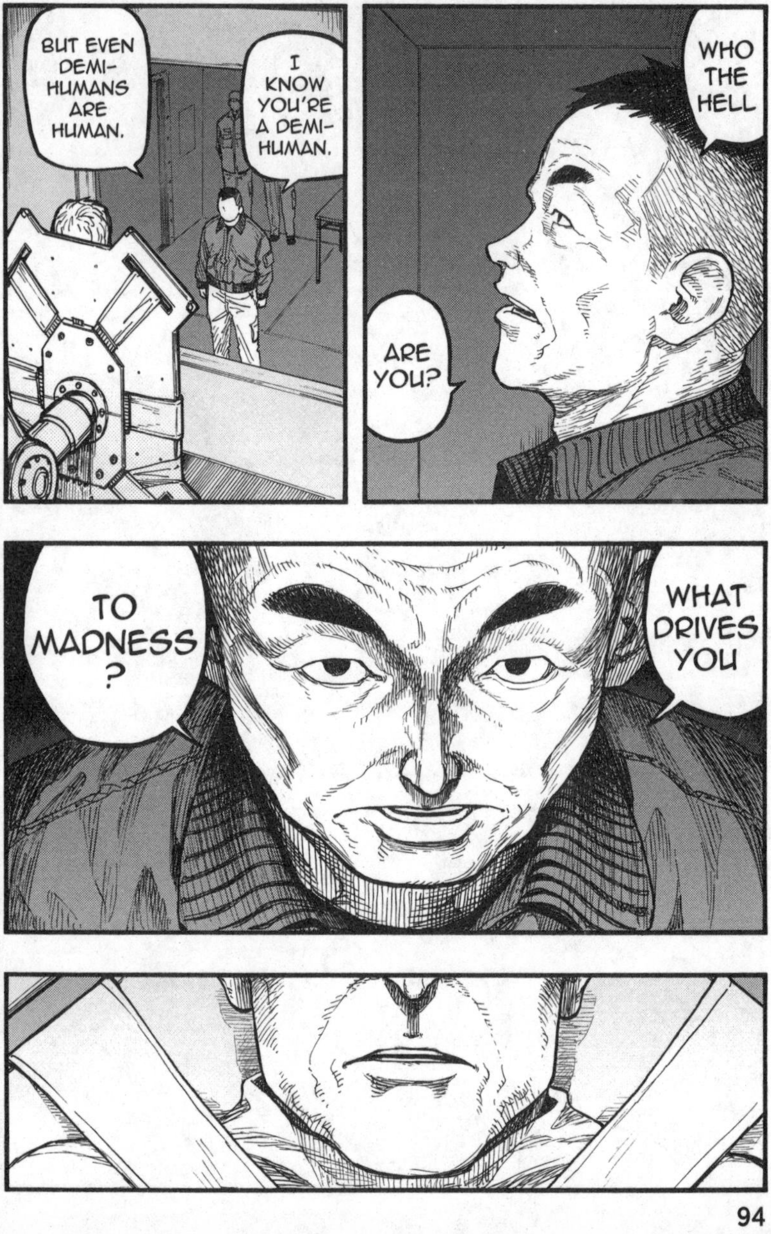
WHO THE HELL
ARE YOU?
I KNOW YOU'RE A DEMI-HUMAN.
BUT EVEN DEMI-HUMANS ARE HUMAN.
WHAT DRIVES YOU
TO MADNESS ?

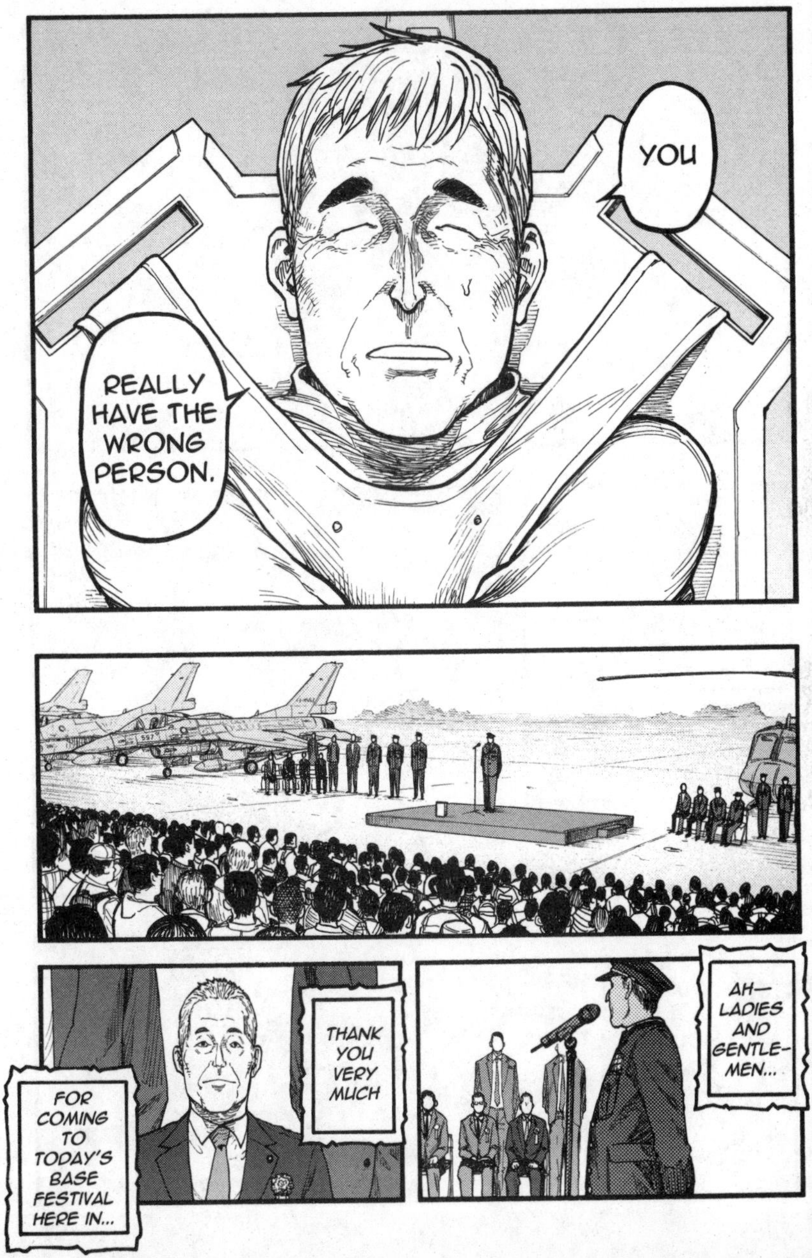

YOU
REALLY HAVE THE WRONG PERSON.
AH— LADIES AND GENTLE-MEN...
THANK YOU VERY MUCH
FOR COMING TO TODAY'S BASE FESTIVAL HERE IN...

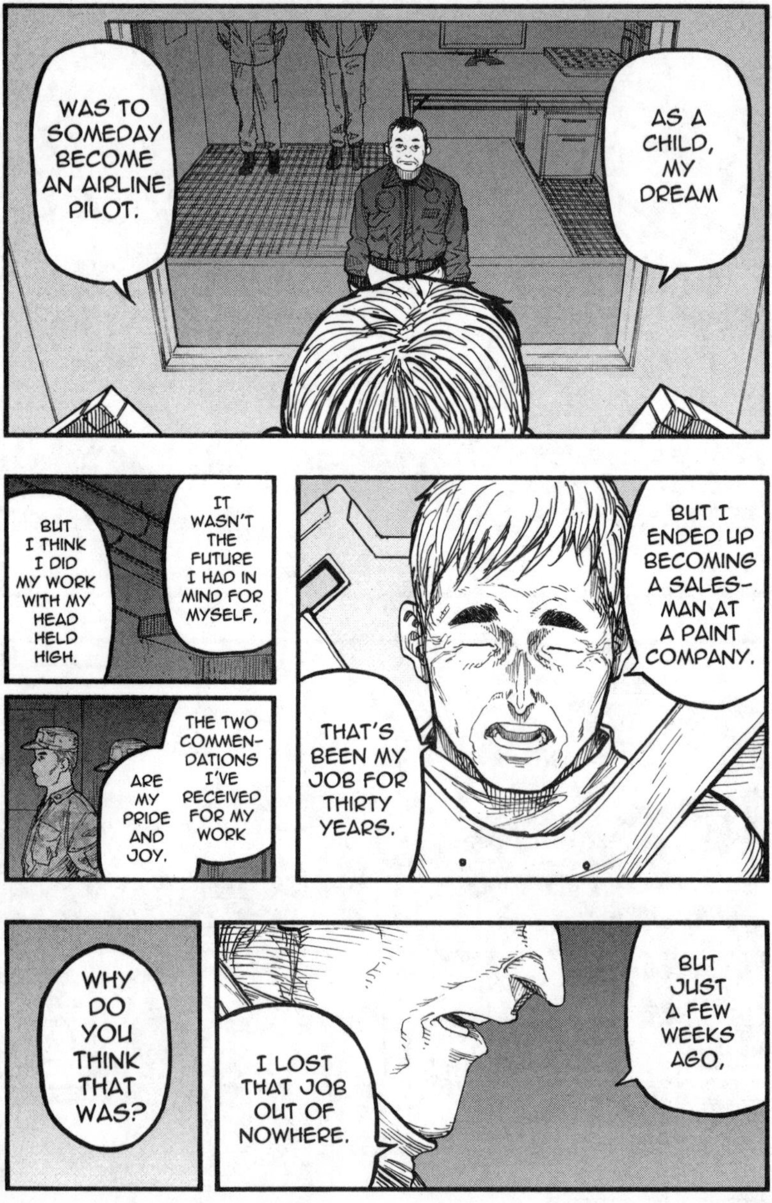
AS A CHILD, MY DREAM
WAS TO SOMEDAY BECOME AN AIRLINE PILOT.
BUT I ENDED UP BECOMING A SALES-MAN AT A PAINT COMPANY.
THAT'S BEEN MY JOB FOR THIRTY YEARS.
IT WASN'T THE FUTURE I HAD IN MIND FOR MYSELF,
BUT I THINK I DID MY WORK WITH MY HEAD HELD HIGH.
THE TWO COMMEN-DATIONS I'VE RECEIVED FOR MY WORK
ARE MY PRIDE AND JOY.
BUT JUST A FEW WEEKS AGO,
I LOST THAT JOB OUT OF NOWHERE.
WHY DO YOU THINK THAT WAS?

NEXT ...

THE PRIME MINISTER WILL BE TAKING THE STAGE.

JUST START THE DAMN THING ALREADY ...

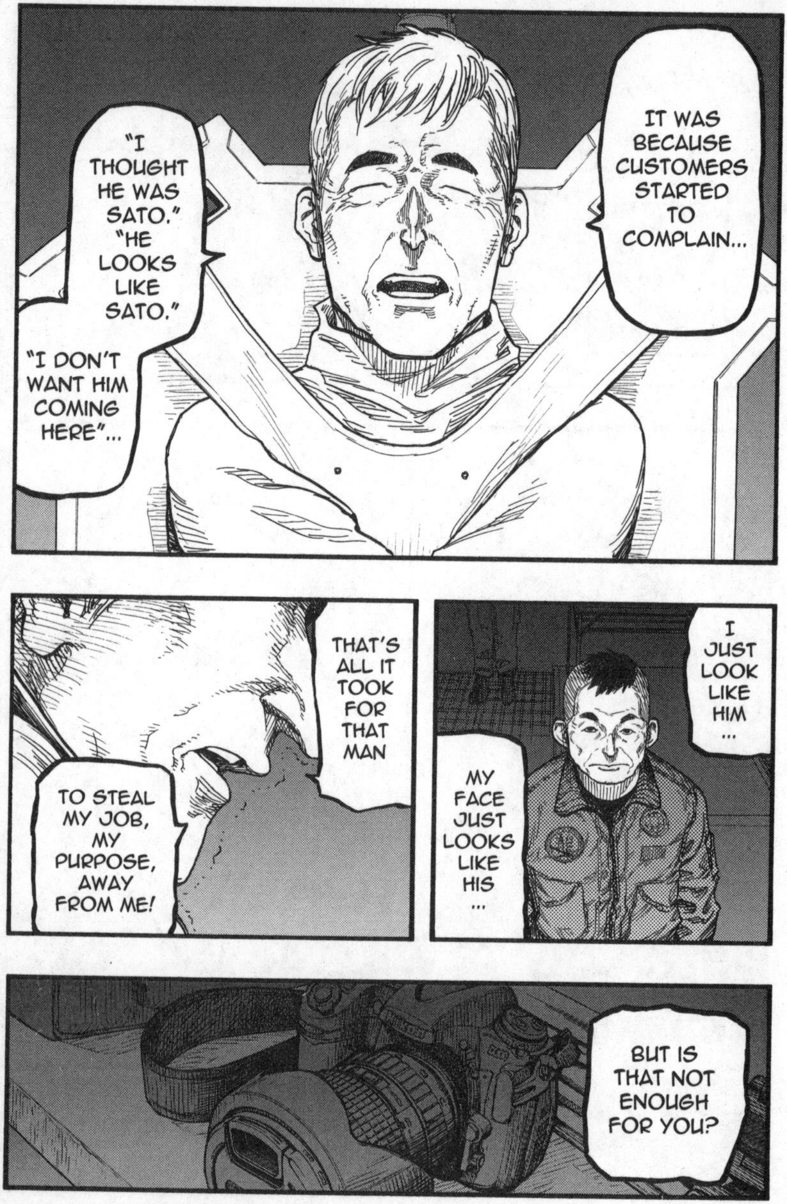
IT WAS BECAUSE CUSTOMERS STARTED TO COMPLAIN...
"I THOUGHT HE WAS SATO." "HE LOOKS LIKE SATO."
"I DON'T WANT HIM COMING HERE"...
I JUST LOOK LIKE HIM ...
MY FACE JUST LOOKS LIKE HIS ...
THAT'S ALL IT TOOK FOR THAT MAN
TO STEAL MY JOB, MY PURPOSE, AWAY FROM ME!
BUT IS THAT NOT ENOUGH FOR YOU?

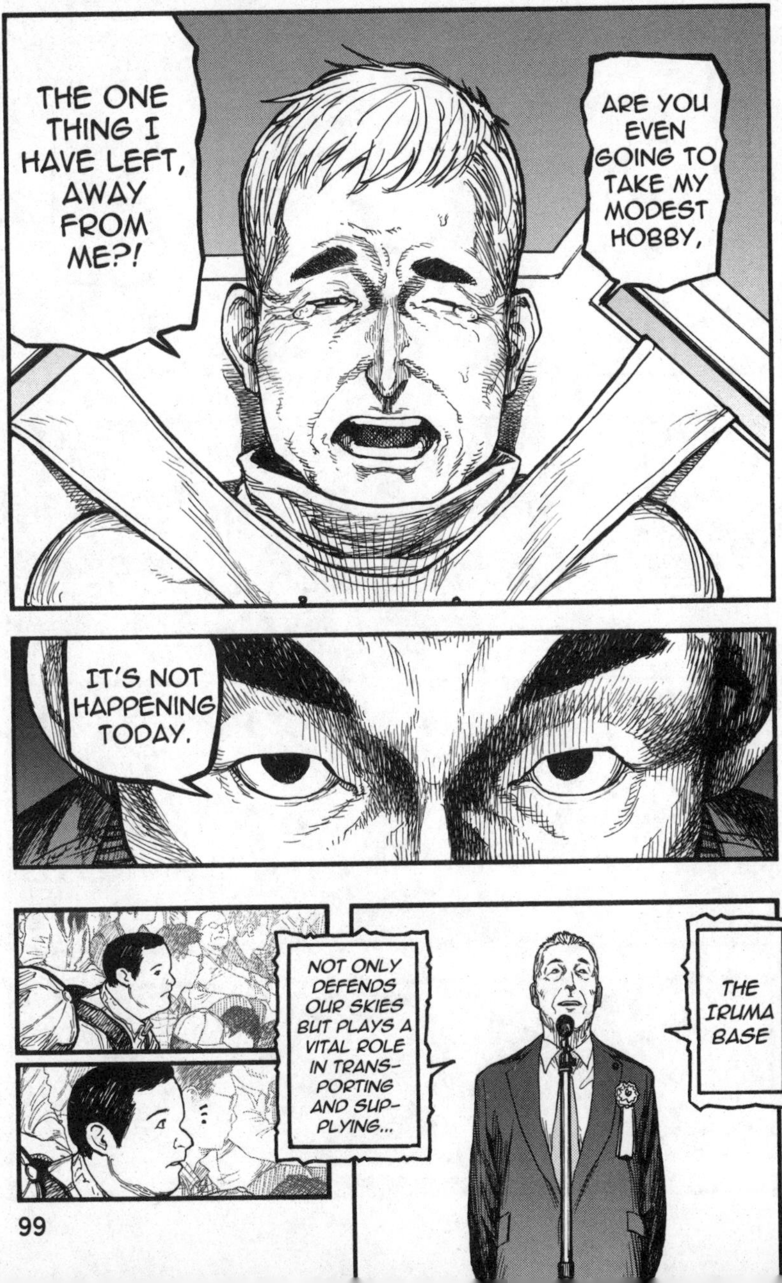
ARE YOU EVEN GOING TO TAKE MY MODEST HOBBY,
THE ONE THING I HAVE LEFT, AWAY FROM ME?!
IT'S NOT HAPPENING TODAY.
THE IRUMA BASE
NOT ONLY DEFENDS OUR SKIES BUT PLAYS A VITAL ROLE IN TRANS-PORTING AND SUP-PLYING...

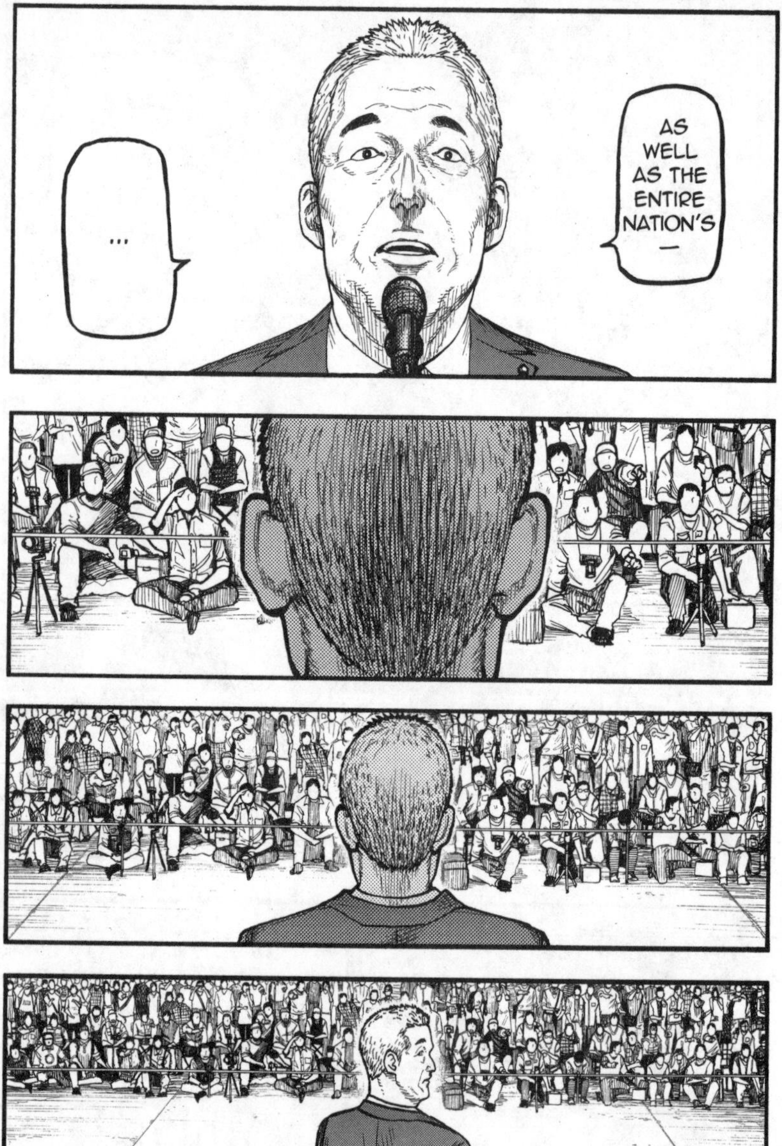
AS WELL AS THE ENTIRE NATION'S —
...

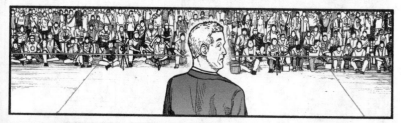

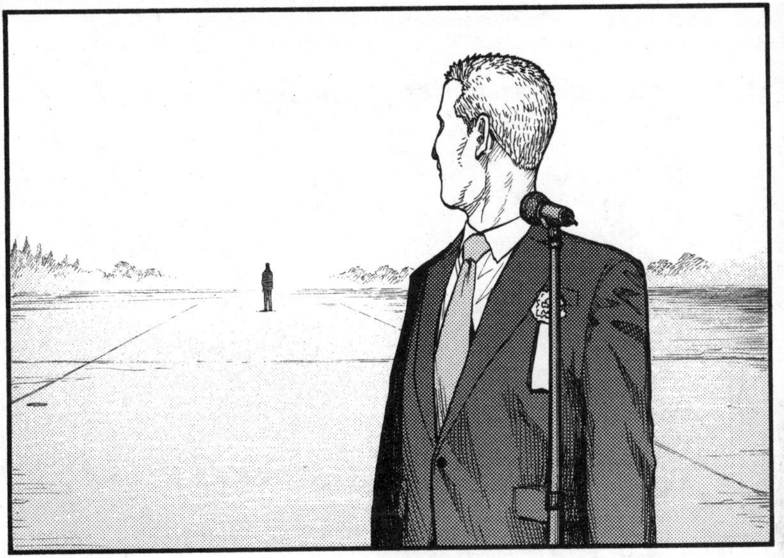

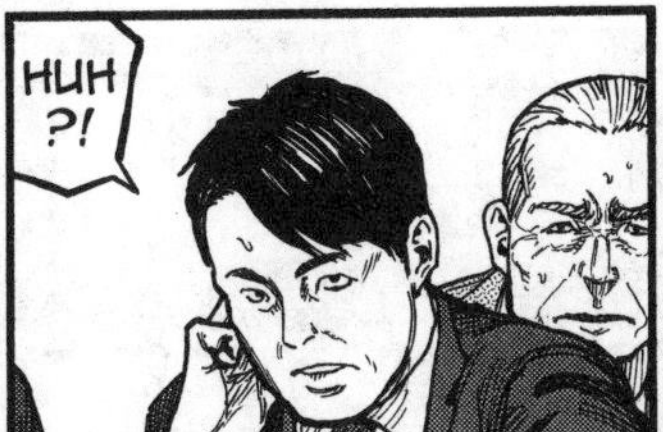
HUH ?!

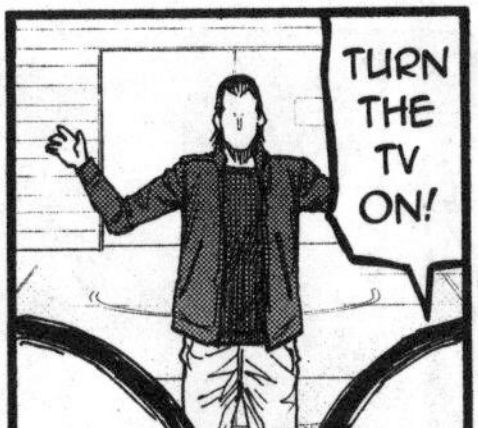
TURN THE TV ON!

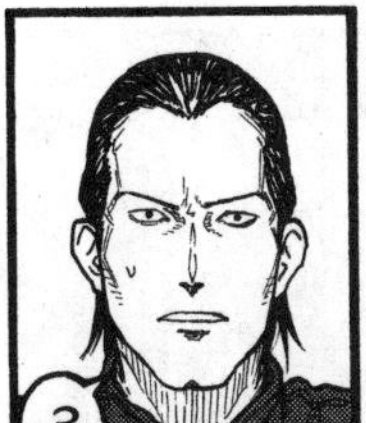
?

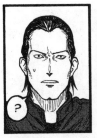

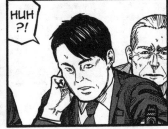

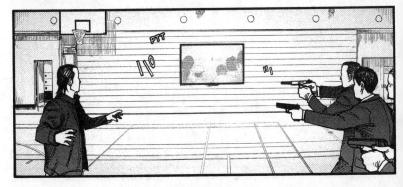

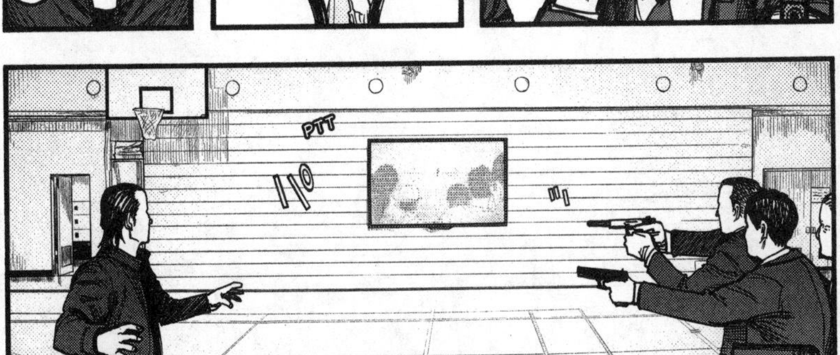
PTT

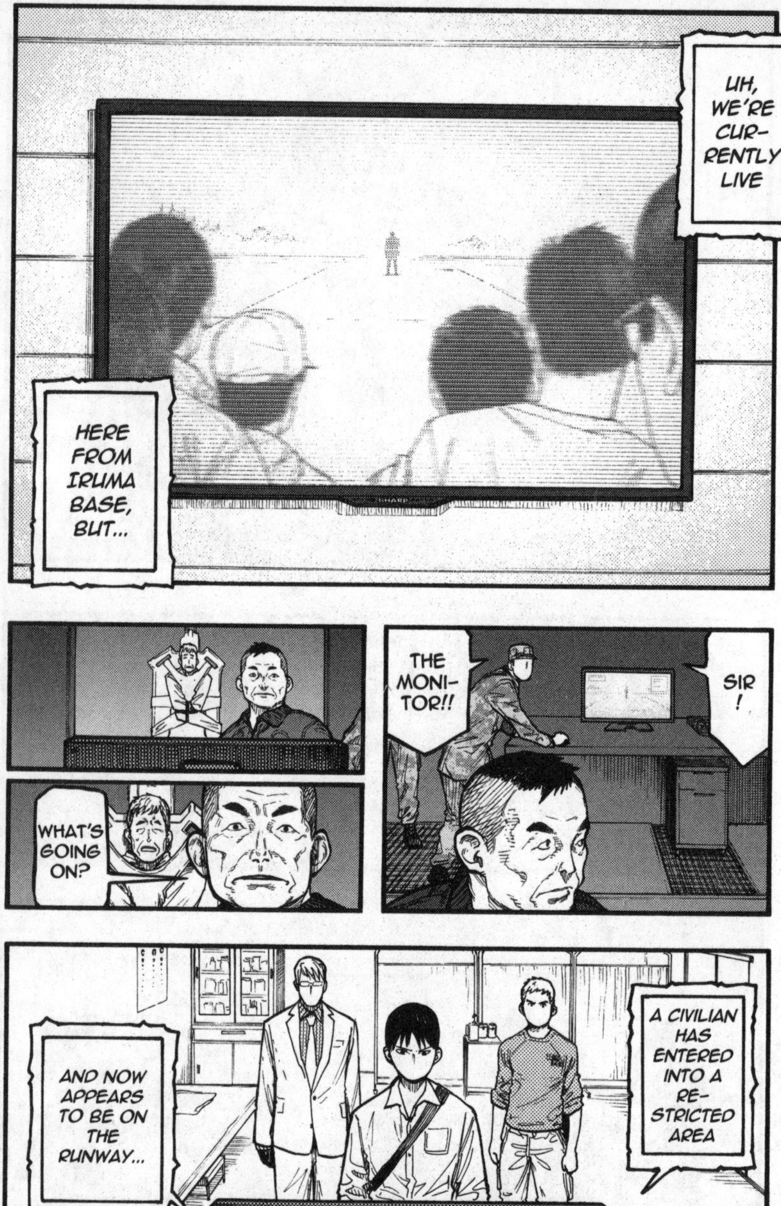
UH, WE'RE CURRENTLY LIVE
HERE FROM IRUMA BASE, BUT...
SIR!
THE MONITOR!!
WHAT'S GOING ON?
A CIVILIAN HAS ENTERED INTO A RESTRICTED AREA
AND NOW APPEARS TO BE ON THE RUNWAY...

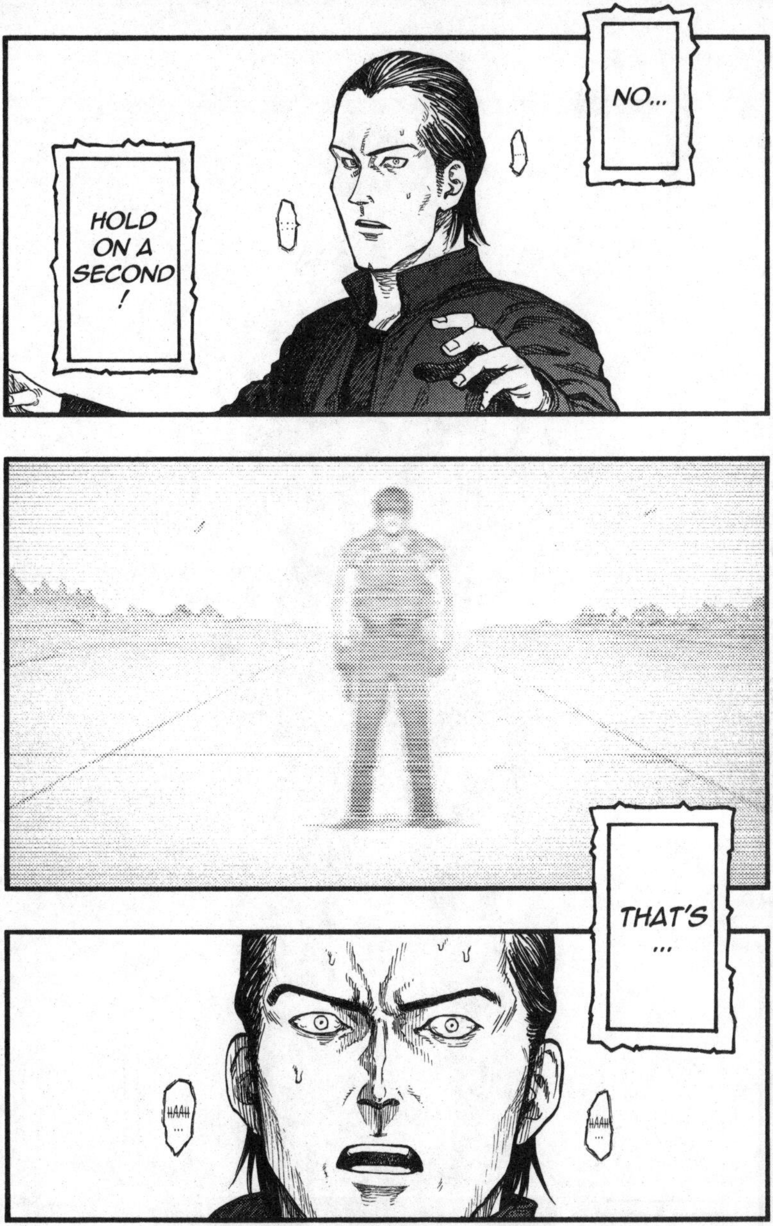
NO...
...
...
HOLD ON A SECOND!
THAT'S ...
HAAH ...
HAAH ...

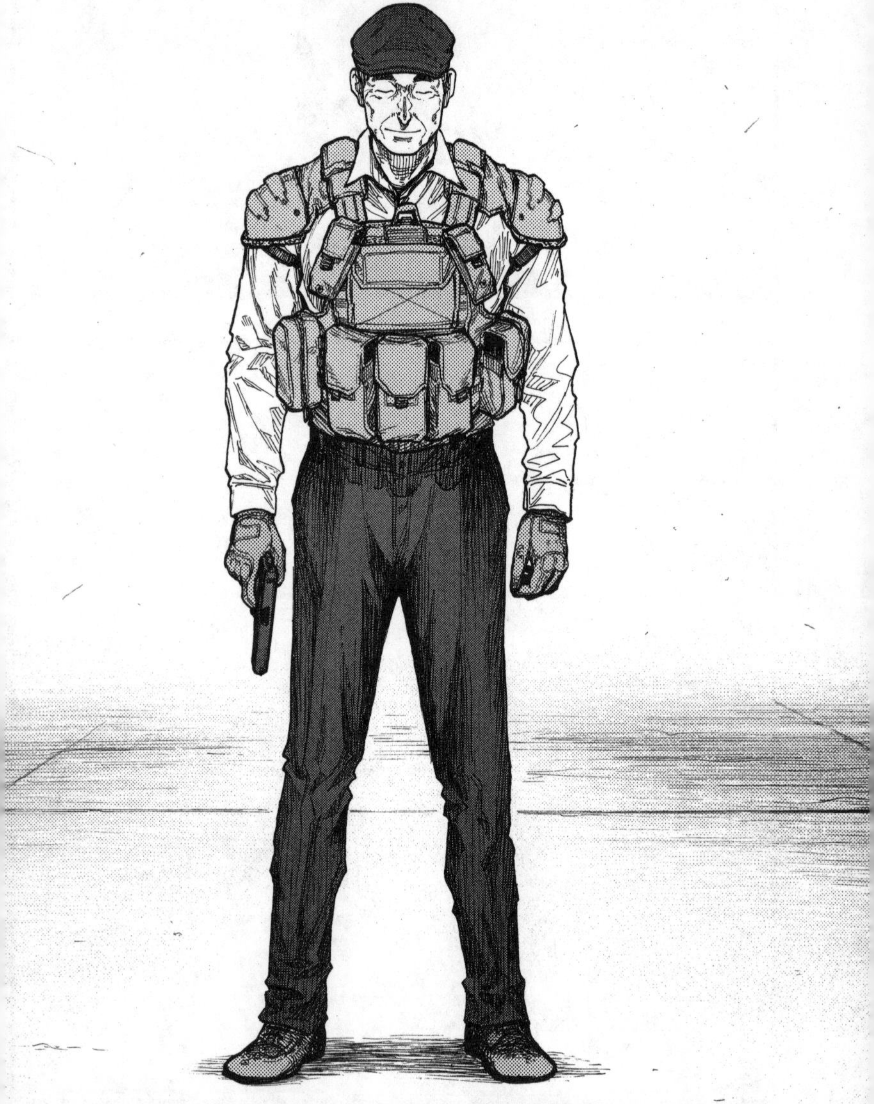

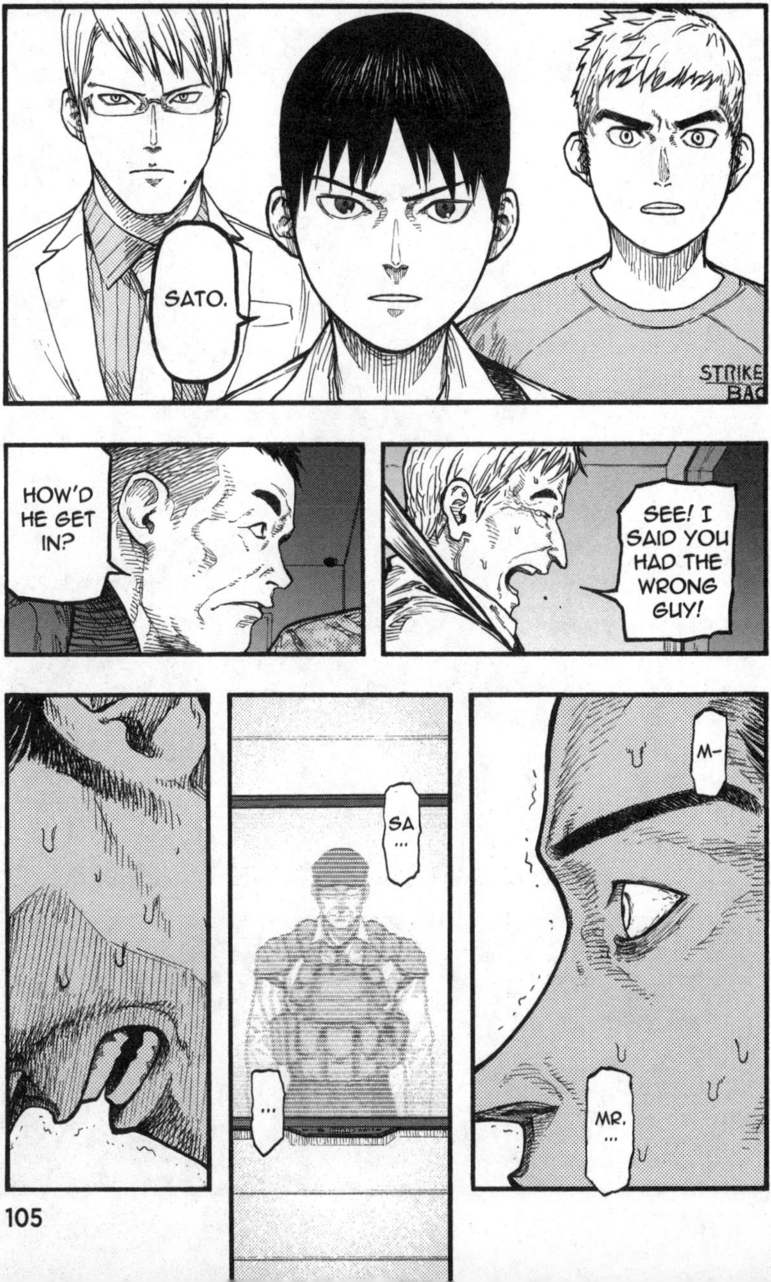
SATO.
STRIKE BAC
SEE! I SAID YOU HAD THE WRONG GUY!
HOW'D HE GET IN?
M-
MR. ...
SA ...
...

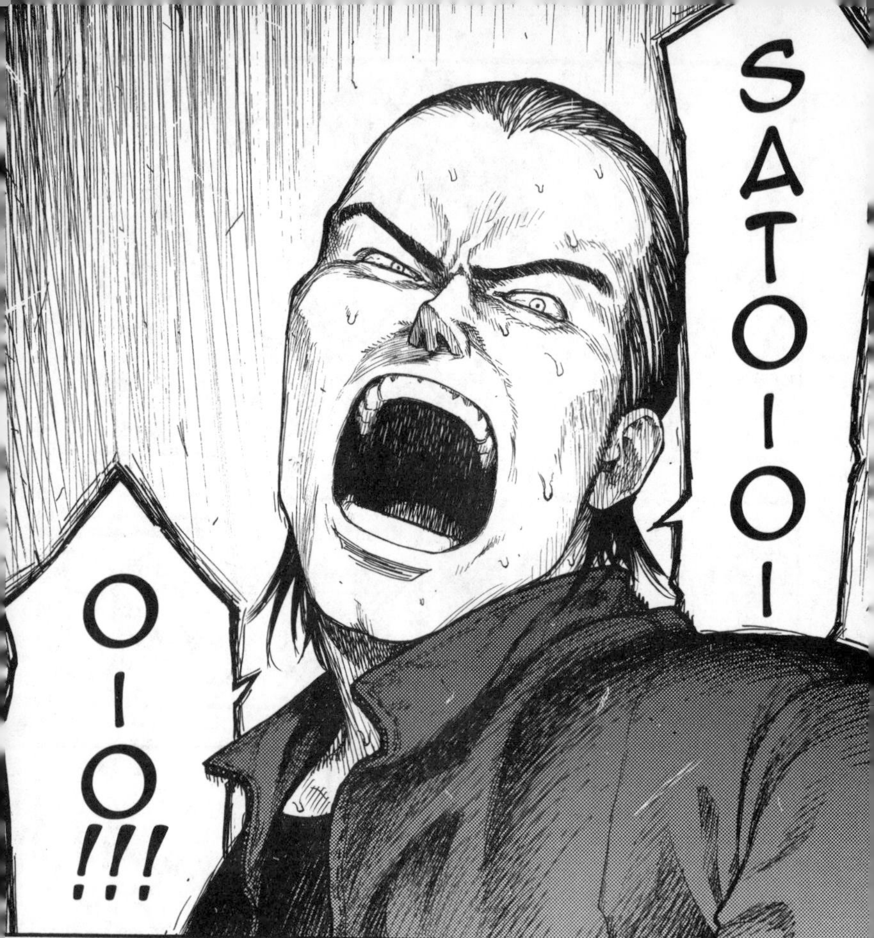
SATO-O-
O-O!!!

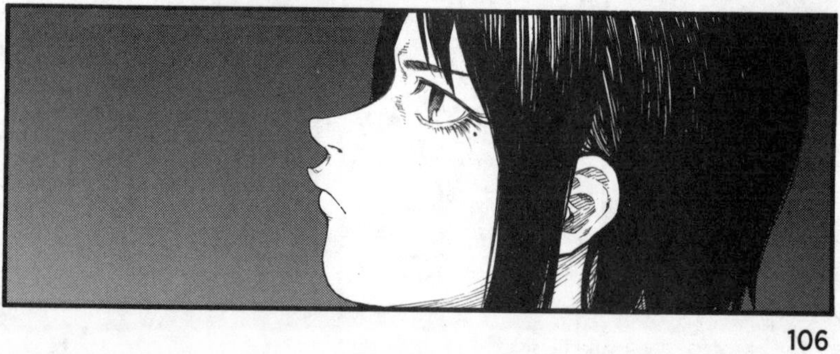

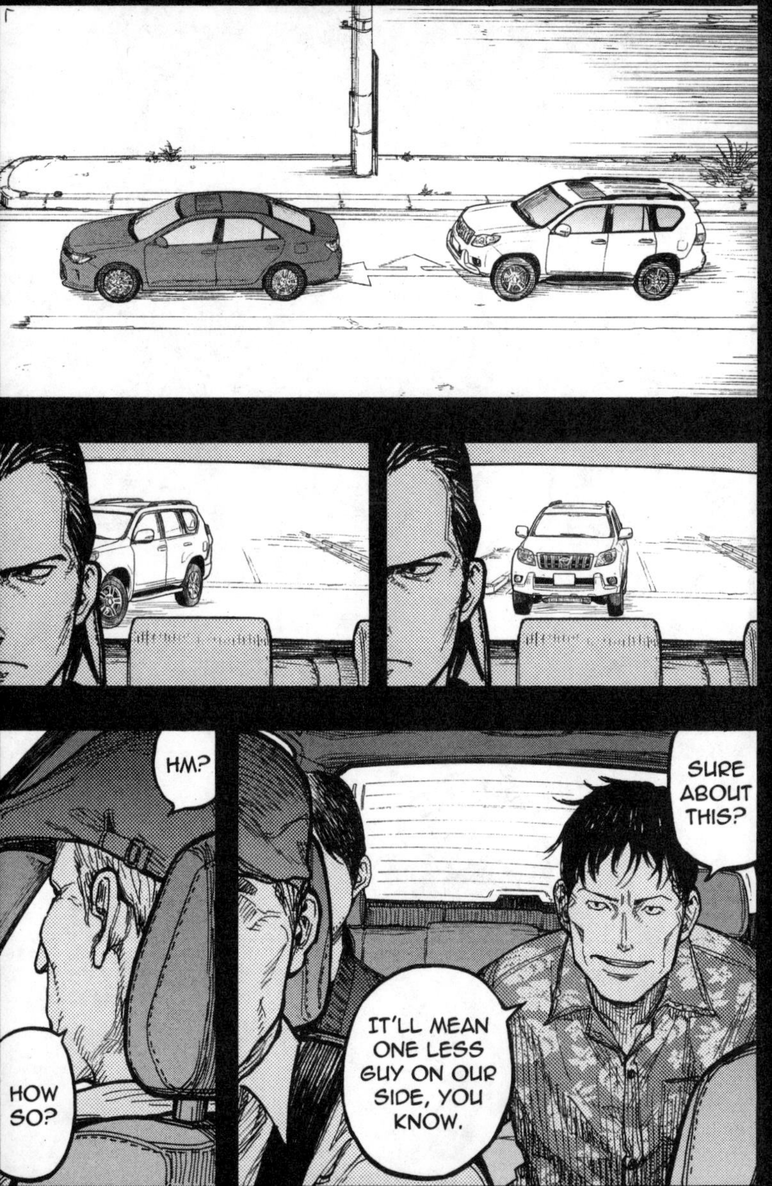
SURE ABOUT THIS?
HM?
IT'LL MEAN ONE LESS GUY ON OUR SIDE, YOU KNOW.
HOW SO?

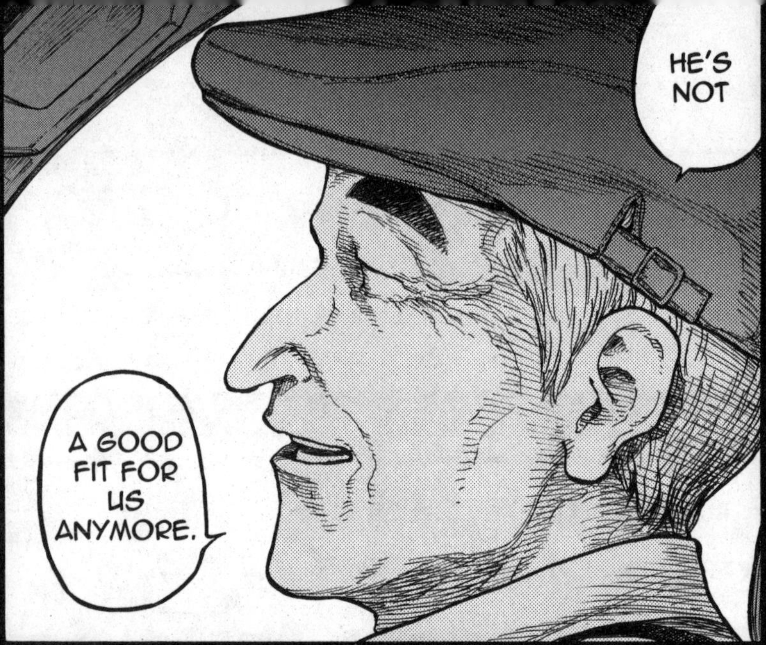
HE'S NOT
A GOOD FIT FOR US ANYMORE.

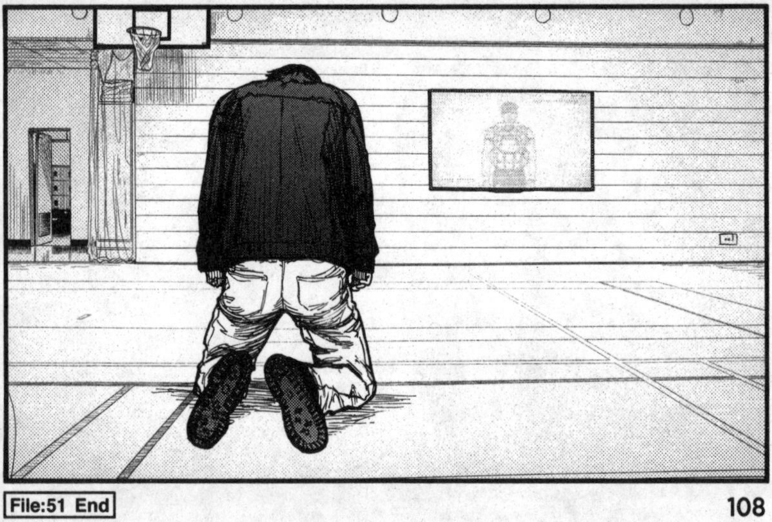

File:51 End

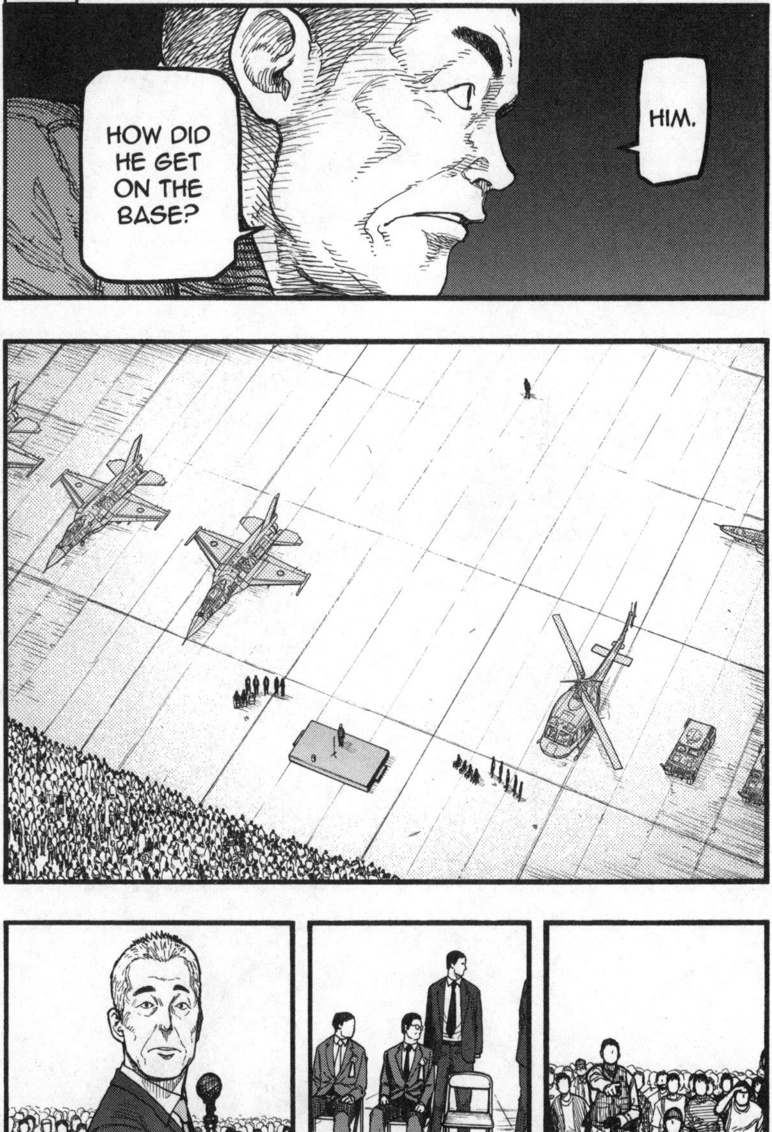
HIM.
HOW DID HE GET ON THE BASE?

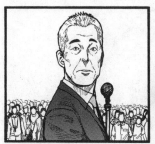

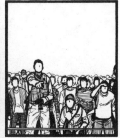

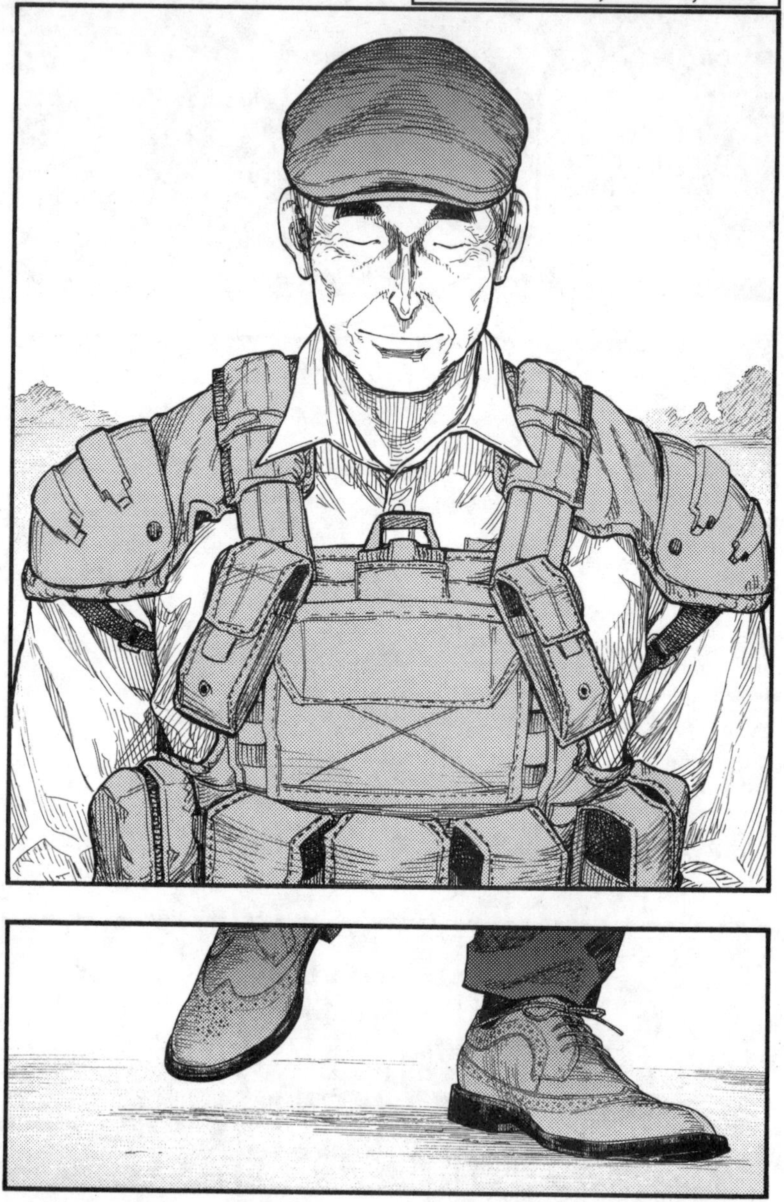

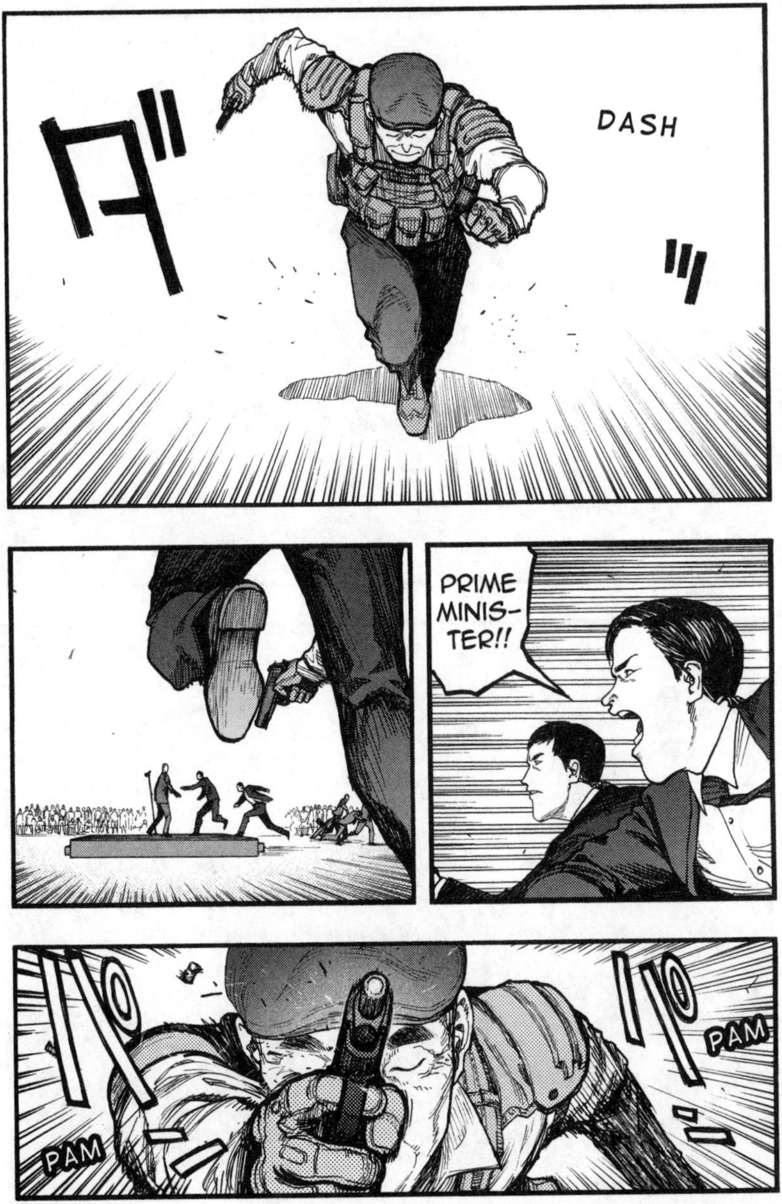
ダッ
DASH
PRIME MINIS-TER!!
PAM
PAM

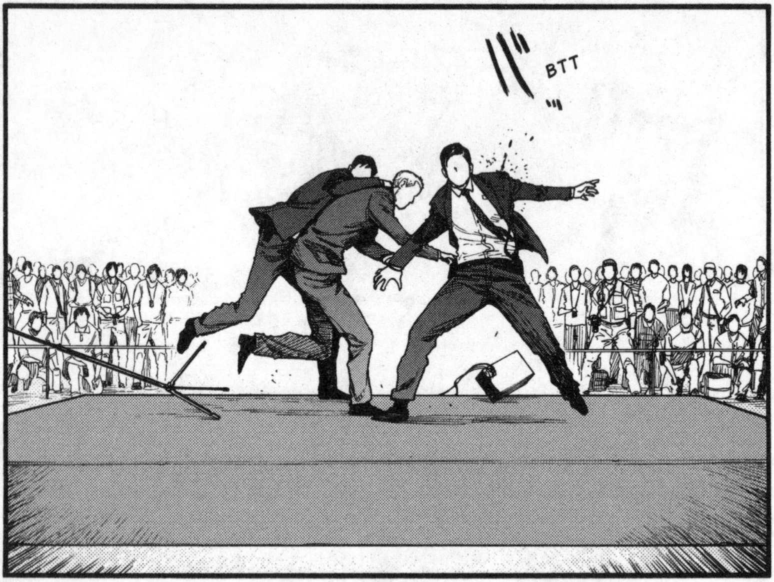
BTT

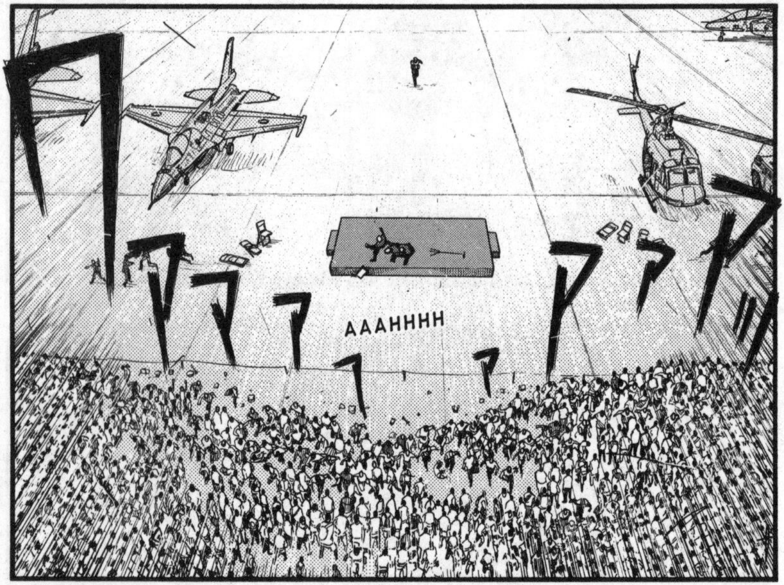
AAAHHHH

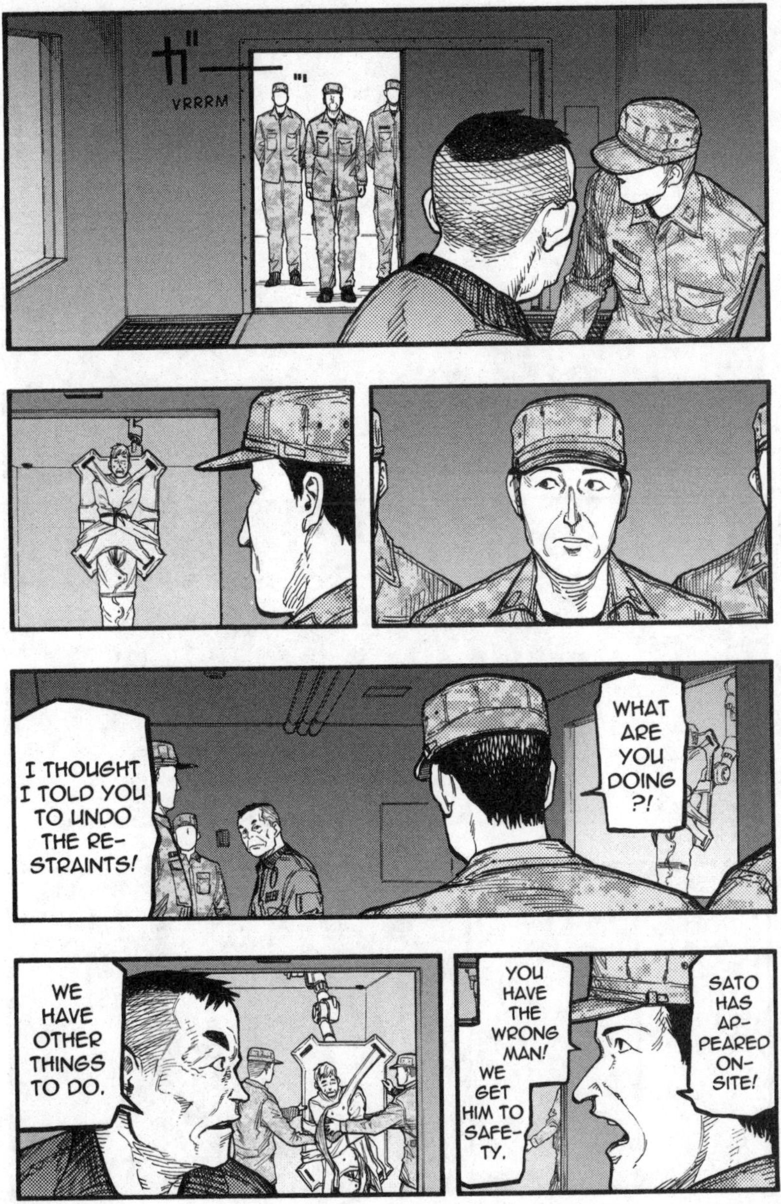
ガー
VRRRM
WHAT ARE YOU DOING?!
I THOUGHT I TOLD YOU TO UNDO THE RESTRAINTS!
SATO HAS APPEARED ON-SITE!
YOU HAVE THE WRONG MAN!
WE GET HIM TO SAFETY.
WE HAVE OTHER THINGS TO DO.

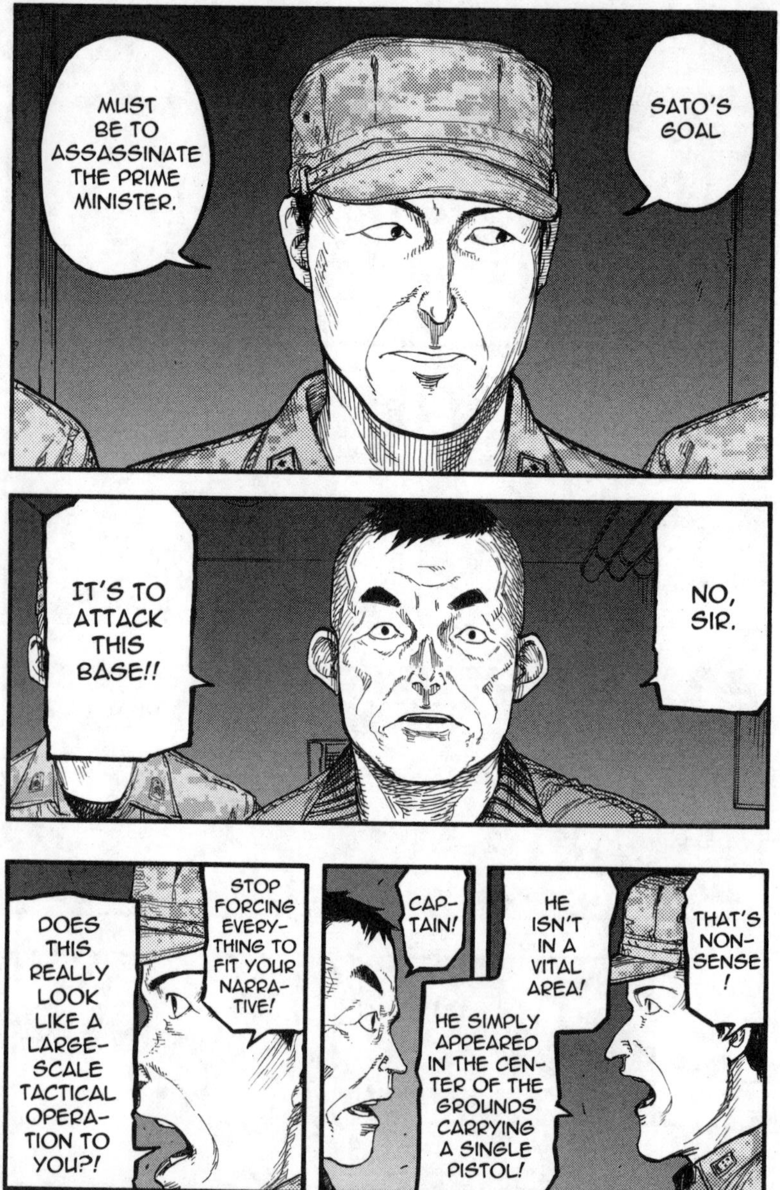
SATO'S GOAL
MUST BE TO ASSASSINATE THE PRIME MINISTER.
NO, SIR.
IT'S TO ATTACK THIS BASE!!
THAT'S NON-SENSE!
HE ISN'T IN A VITAL AREA!
HE SIMPLY APPEARED IN THE CEN-TER OF THE GROUNDS CARRYING A SINGLE PISTOL!
CAP-TAIN!
STOP FORCING EVERY-THING TO FIT YOUR NARRA-TIVE!
DOES THIS REALLY LOOK LIKE A LARGE-SCALE TACTICAL OPERA-TION TO YOU?!

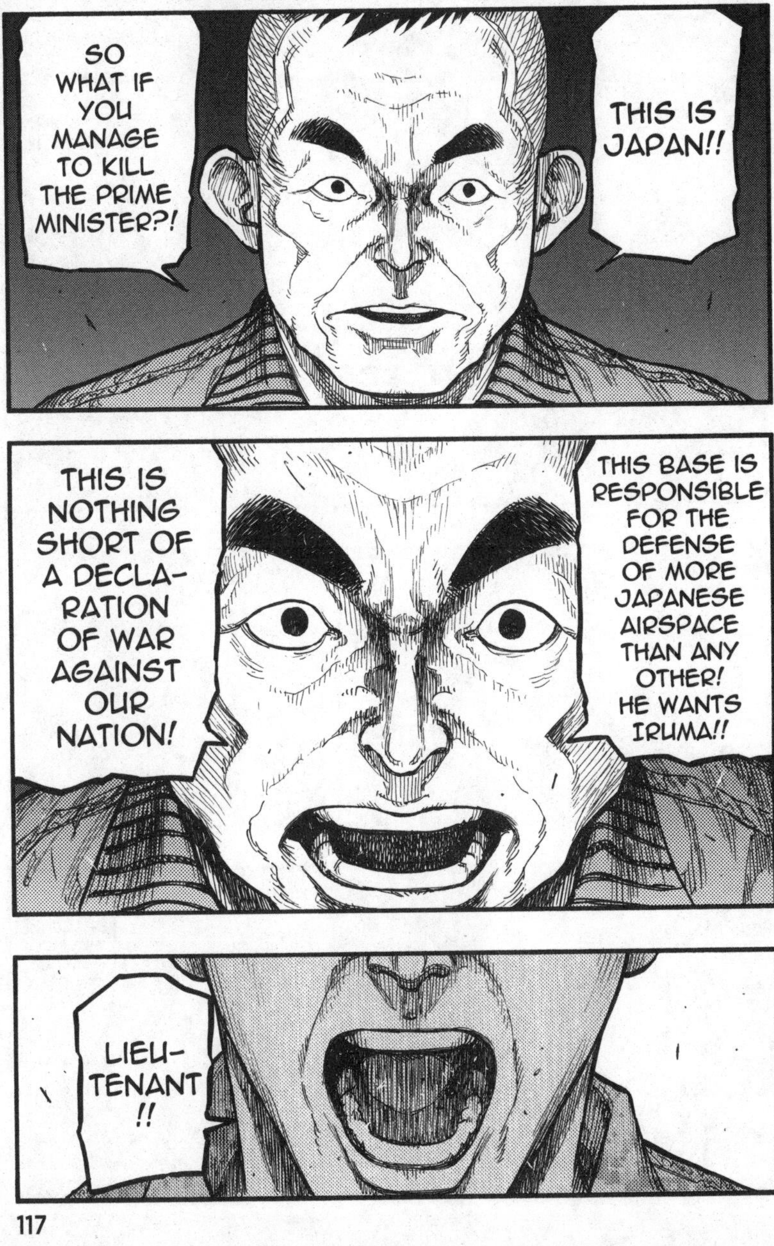
SO WHAT IF YOU MANAGE TO KILL THE PRIME MINISTER?!
THIS IS JAPAN!!
THIS IS NOTHING SHORT OF A DECLA-RATION OF WAR AGAINST OUR NATION!
THIS BASE IS RESPONSIBLE FOR THE DEFENSE OF MORE JAPANESE AIRSPACE THAN ANY OTHER! HE WANTS IRUMA!!
LIEU-TENANT!!

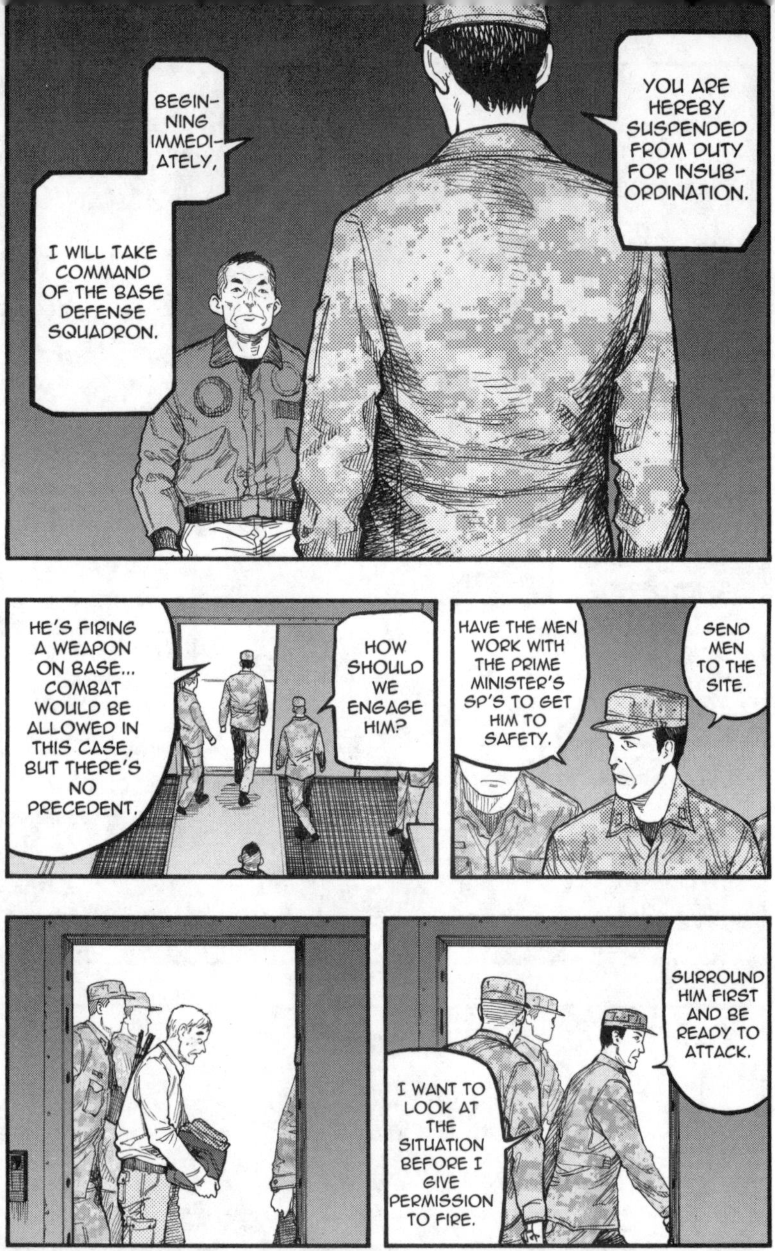
YOU ARE HEREBY SUSPENDED FROM DUTY FOR INSUBORDINATION.
BEGINNING IMMEDIATELY,
I WILL TAKE COMMAND OF THE BASE DEFENSE SQUADRON.
SEND MEN TO THE SITE.
HAVE THE MEN WORK WITH THE PRIME MINISTER'S SP'S TO GET HIM TO SAFETY.
HOW SHOULD WE ENGAGE HIM?
HE'S FIRING A WEAPON ON BASE... COMBAT WOULD BE ALLOWED IN THIS CASE, BUT THERE'S NO PRECEDENT.
SURROUND HIM FIRST AND BE READY TO ATTACK.
I WANT TO LOOK AT THE SITUATION BEFORE I GIVE PERMISSION TO FIRE.

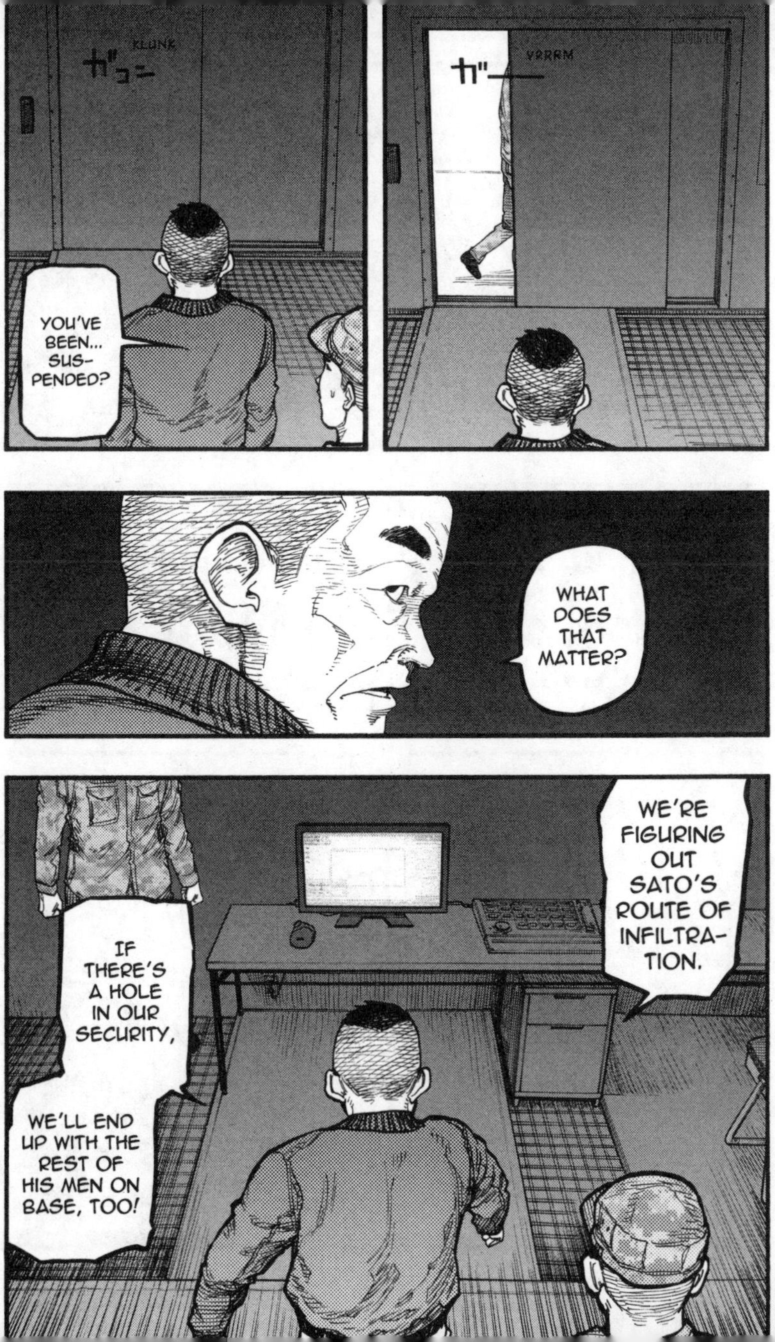
ガー
VRRRM
KLUNK
YOU'VE BEEN... SUS-PENDED?
WHAT DOES THAT MATTER?
WE'RE FIGURING OUT SATO'S ROUTE OF INFILTRA-TION.
IF THERE'S A HOLE IN OUR SECURITY,
WE'LL END UP WITH THE REST OF HIS MEN ON BASE, TOO!

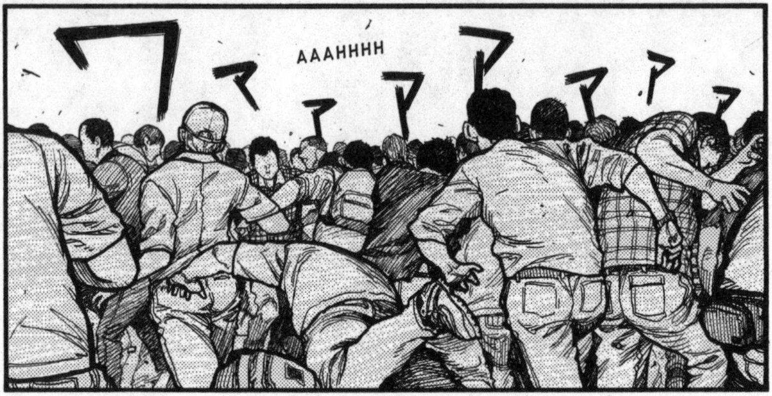
AAAHHHH
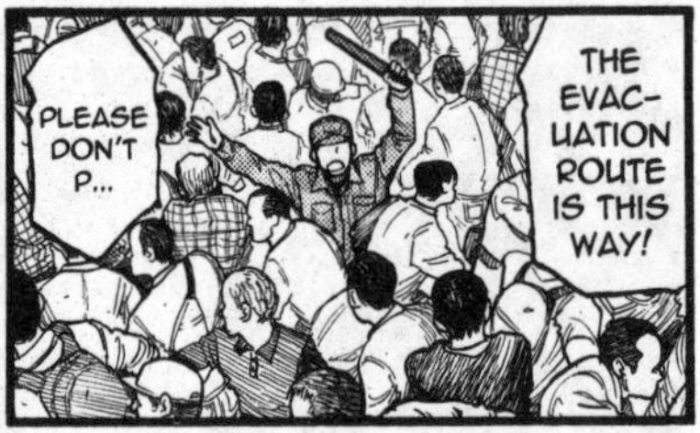
THE EVAC-UATION ROUTE IS THIS WAY!
PLEASE DON'T P...
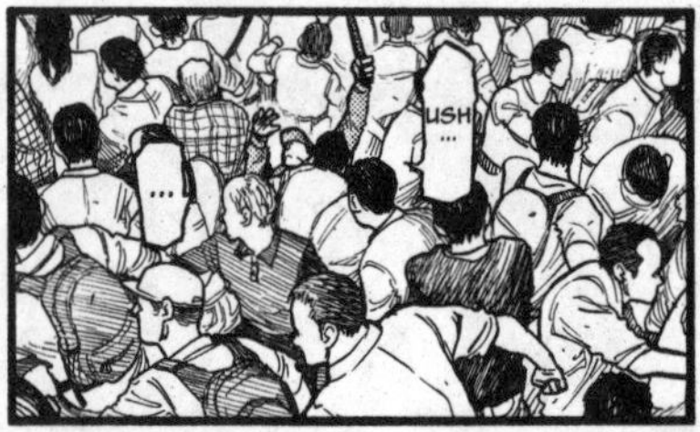
USH ...
...
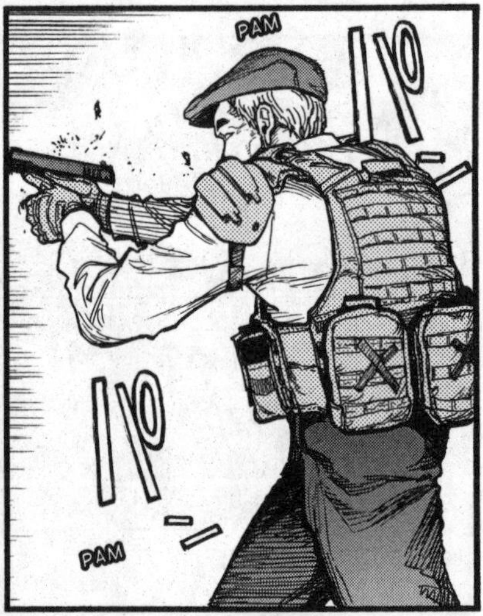
PAM
PAM
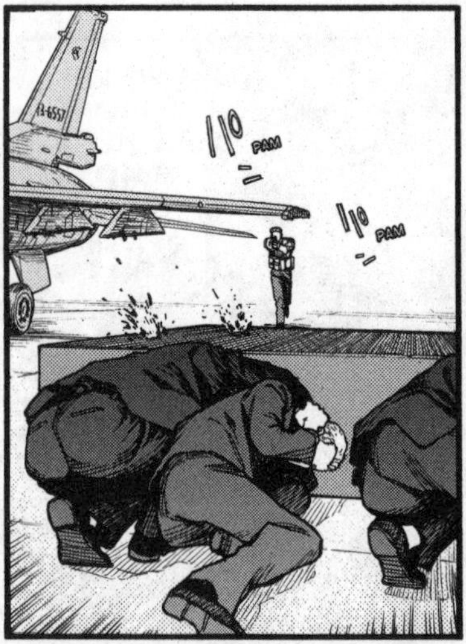
PAM
PAM

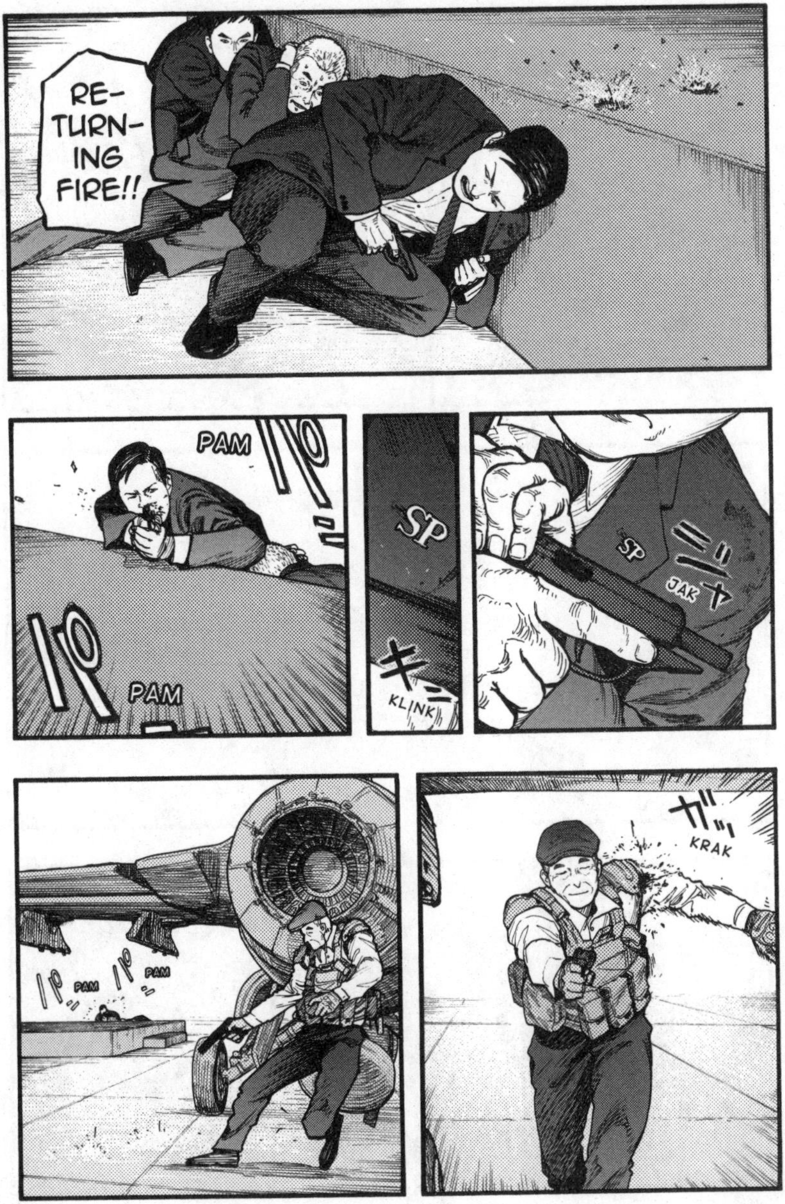
RE-
TURN-
ING
FIRE!!
SP
JAK
SP
KLINK
PAM
PAM
KRAK
PAM
PAM

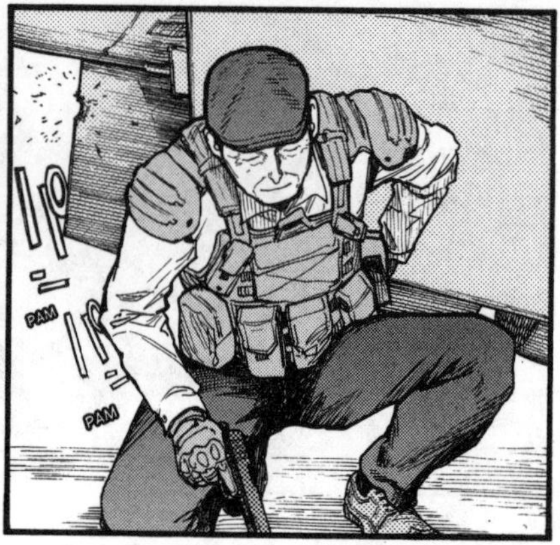
PAM
PAM
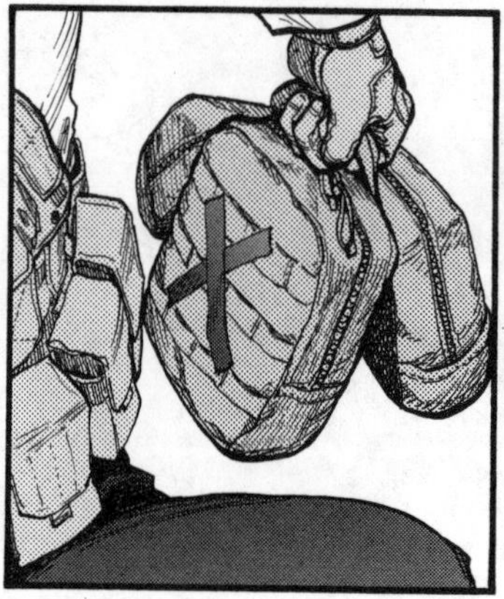
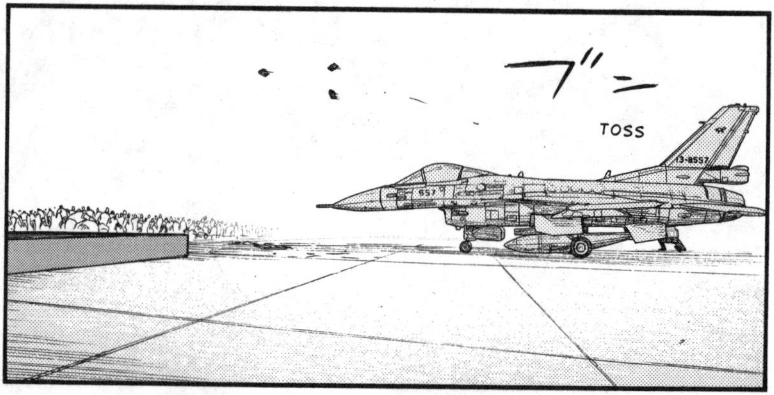
ブン
TOSS
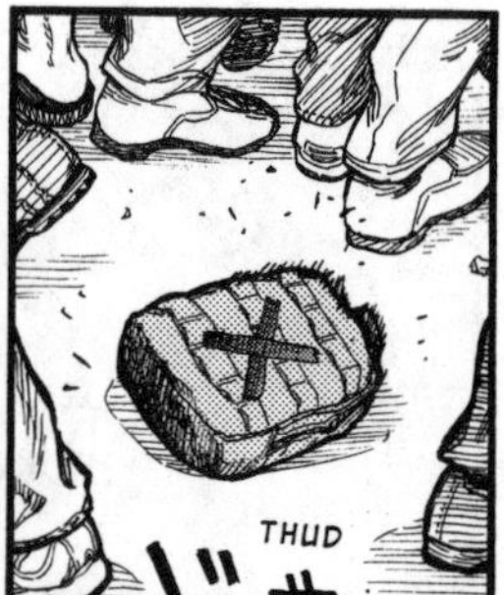
THUD
ドサッ
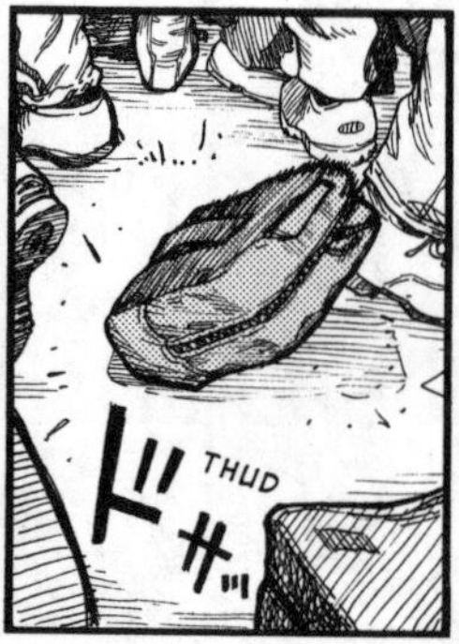
ドサッ
THUD
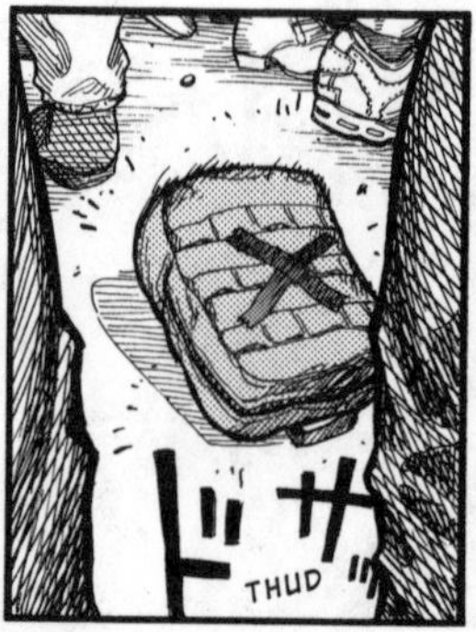
ドザッ
THUD

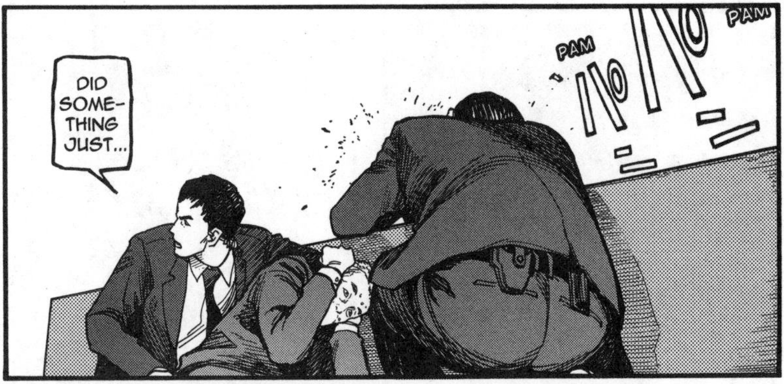
PAM
PAM
DID SOMETHING JUST...

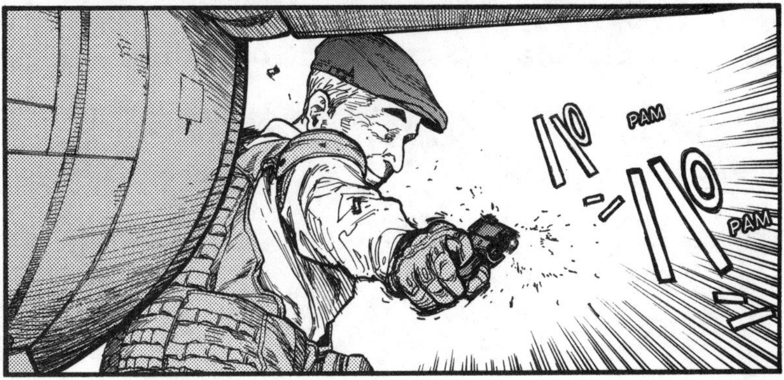
PAM
PAM

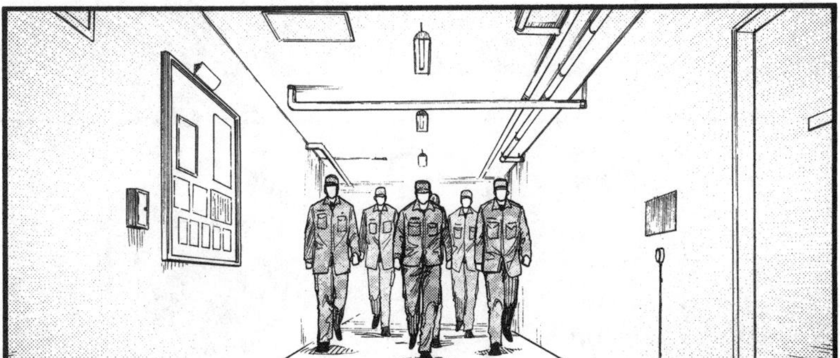

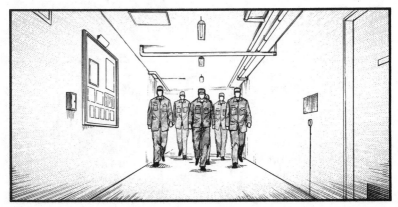

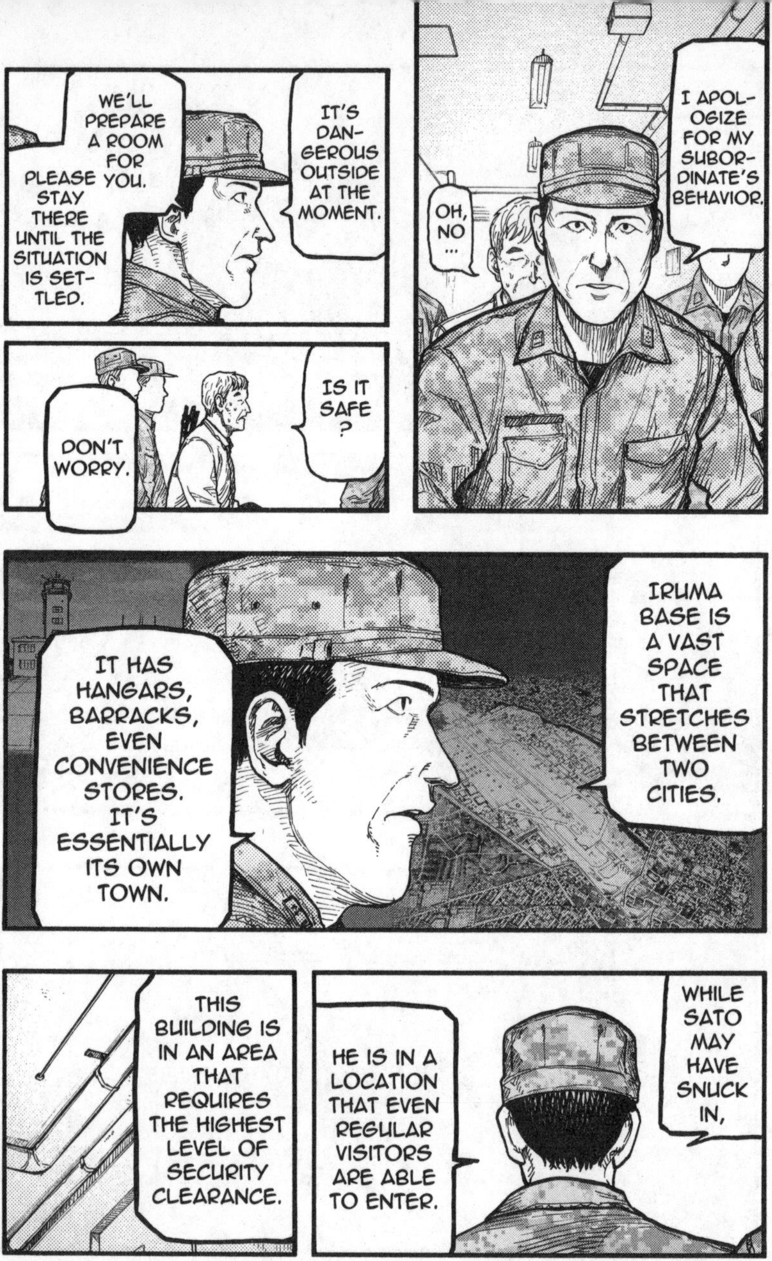
I APOLOGIZE FOR MY SUBORDINATE'S BEHAVIOR.
OH, NO ...
IT'S DANGEROUS OUTSIDE AT THE MOMENT.
WE'LL PREPARE A ROOM FOR YOU. PLEASE STAY THERE UNTIL THE SITUATION IS SETTLED.
IS IT SAFE?
DON'T WORRY.
IRUMA BASE IS A VAST SPACE THAT STRETCHES BETWEEN TWO CITIES.
IT HAS HANGARS, BARRACKS, EVEN CONVENIENCE STORES. IT'S ESSENTIALLY ITS OWN TOWN.
WHILE SATO MAY HAVE SNUCK IN,
HE IS IN A LOCATION THAT EVEN REGULAR VISITORS ARE ABLE TO ENTER.
THIS BUILDING IS IN AN AREA THAT REQUIRES THE HIGHEST LEVEL OF SECURITY CLEARANCE.

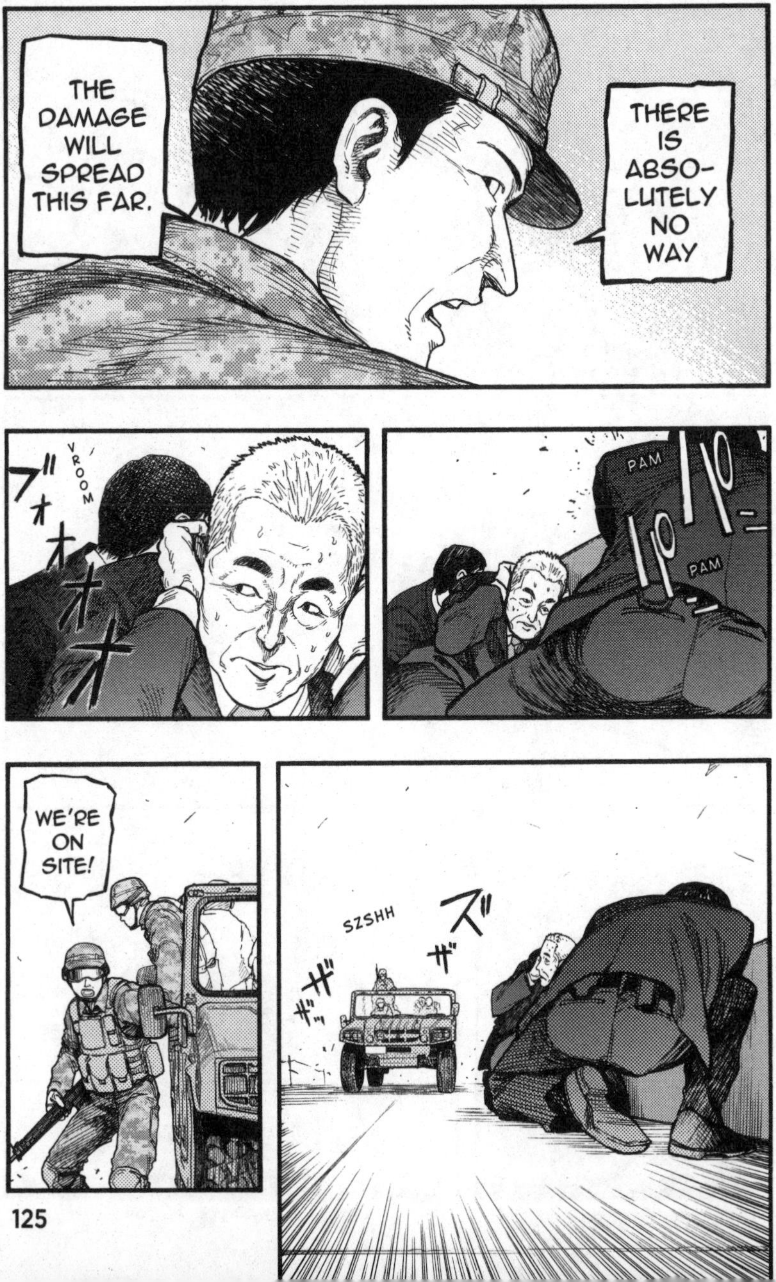
THERE IS ABSO-LUTELY NO WAY
THE DAMAGE WILL SPREAD THIS FAR.
PAM
PAM
VROOM
SZSHH
WE'RE ON SITE!

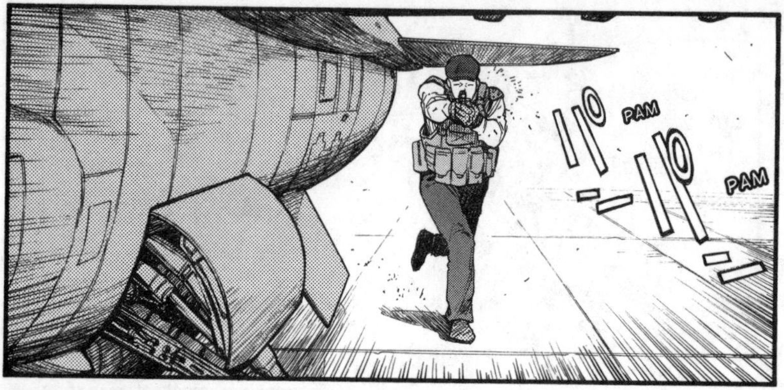
PAM
PAM
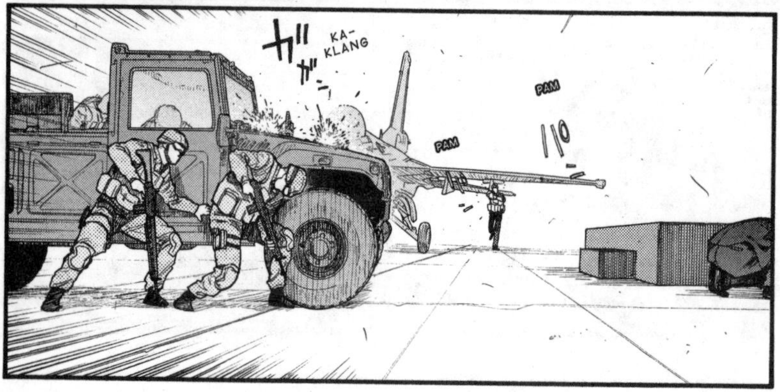
KA-KLANG
PAM
PAM
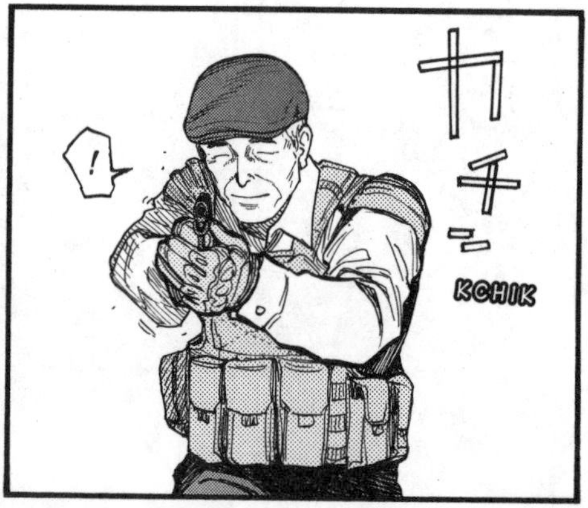
!
KCHIK
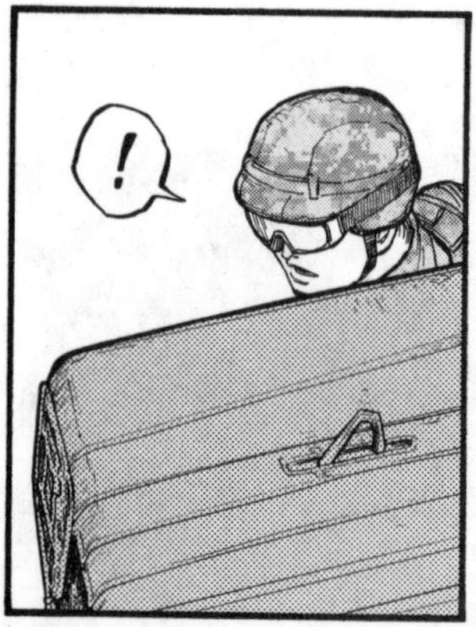
!

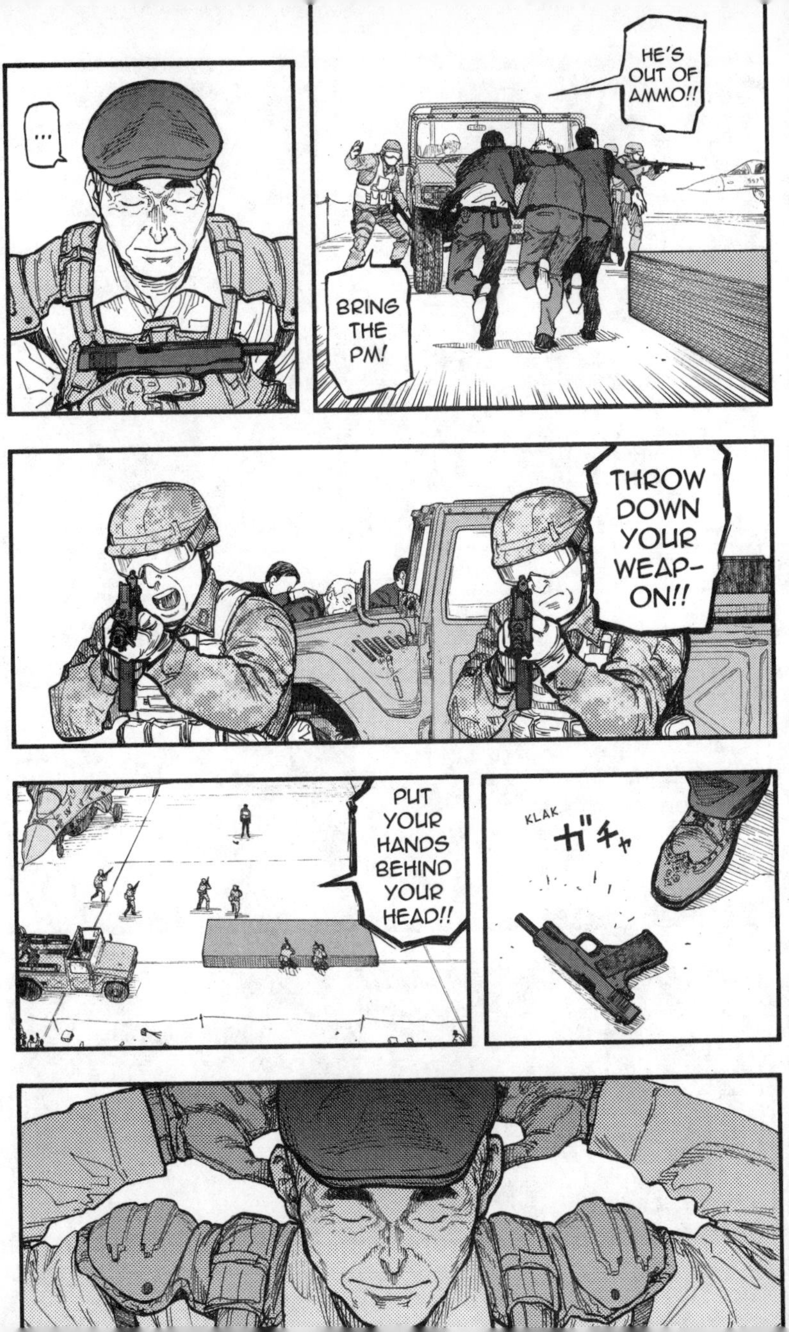
HE'S OUT OF AMMO!!
BRING THE PM!
...
THROW DOWN YOUR WEAP-ON!!
KLAK
ガチャ
PUT YOUR HANDS BEHIND YOUR HEAD!!

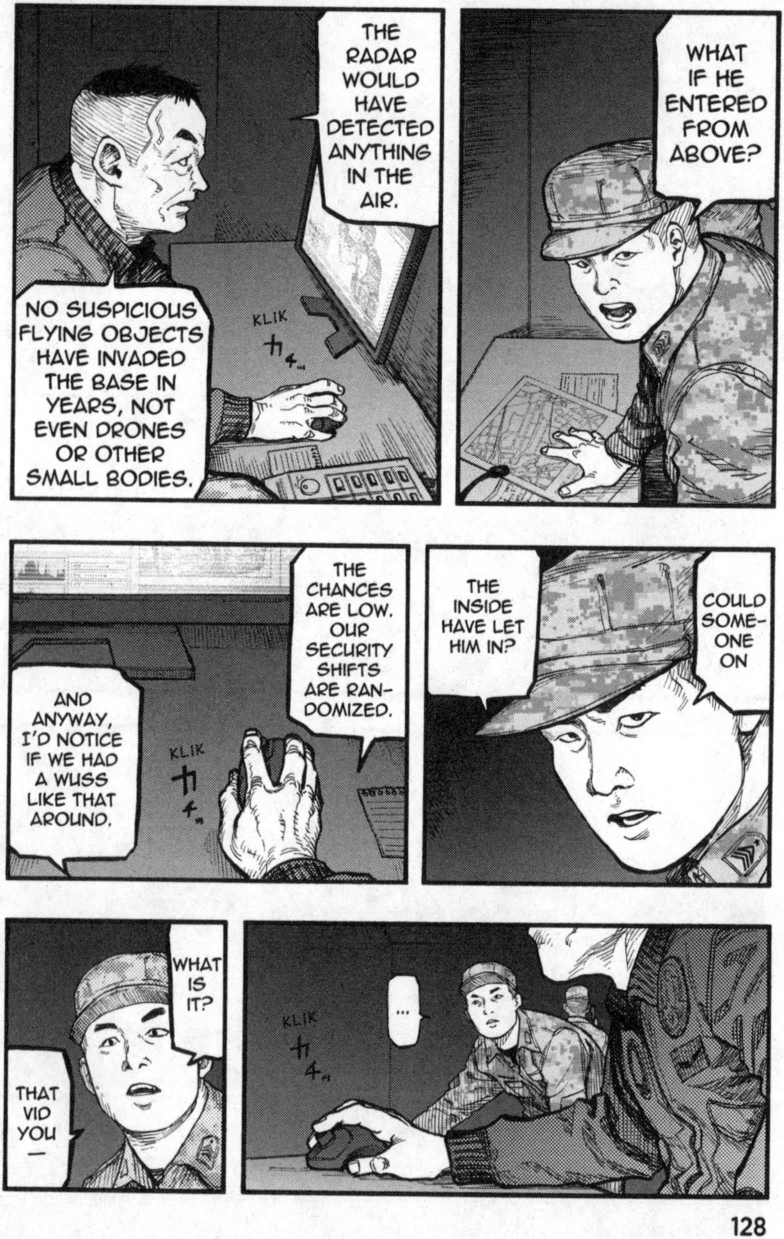
WHAT IF HE ENTERED FROM ABOVE?
THE RADAR WOULD HAVE DETECTED ANYTHING IN THE AIR.
KLIK
NO SUSPICIOUS FLYING OBJECTS HAVE INVADED THE BASE IN YEARS, NOT EVEN DRONES OR OTHER SMALL BODIES.
COULD SOME-ONE ON
THE INSIDE HAVE LET HIM IN?
THE CHANCES ARE LOW. OUR SECURITY SHIFTS ARE RAN-DOMIZED.
KLIK
AND ANYWAY, I'D NOTICE IF WE HAD A WUSS LIKE THAT AROUND.
...
KLIK
WHAT IS IT?
THAT VID YOU —

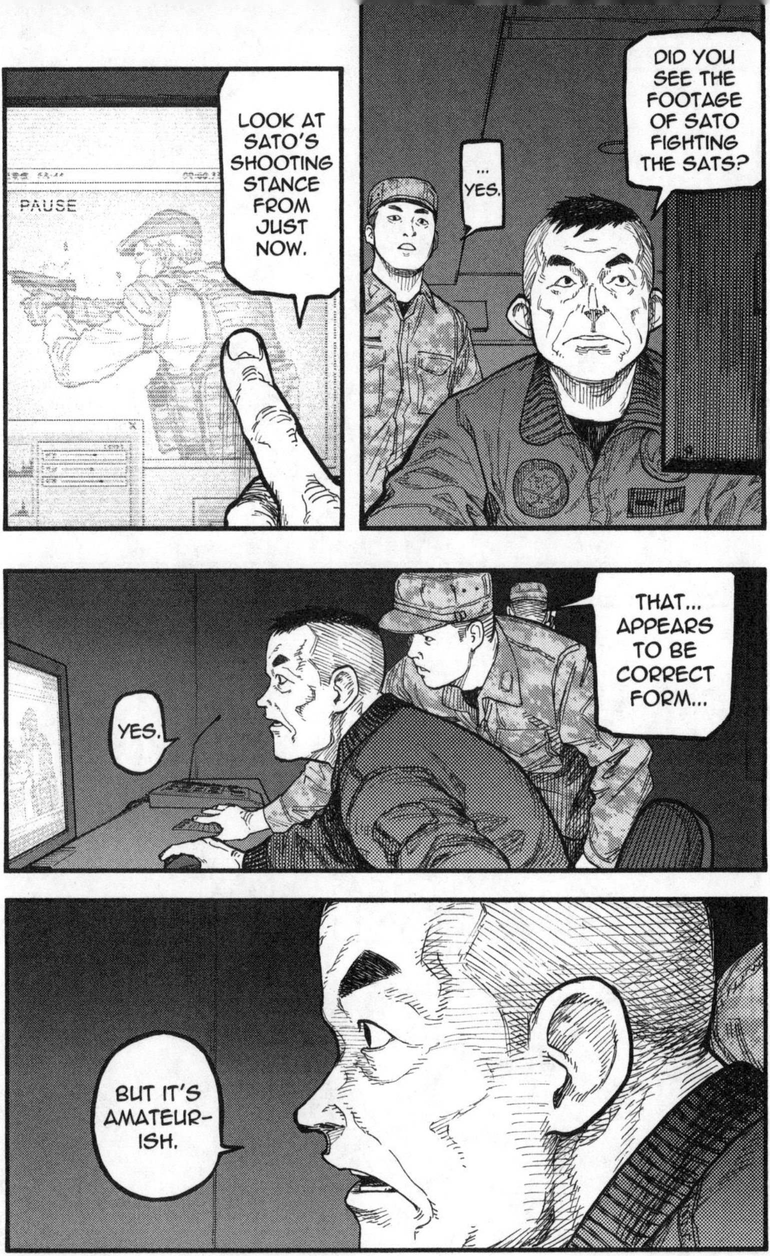
DID YOU SEE THE FOOTAGE OF SATO FIGHTING THE SATS?
... YES.
LOOK AT SATO'S SHOOTING STANCE FROM JUST NOW.
PAUSE
THAT... APPEARS TO BE CORRECT FORM...
YES.
BUT IT'S AMATEUR-ISH.

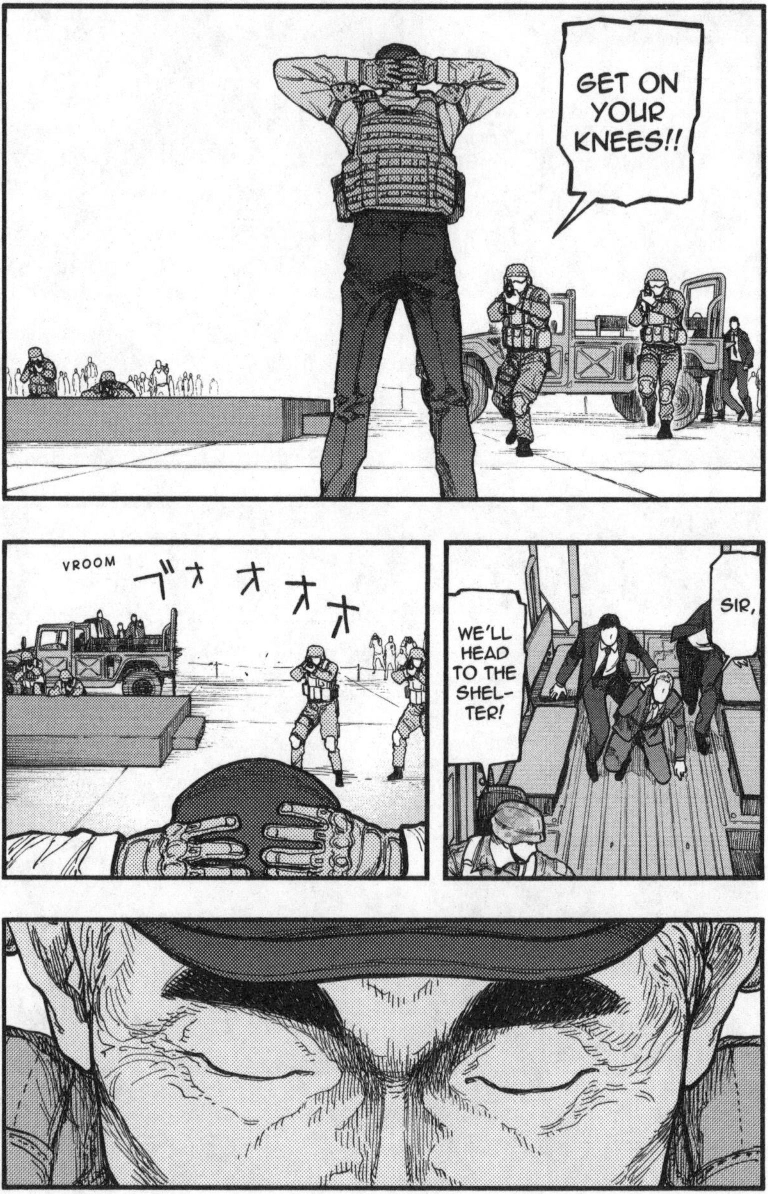
GET ON YOUR KNEES!!
SIR,
WE'LL HEAD TO THE SHEL-TER!
VROOM
ブォオオオ

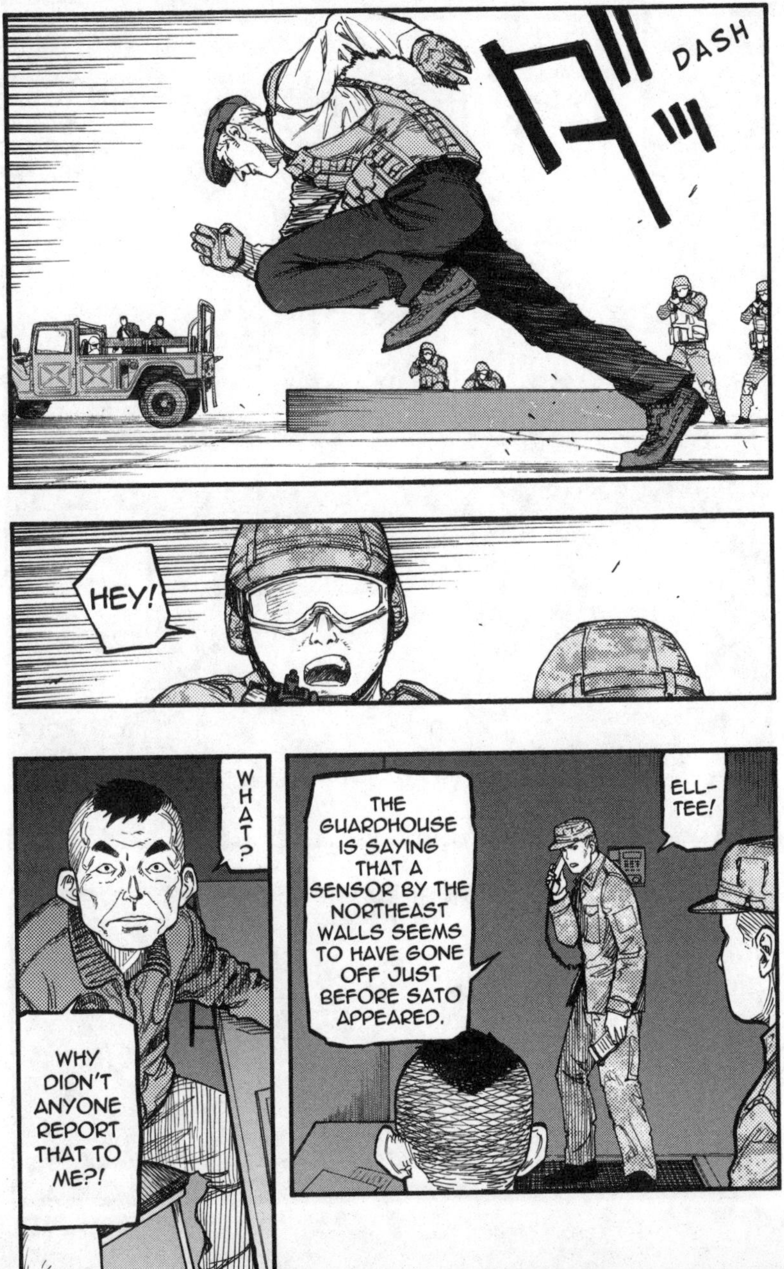
ダッ
DASH
HEY!
ELL-TEE!
THE GUARDHOUSE IS SAYING THAT A SENSOR BY THE NORTHEAST WALLS SEEMS TO HAVE GONE OFF JUST BEFORE SATO APPEARED.
WHAT?
WHY DIDN'T ANYONE REPORT THAT TO ME?!

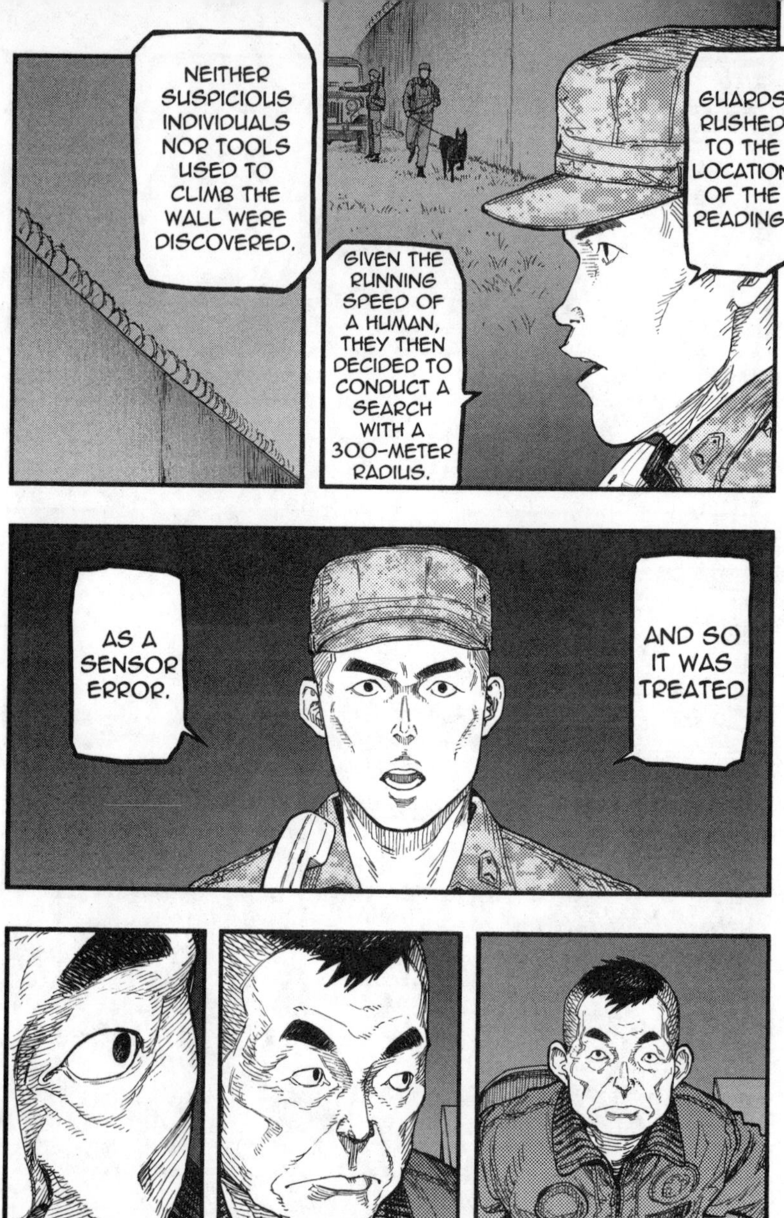
GUARDS RUSHED TO THE LOCATION OF THE READING.
GIVEN THE RUNNING SPEED OF A HUMAN, THEY THEN DECIDED TO CONDUCT A SEARCH WITH A 300-METER RADIUS.
NEITHER SUSPICIOUS INDIVIDUALS NOR TOOLS USED TO CLIMB THE WALL WERE DISCOVERED.
AND SO IT WAS TREATED
AS A SENSOR ERROR.

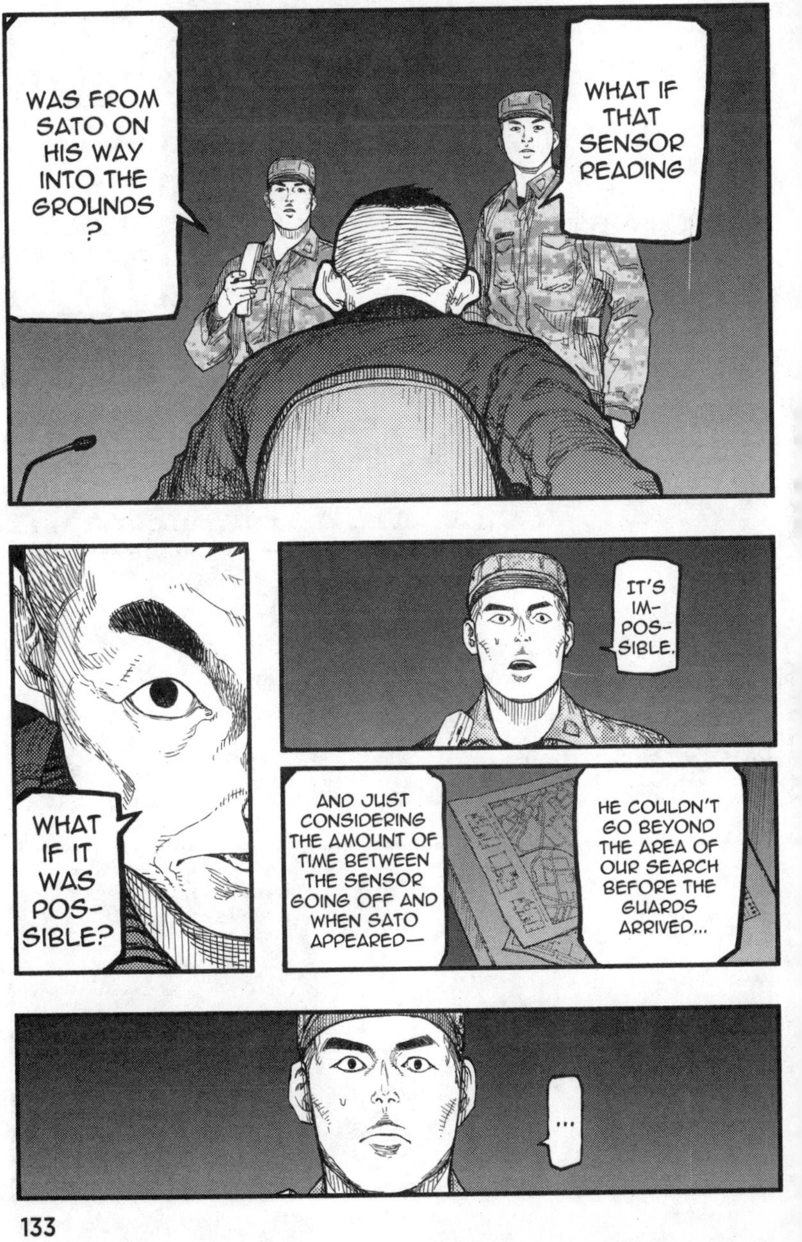
WHAT IF THAT SENSOR READING
WAS FROM SATO ON HIS WAY INTO THE GROUNDS ?
IT'S IM-POS-SIBLE.
HE COULDN'T GO BEYOND THE AREA OF OUR SEARCH BEFORE THE GUARDS ARRIVED...
AND JUST CONSIDERING THE AMOUNT OF TIME BETWEEN THE SENSOR GOING OFF AND WHEN SATO APPEARED—
WHAT IF IT WAS POS-SIBLE?
...

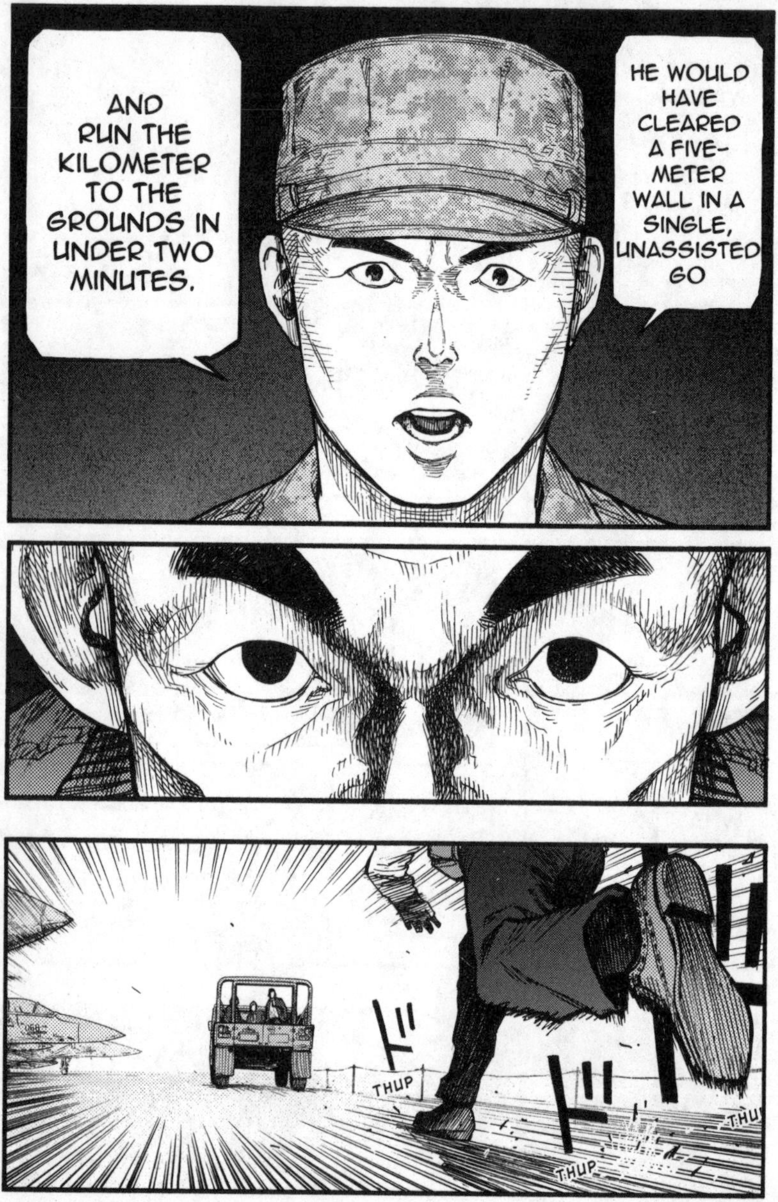
HE WOULD HAVE CLEARED A FIVE-METER WALL IN A SINGLE, UNASSISTED GO
AND RUN THE KILOMETER TO THE GROUNDS IN UNDER TWO MINUTES.
THU
THUP
THUP

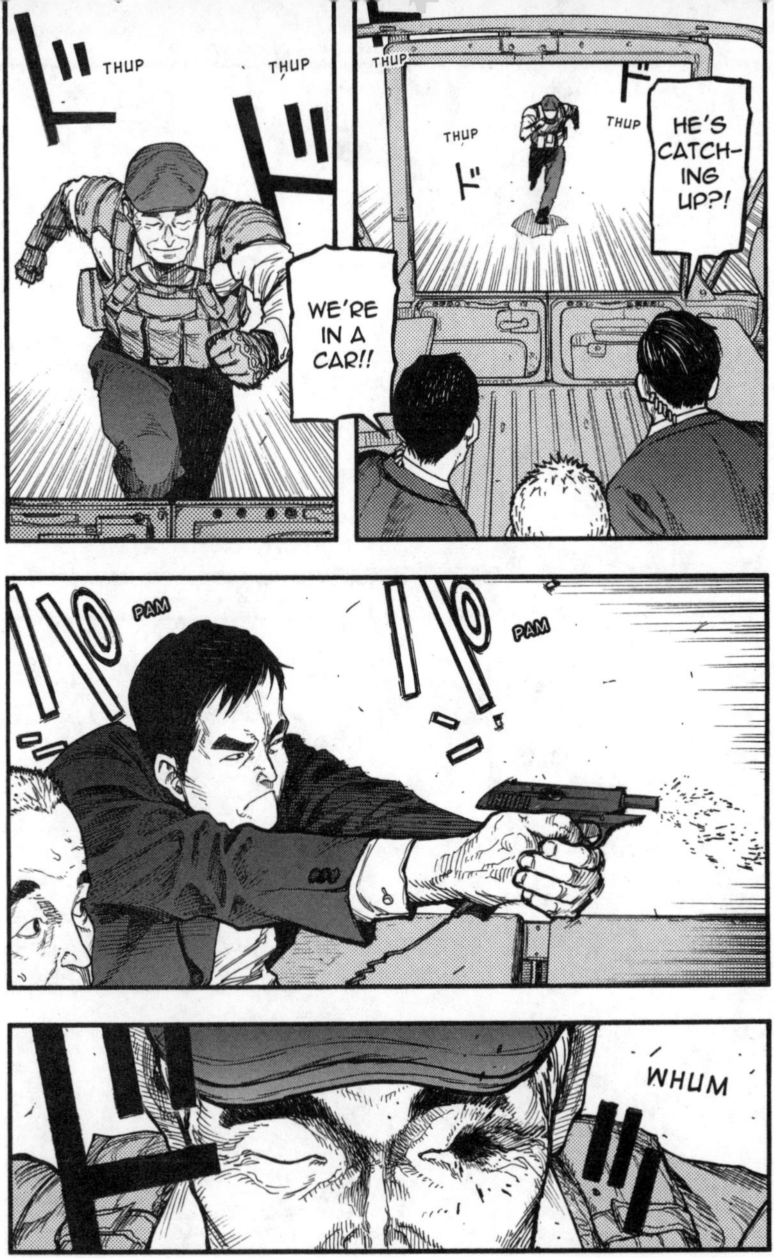
HE'S CATCHING-UP?!
THUP
THUP
THUP
WE'RE IN A CAR!!
THUP
THUP
PAM
PAM
WHUM

BOM
ド
KA
ガ
KLANK
ガ

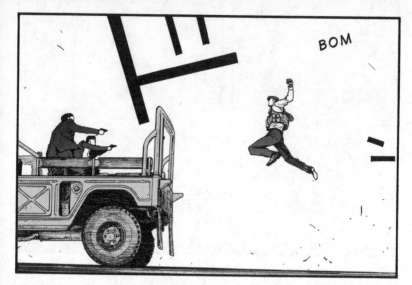

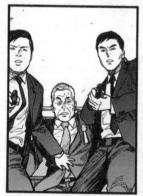

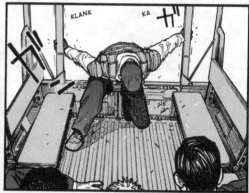

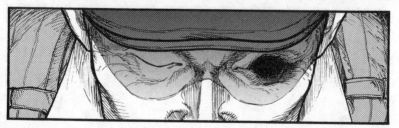

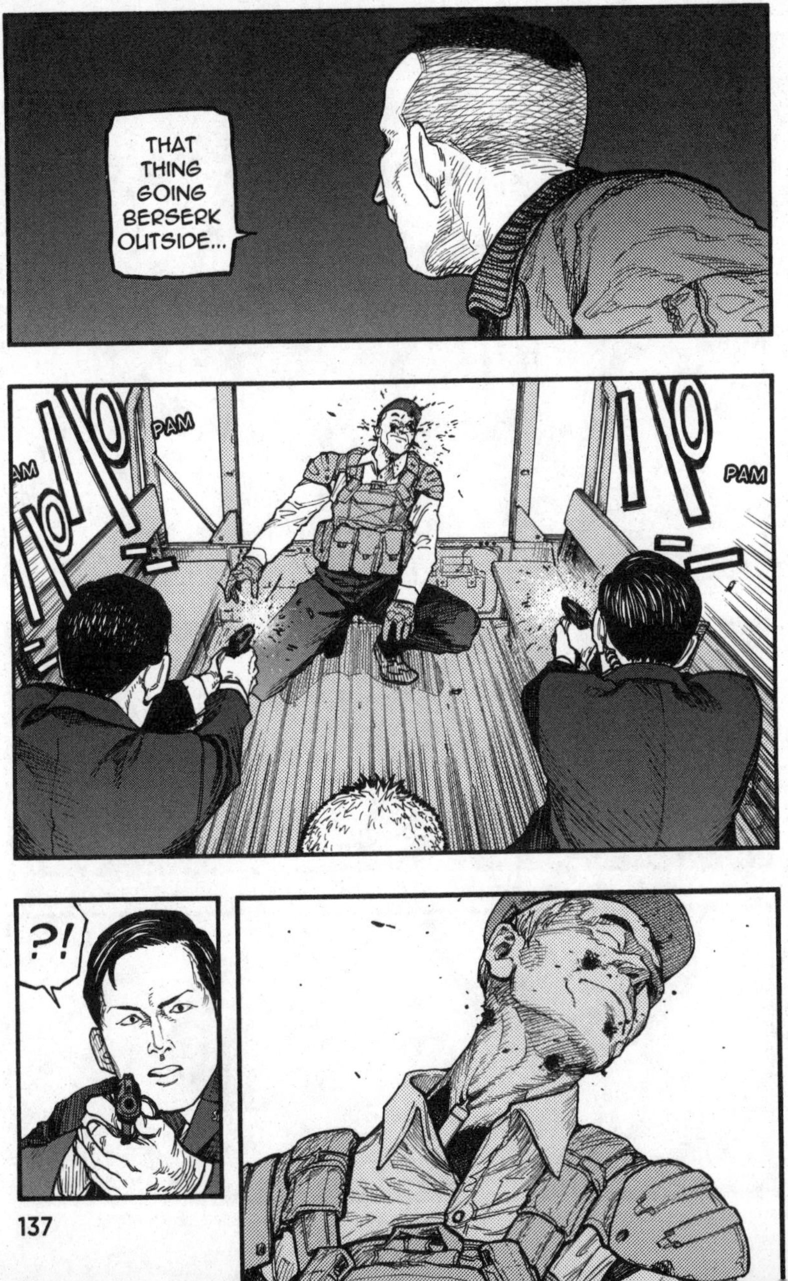
THAT THING GOING BERSERK OUTSIDE...
PAM
PAM
?!

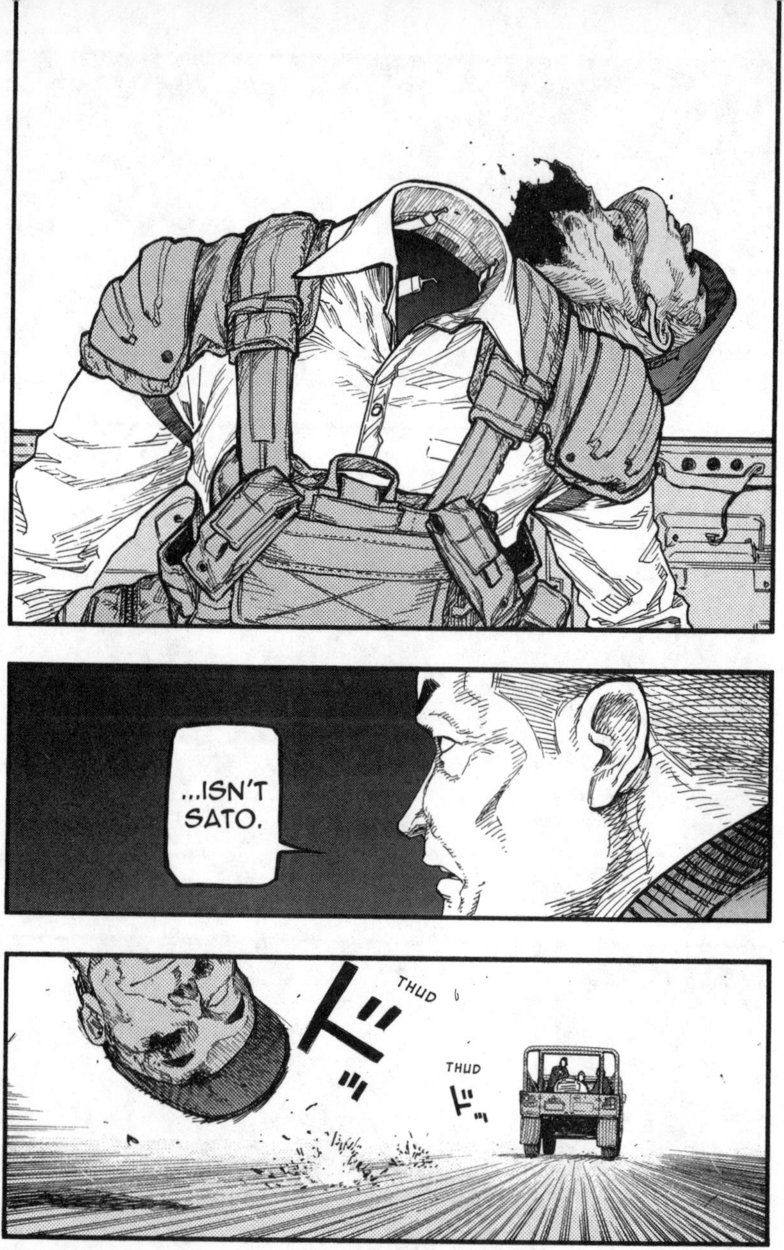
...ISN'T SATO.
ドッ
THUD
ドッ
THUD

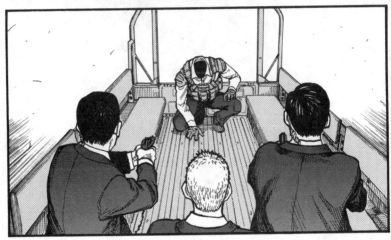

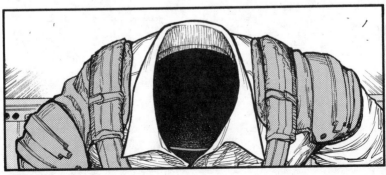

139

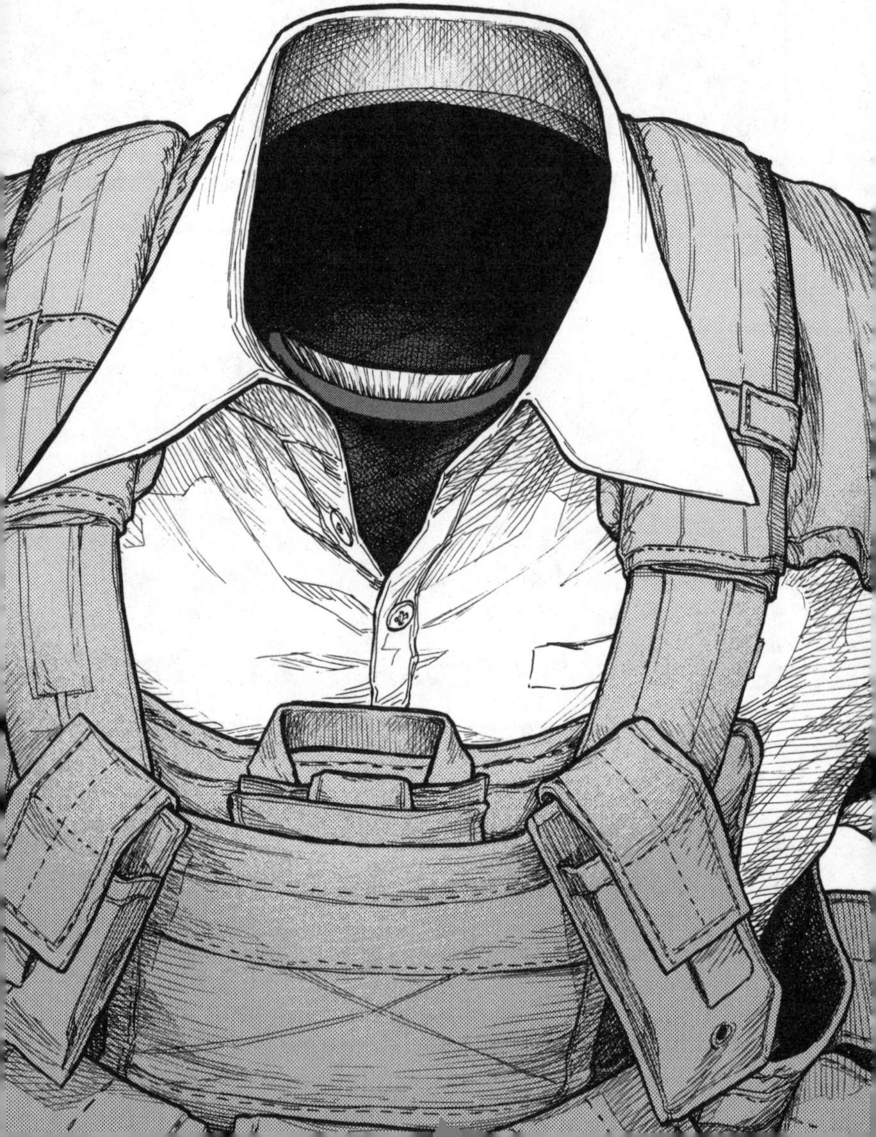

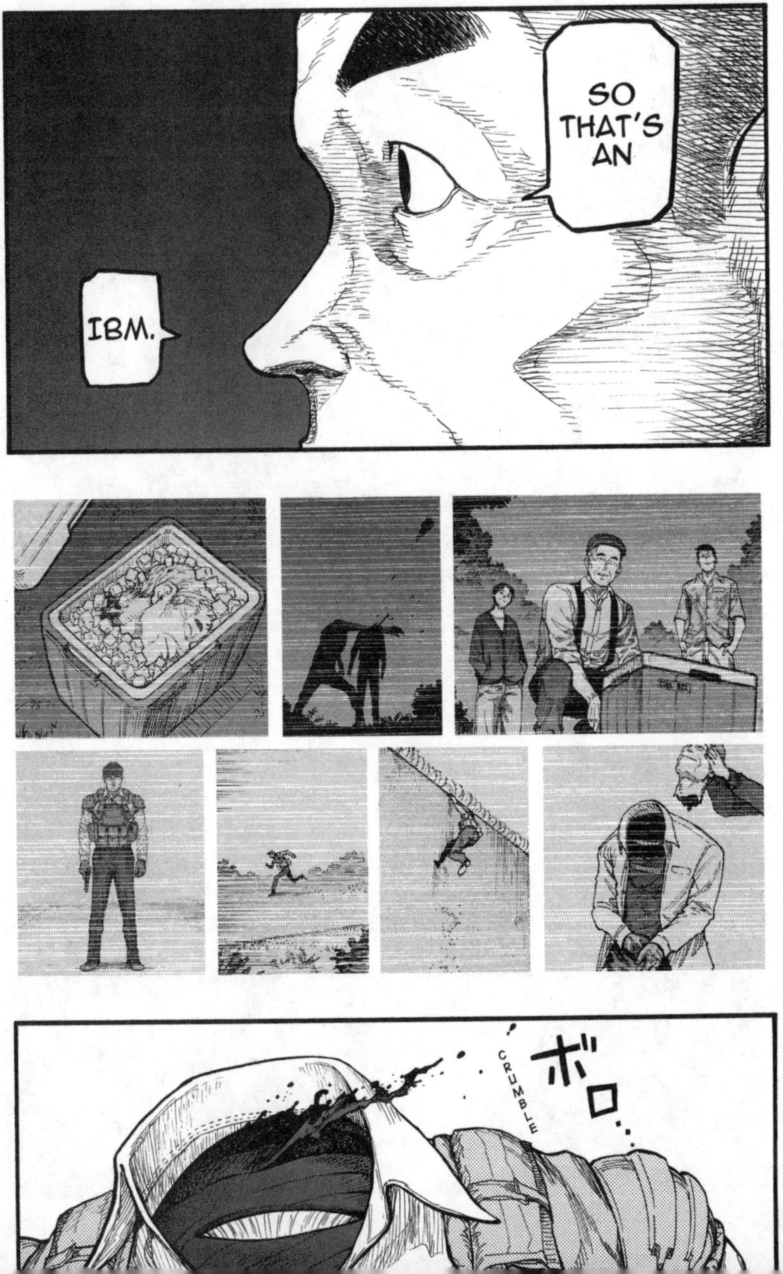
SO THAT'S AN
IBM.
ボロ…
CRUMBLE

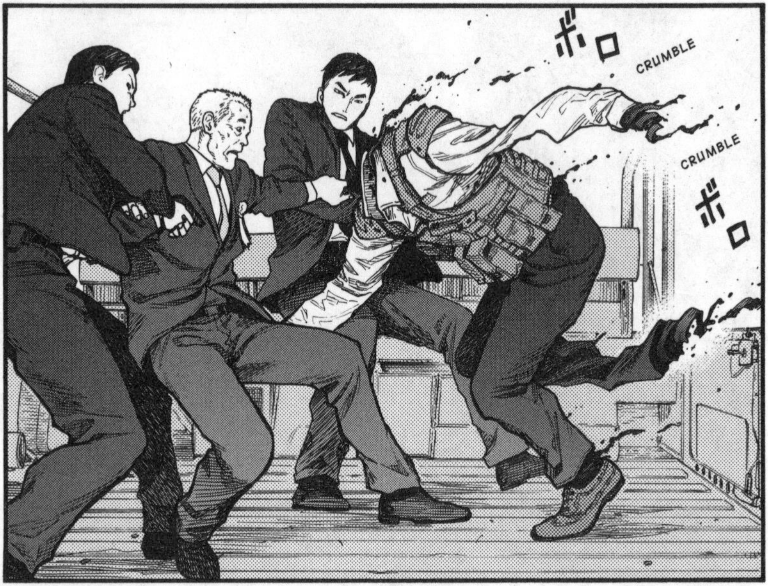
ボロ
CRUMBLE
CRUMBLE
ボロ
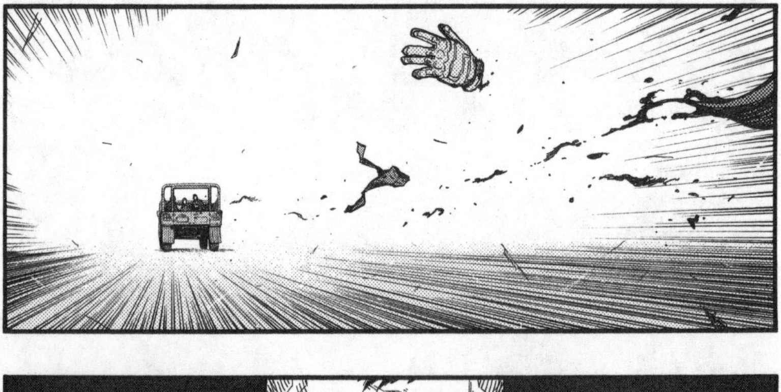
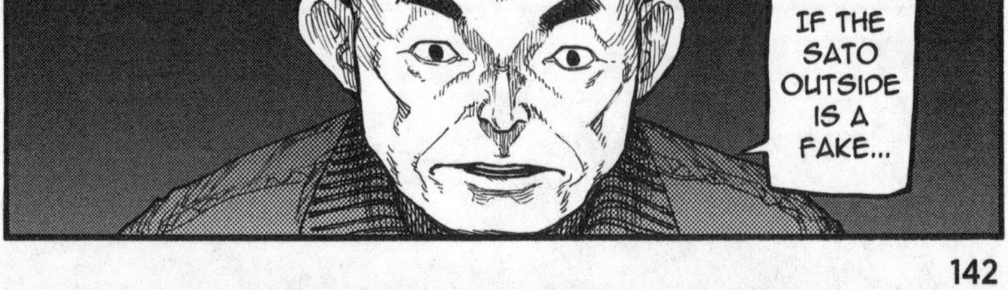
IF THE SATO OUTSIDE IS A FAKE...

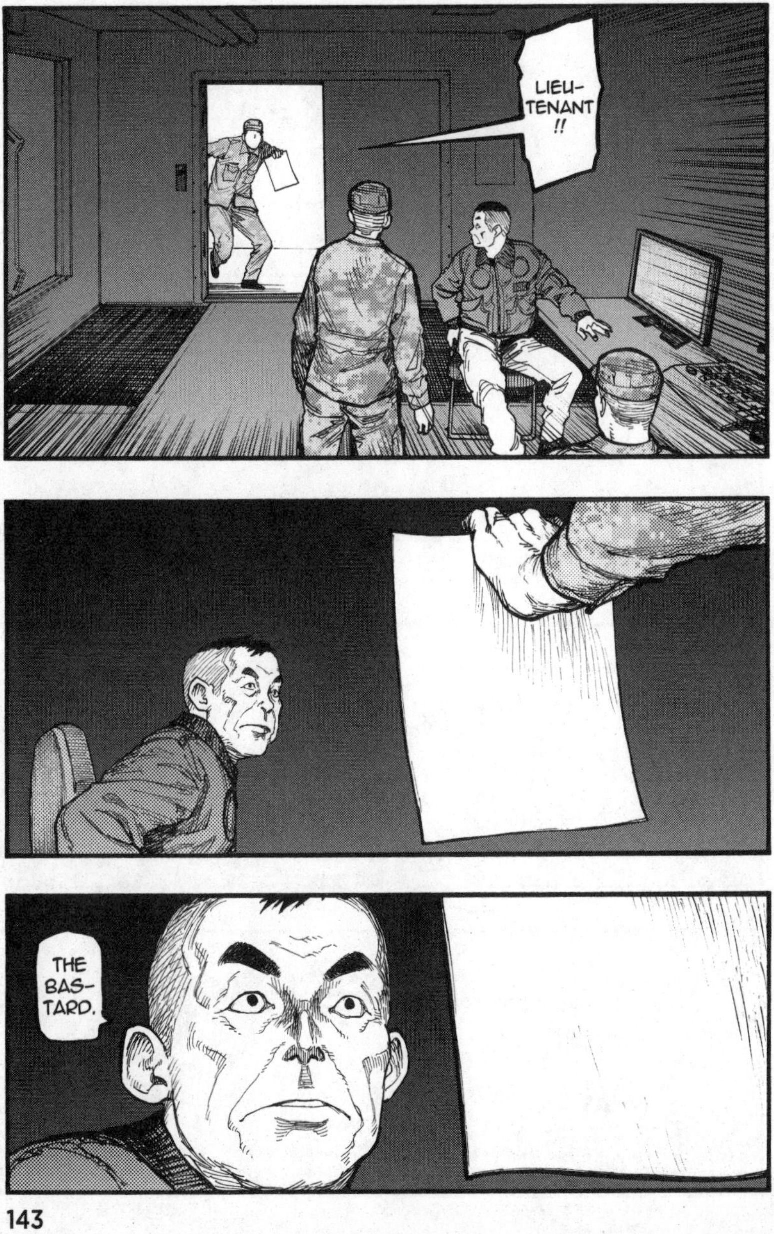
LIEU-
TENANT
!!
THE BAS-TARD.

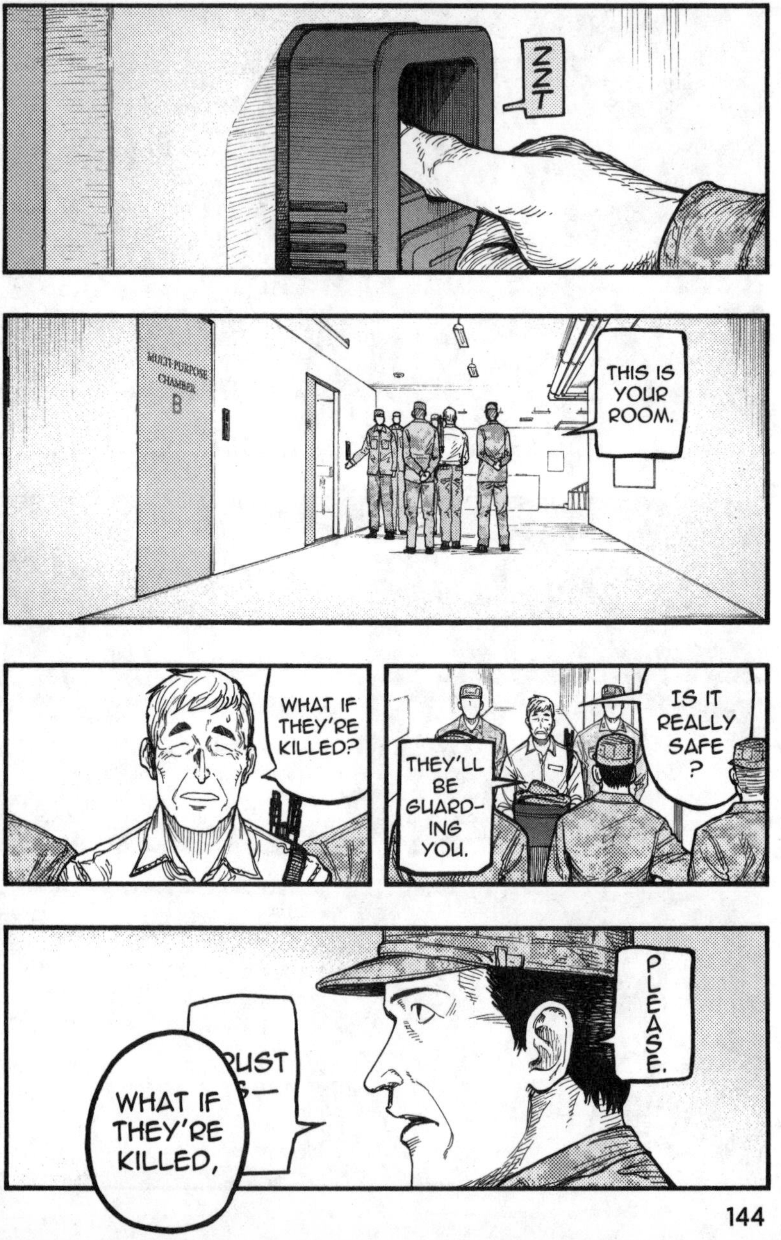
ZZT
MULTI-PURPOSE CHAMBER B
THIS IS YOUR ROOM.
IS IT REALLY SAFE?
THEY'LL BE GUARDING YOU.
WHAT IF THEY'RE KILLED?
PLEASE.
WHAT IF THEY'RE KILLED,

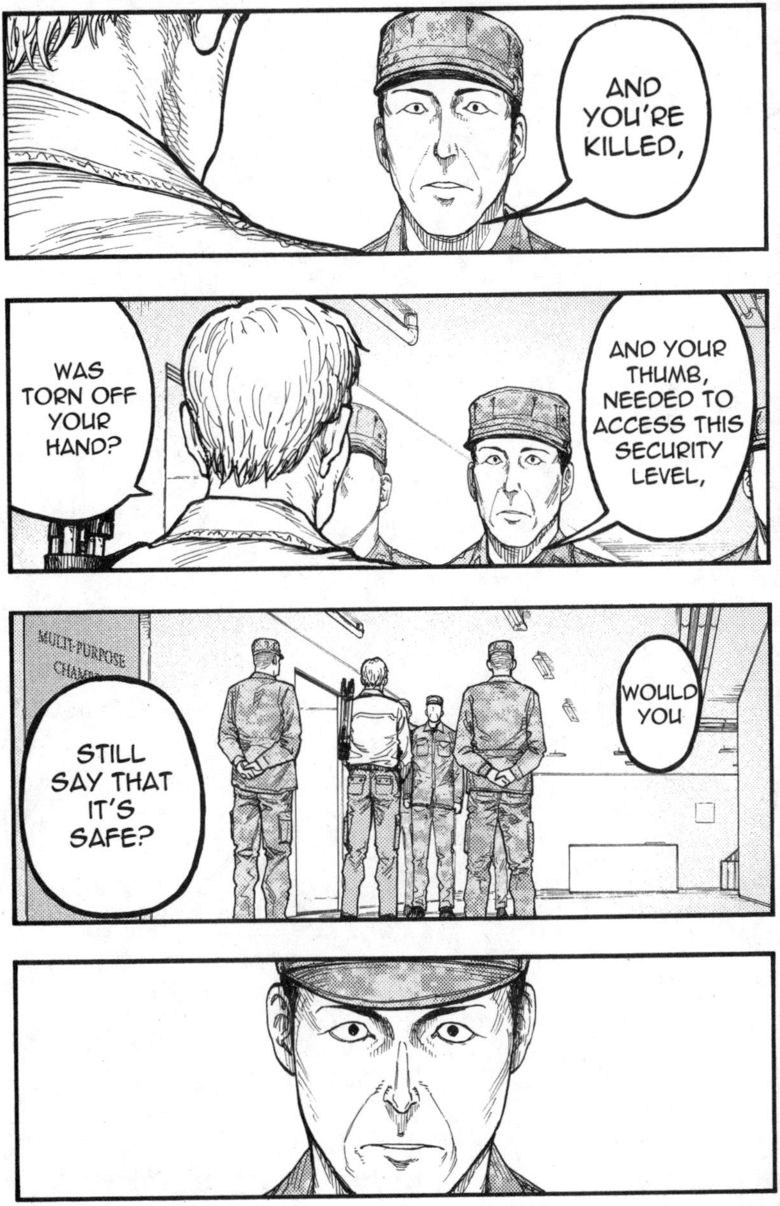
AND YOU'RE KILLED,
AND YOUR THUMB, NEEDED TO ACCESS THIS SECURITY LEVEL,
WAS TORN OFF YOUR HAND?
WOULD YOU
MULTI-PURPOSE
STILL SAY THAT IT'S SAFE?

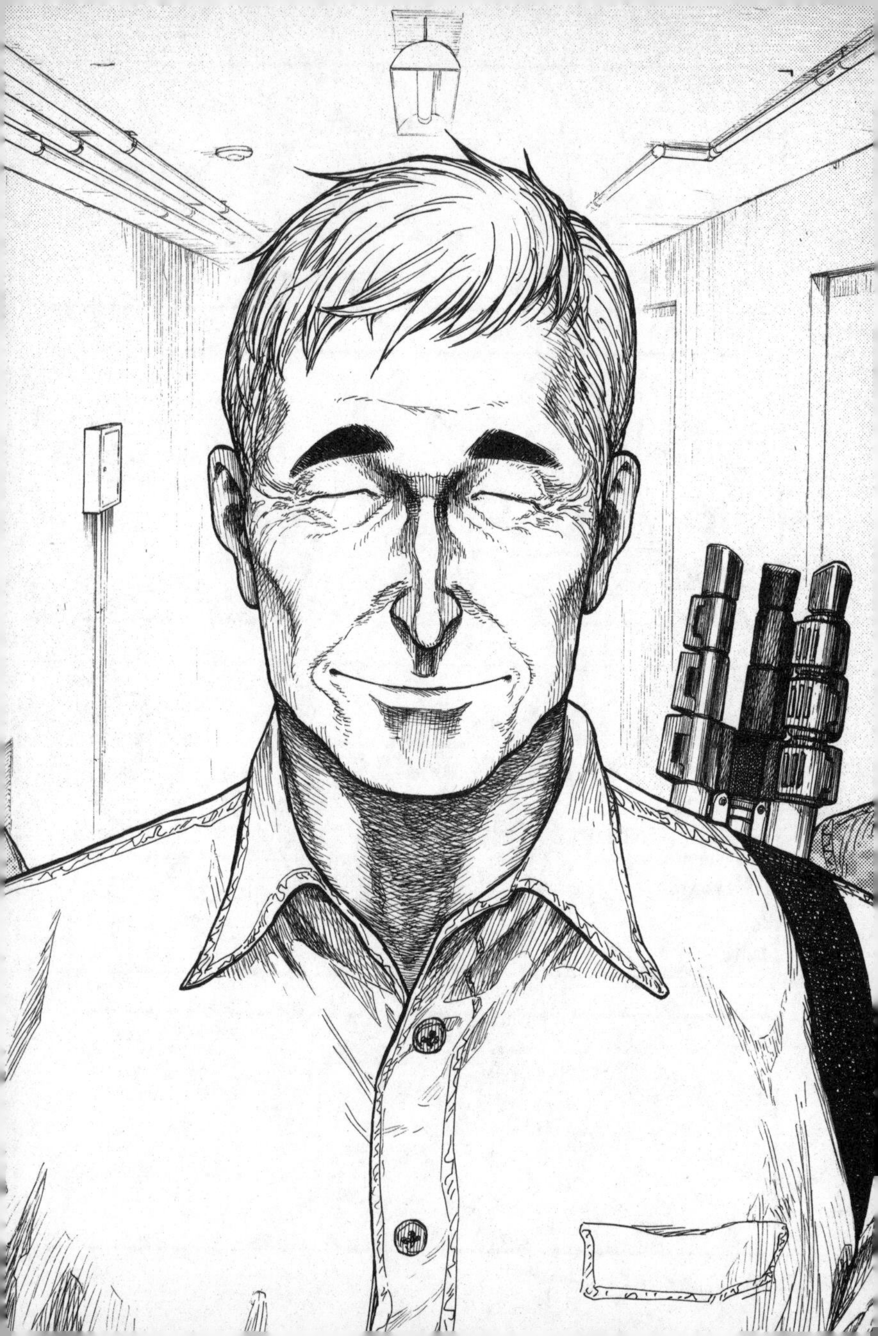

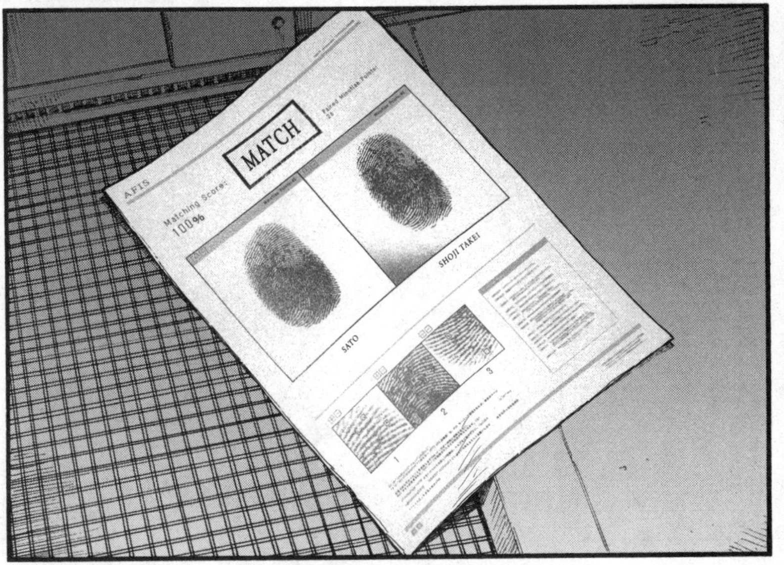
AFIS
Matching Score:
100%
MATCH
SHOJI TAKEI
SATO

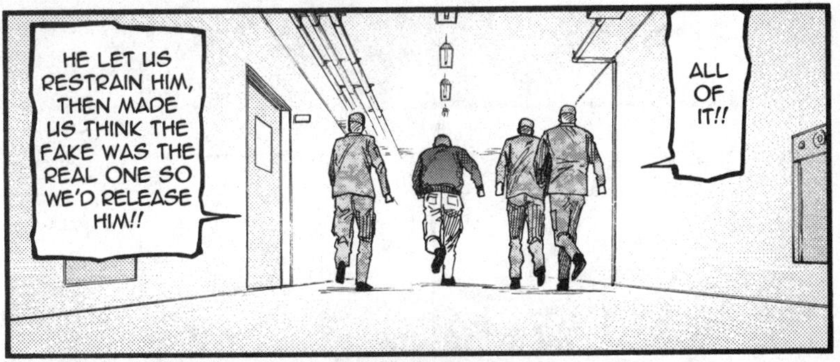
ALL OF IT!!
HE LET US RESTRAIN HIM, THEN MADE US THINK THE FAKE WAS THE REAL ONE SO WE'D RELEASE HIM!!

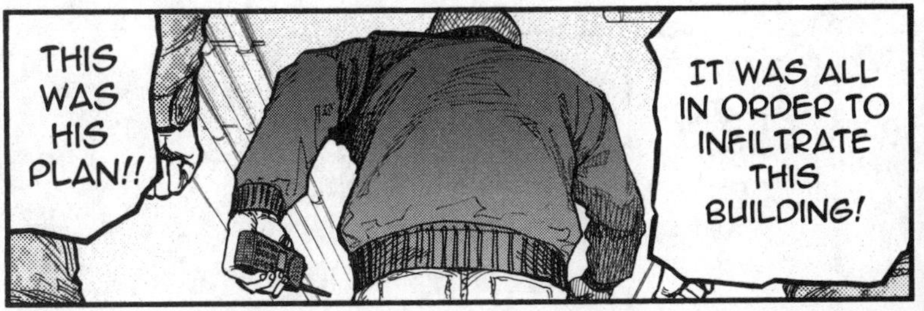
IT WAS ALL IN ORDER TO INFILTRATE THIS BUILDING!
THIS WAS HIS PLAN!!

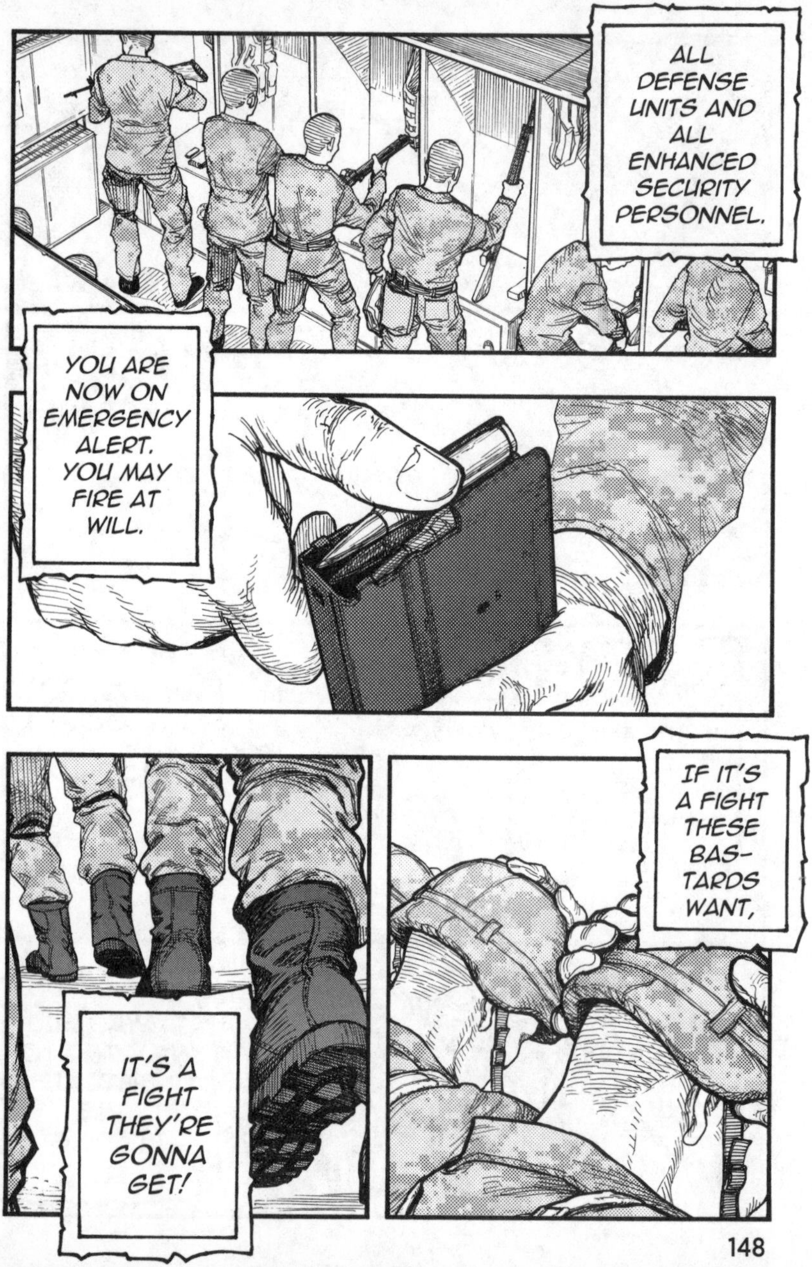
ALL DEFENSE UNITS AND ALL ENHANCED SECURITY PERSONNEL.
YOU ARE NOW ON EMERGENCY ALERT. YOU MAY FIRE AT WILL.
IF IT'S A FIGHT THESE BAS-TARDS WANT,
IT'S A FIGHT THEY'RE GONNA GET!

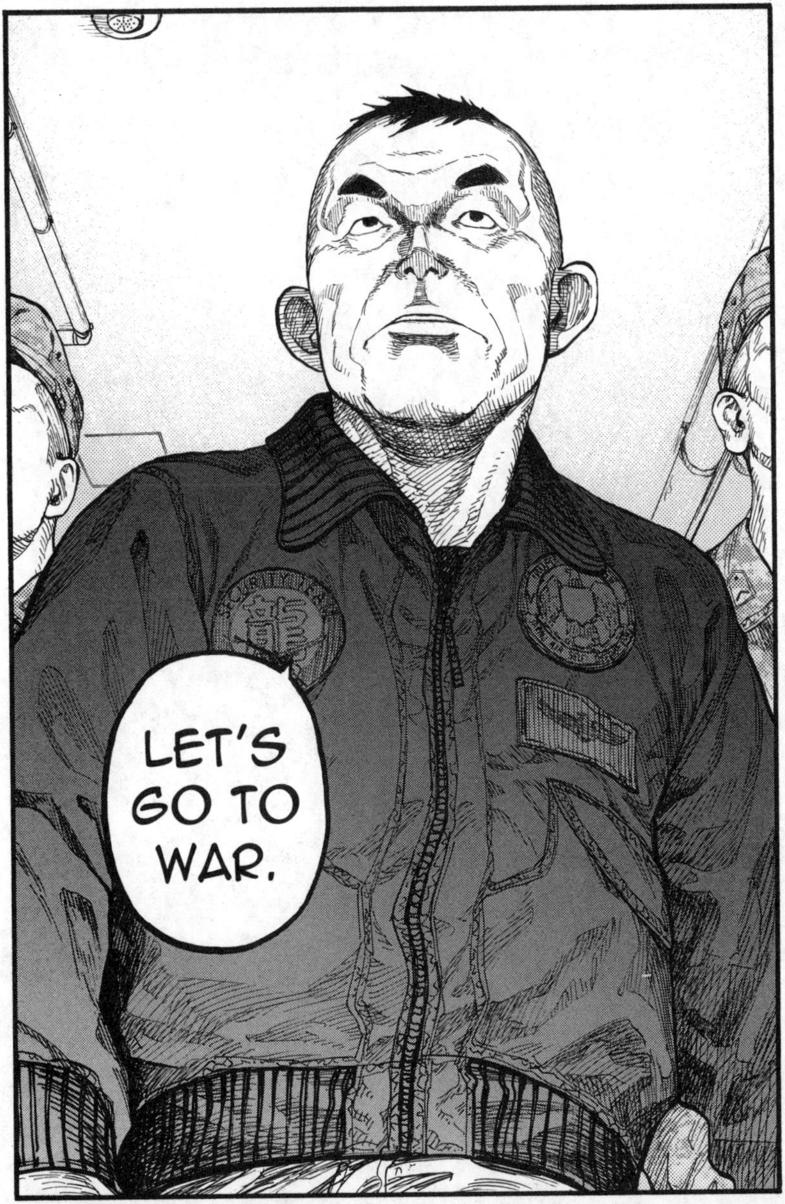
LET'S GO TO WAR.

File:52 End

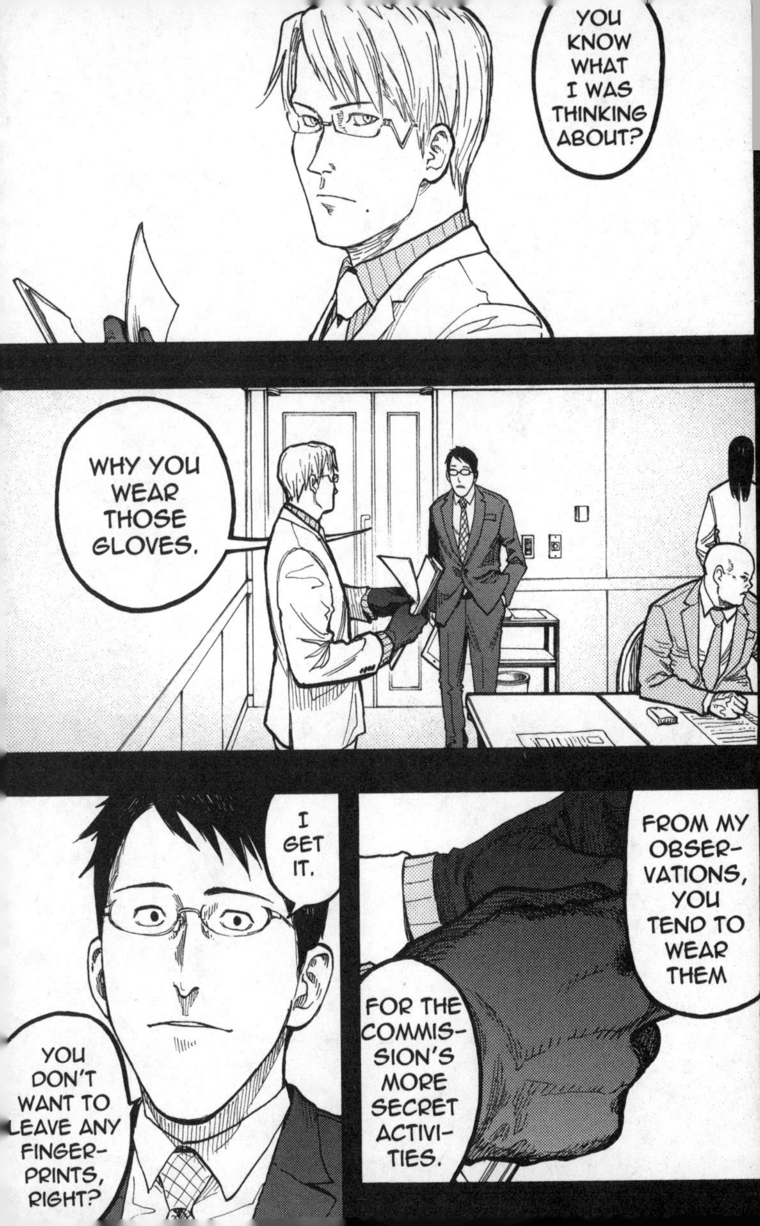
YOU KNOW WHAT I WAS THINKING ABOUT?
WHY YOU WEAR THOSE GLOVES.
FROM MY OBSERVATIONS, YOU TEND TO WEAR THEM
FOR THE COMMISSION'S MORE SECRET ACTIVITIES.
I GET IT.
YOU DON'T WANT TO LEAVE ANY FINGERPRINTS, RIGHT?

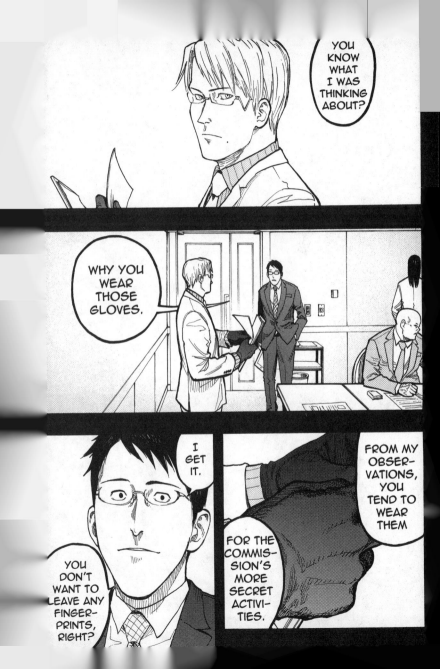

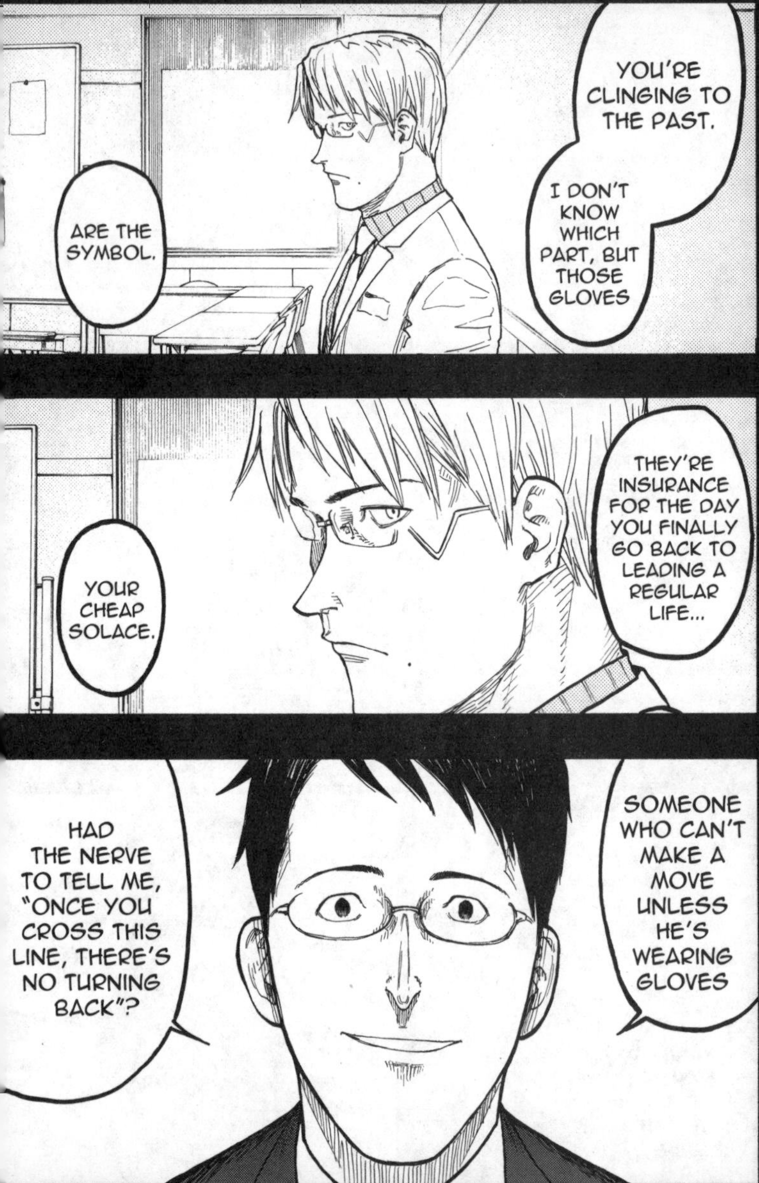
YOU'RE CLINGING TO THE PAST.
I DON'T KNOW WHICH PART, BUT THOSE GLOVES
ARE THE SYMBOL.
THEY'RE INSURANCE FOR THE DAY YOU FINALLY GO BACK TO LEADING A REGULAR LIFE...
YOUR CHEAP SOLACE.
SOMEONE WHO CAN'T MAKE A MOVE UNLESS HE'S WEARING GLOVES
HAD THE NERVE TO TELL ME, "ONCE YOU CROSS THIS LINE, THERE'S NO TURNING BACK"?

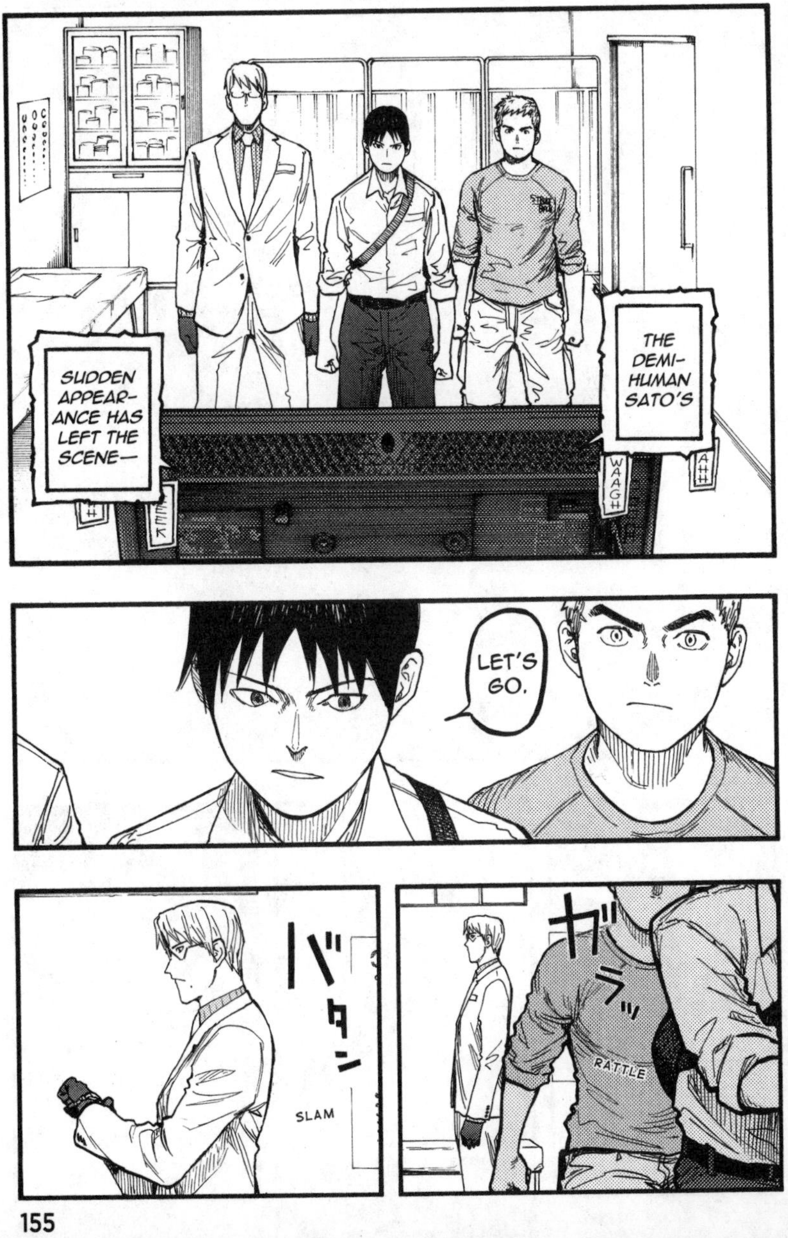
THE DEMI-HUMAN SATO'S
SUDDEN APPEARANCE HAS LEFT THE SCENE—
AHH
WAAGH
EEK
LET'S GO.
ガラッ
RATTLE
バタン
SLAM

File 53: Conviction

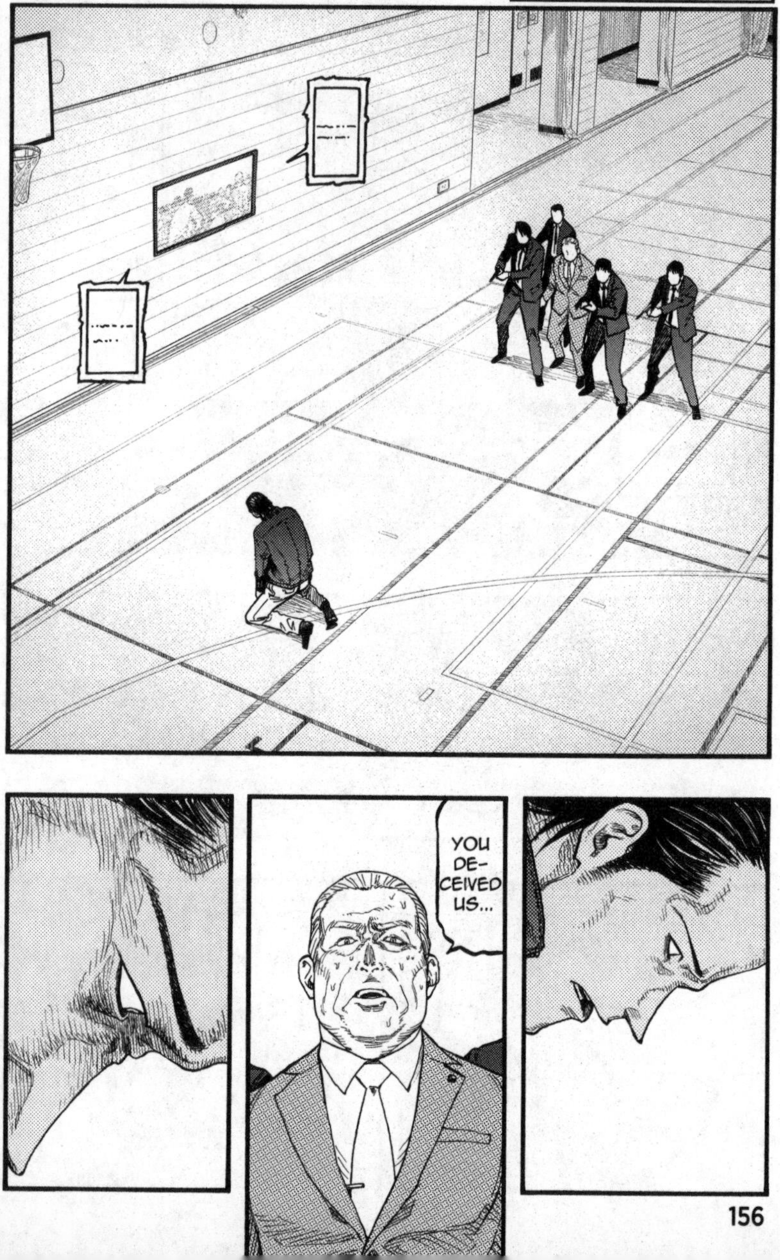
YOU DE-CEIVED US...

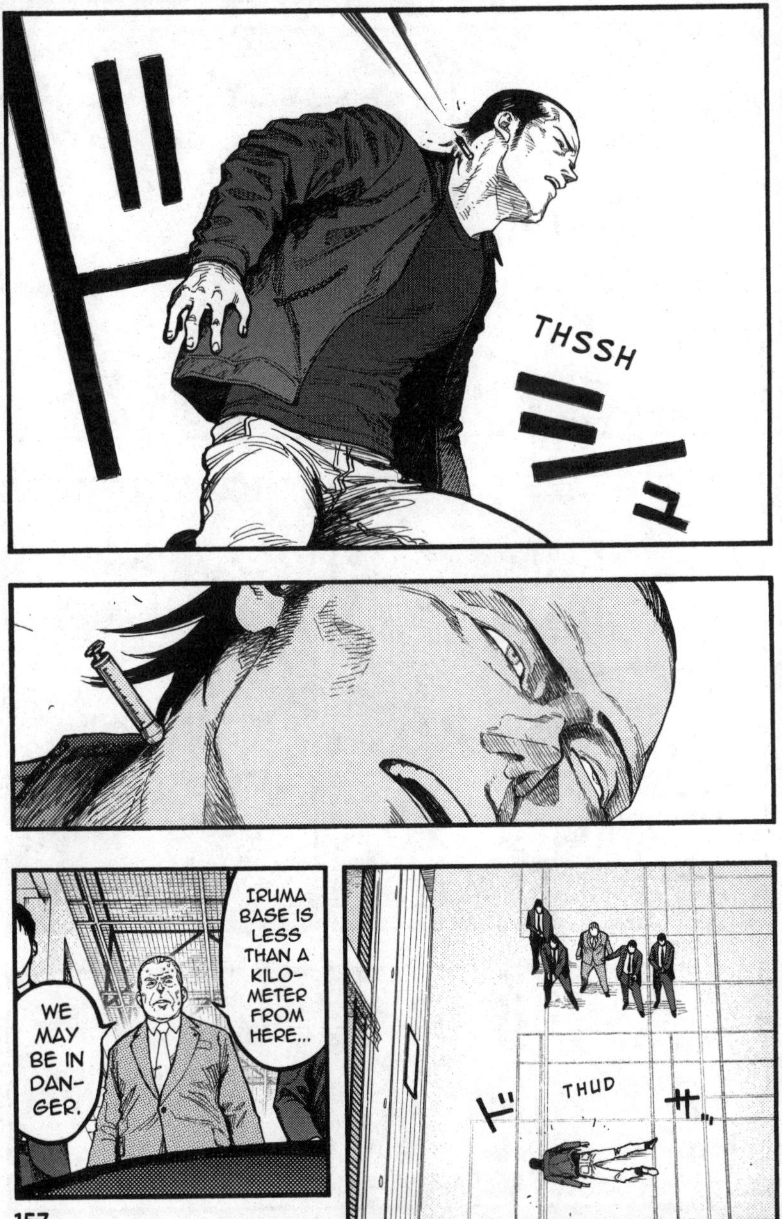
THSSH
THUD
IRUMA BASE IS LESS THAN A KILO-METER FROM HERE...
WE MAY BE IN DAN-GER.

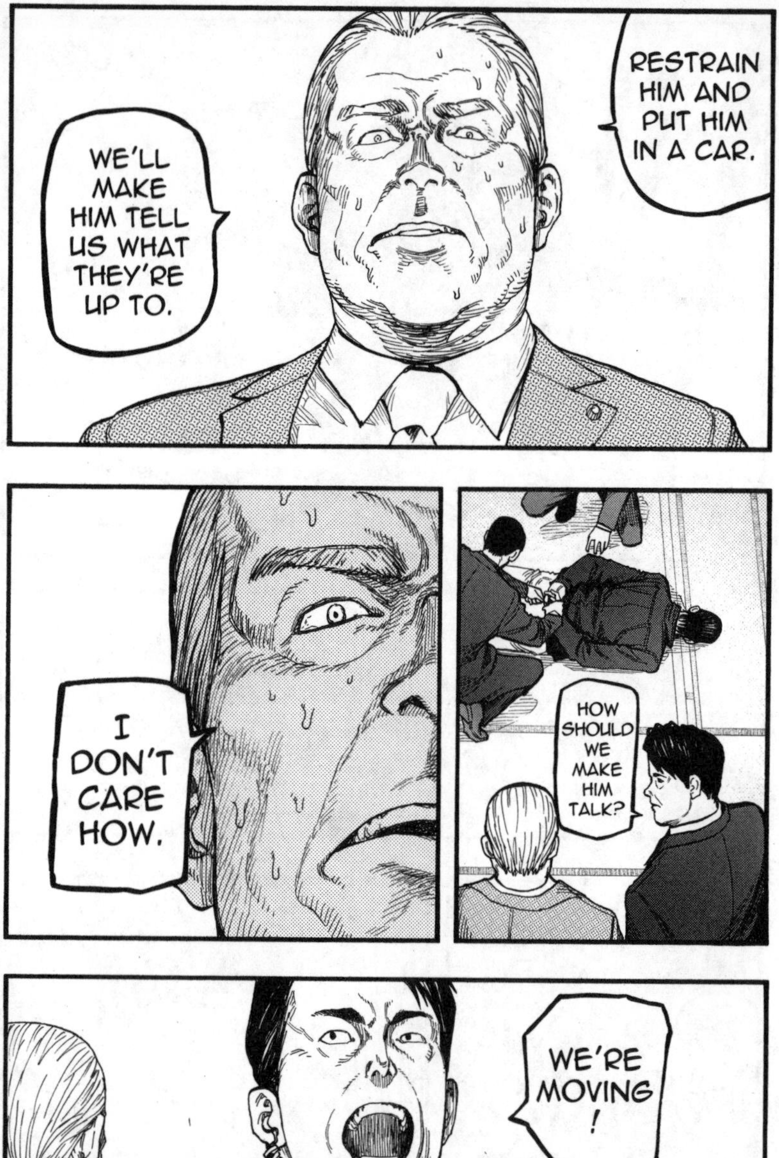
RESTRAIN HIM AND PUT HIM IN A CAR.
WE'LL MAKE HIM TELL US WHAT THEY'RE UP TO.
HOW SHOULD WE MAKE HIM TALK?
I DON'T CARE HOW.
WE'RE MOVING!

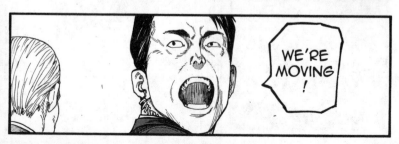

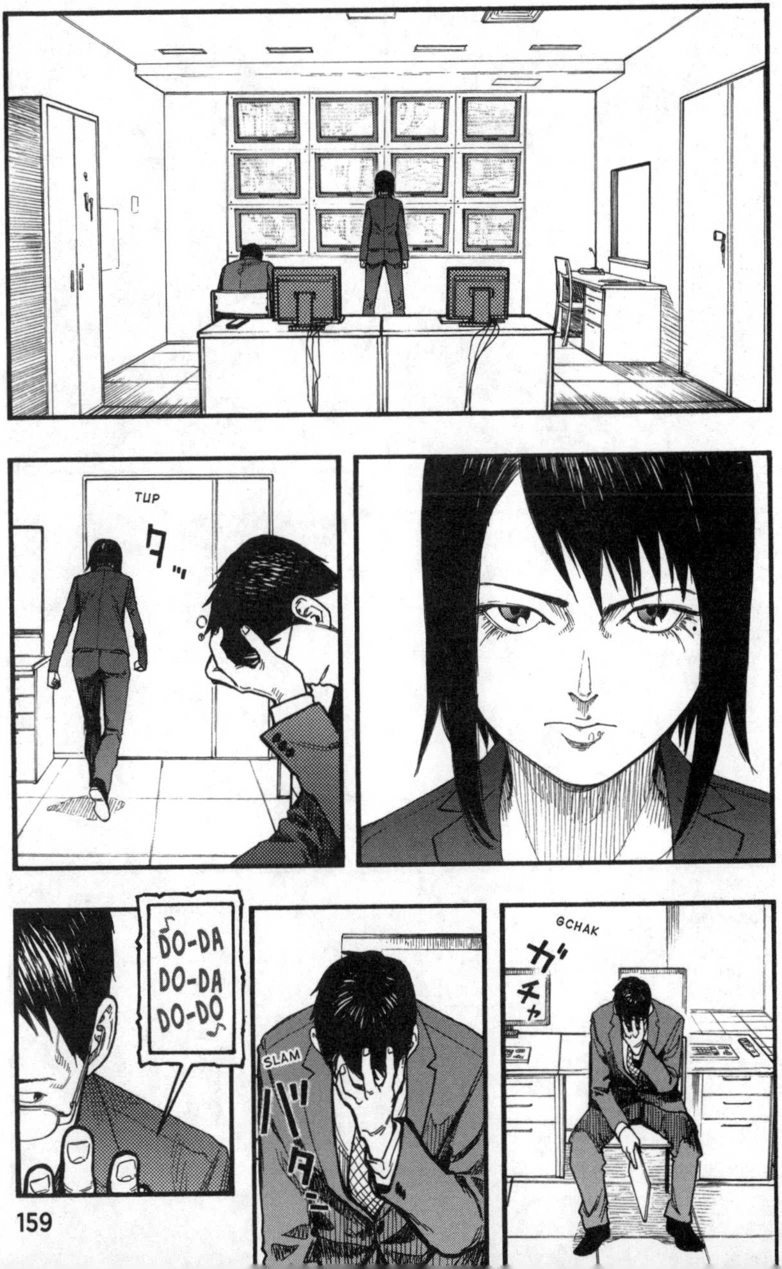
TUP
タッ
GCHAK
ガチャ
SLAM
DO-DA
DO-DA
DO-DO

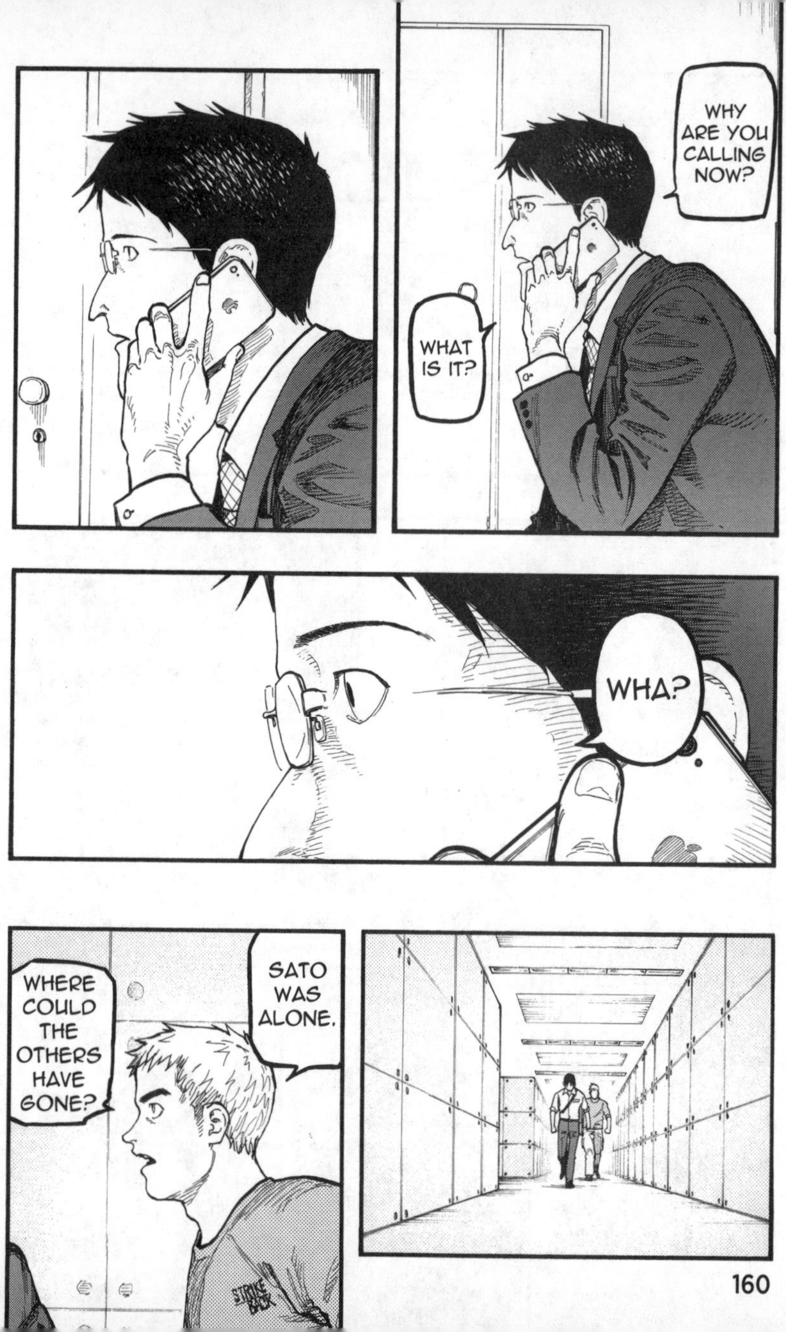
WHY ARE YOU CALLING NOW?
WHAT IS IT?
WHA?
SATO WAS ALONE.
WHERE COULD THE OTHERS HAVE GONE?

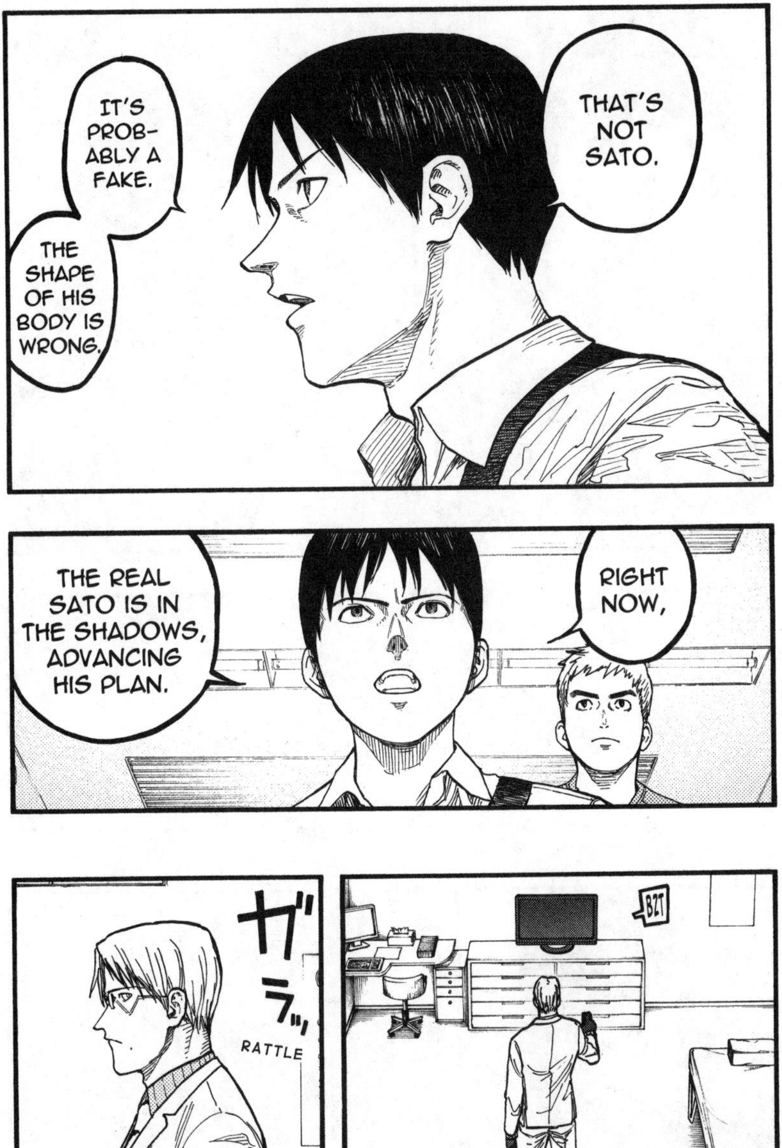
THAT'S NOT SATO.
IT'S PROBABLY A FAKE.
THE SHAPE OF HIS BODY IS WRONG.
RIGHT NOW,
THE REAL SATO IS IN THE SHADOWS, ADVANCING HIS PLAN.
BZT
ガラッ
RATTLE

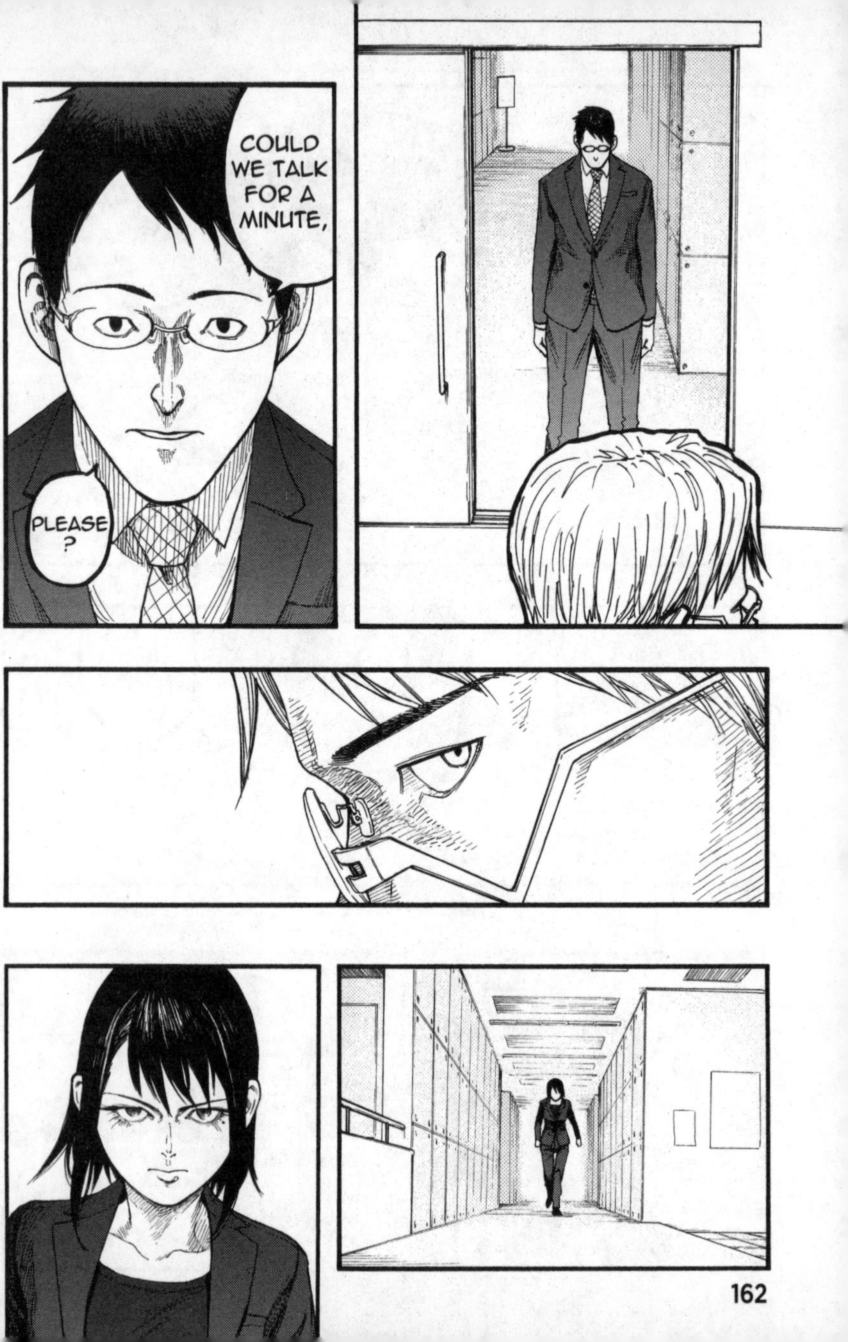
COULD WE TALK FOR A MINUTE,
PLEASE ?

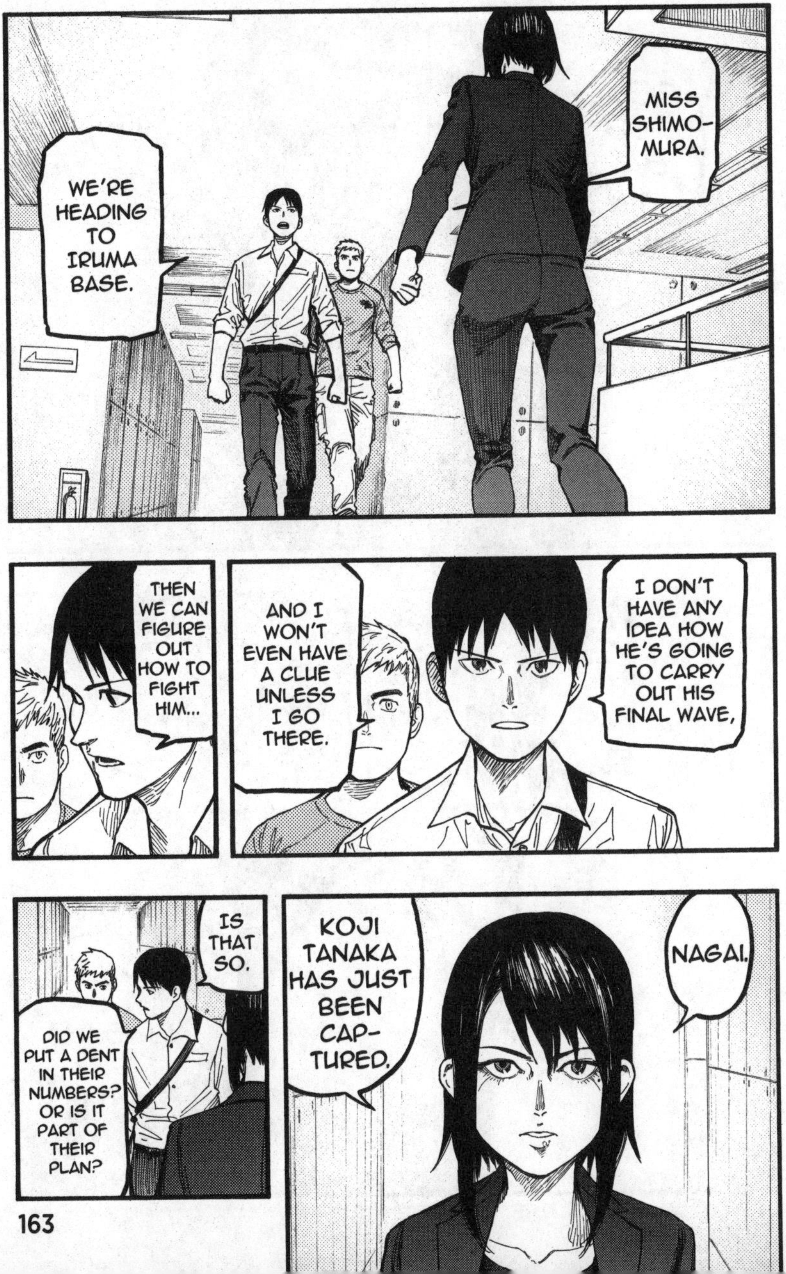
MISS SHIMOMURA.
WE'RE HEADING TO IRUMA BASE.
I DON'T HAVE ANY IDEA HOW HE'S GOING TO CARRY OUT HIS FINAL WAVE,
AND I WON'T EVEN HAVE A CLUE UNLESS I GO THERE.
THEN WE CAN FIGURE OUT HOW TO FIGHT HIM...
NAGAI.
KOJI TANAKA HAS JUST BEEN CAPTURED.
IS THAT SO.
DID WE PUT A DENT IN THEIR NUMBERS? OR IS IT PART OF THEIR PLAN?

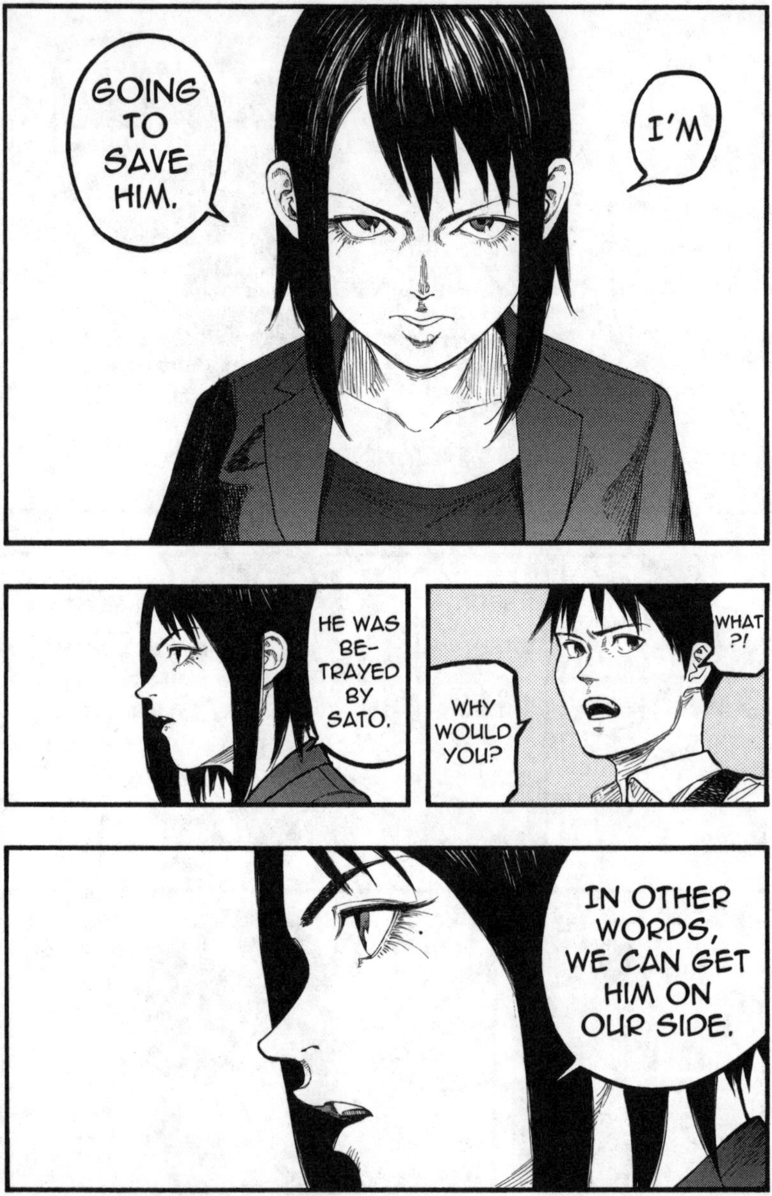
I'M
GOING TO SAVE HIM.
WHAT?!
WHY WOULD YOU?
HE WAS BE-TRAYED BY SATO.
IN OTHER WORDS, WE CAN GET HIM ON OUR SIDE.

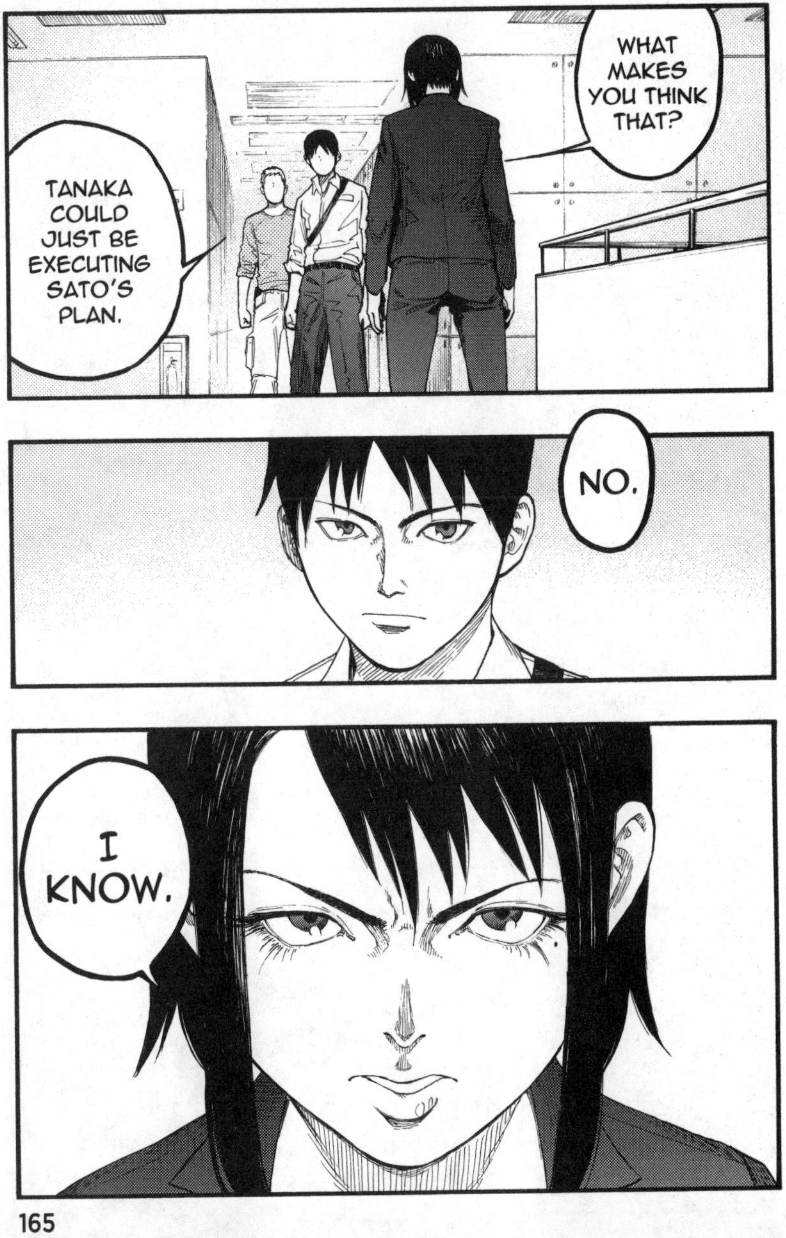
WHAT MAKES YOU THINK THAT?
TANAKA COULD JUST BE EXECUTING SATO'S PLAN.
NO.
I KNOW.

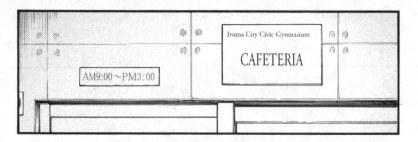

Iruma City Civic Gymnasium

CAFETERIA

AM9:00～PM3:00

MY SECRETARY JUST CONTACTED ME.

THAT'S RIGHT. I HIRED A SECRETARY.

THEY FOUND SIGNS THAT TOP-SECRET DHCC DATA

HAS BEEN RETRIEVED WITHOUT AUTHORI-ZATION.

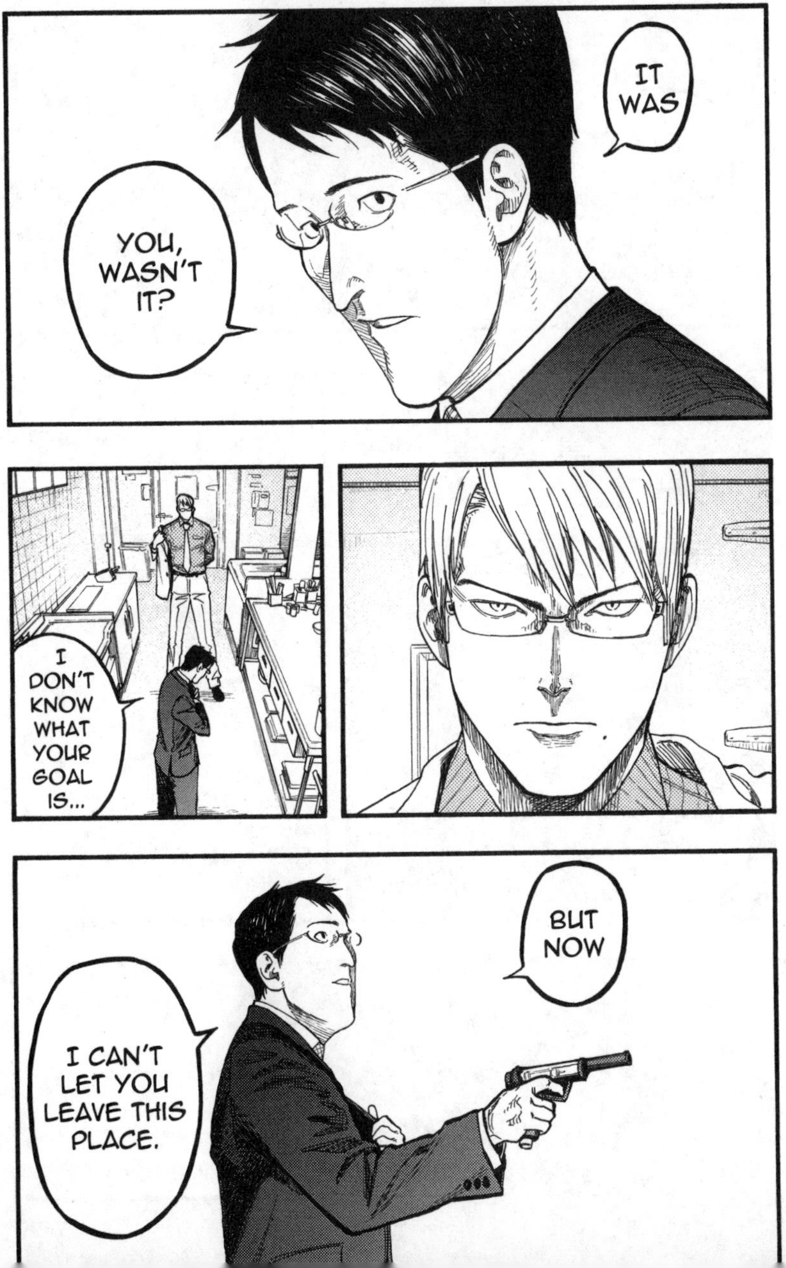
IT WAS
YOU, WASN'T IT?
I DON'T KNOW WHAT YOUR GOAL IS...
BUT NOW
I CAN'T LET YOU LEAVE THIS PLACE.

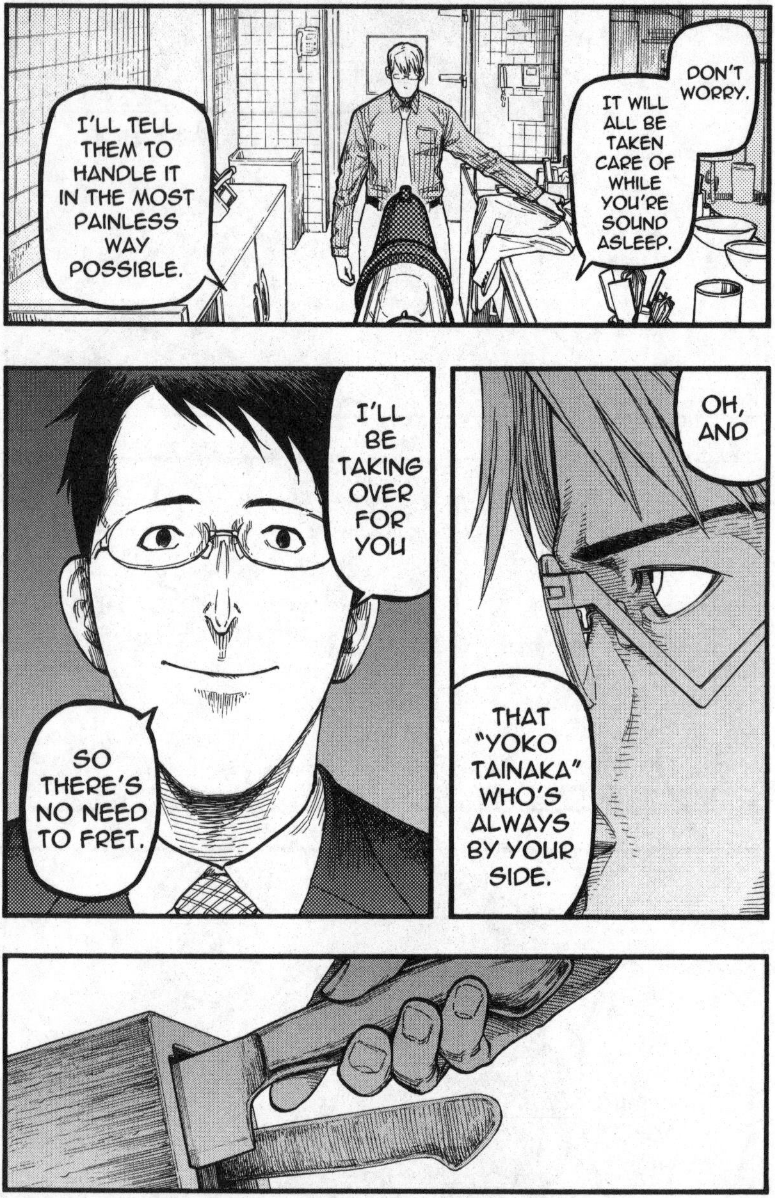
DON'T WORRY.
IT WILL ALL BE TAKEN CARE OF WHILE YOU'RE SOUND ASLEEP.
I'LL TELL THEM TO HANDLE IT IN THE MOST PAINLESS WAY POSSIBLE.
OH, AND
THAT "YOKO TAINAKA" WHO'S ALWAYS BY YOUR SIDE.
I'LL BE TAKING OVER FOR YOU
SO THERE'S NO NEED TO FRET.

HAH

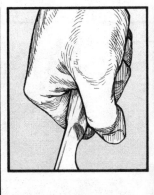

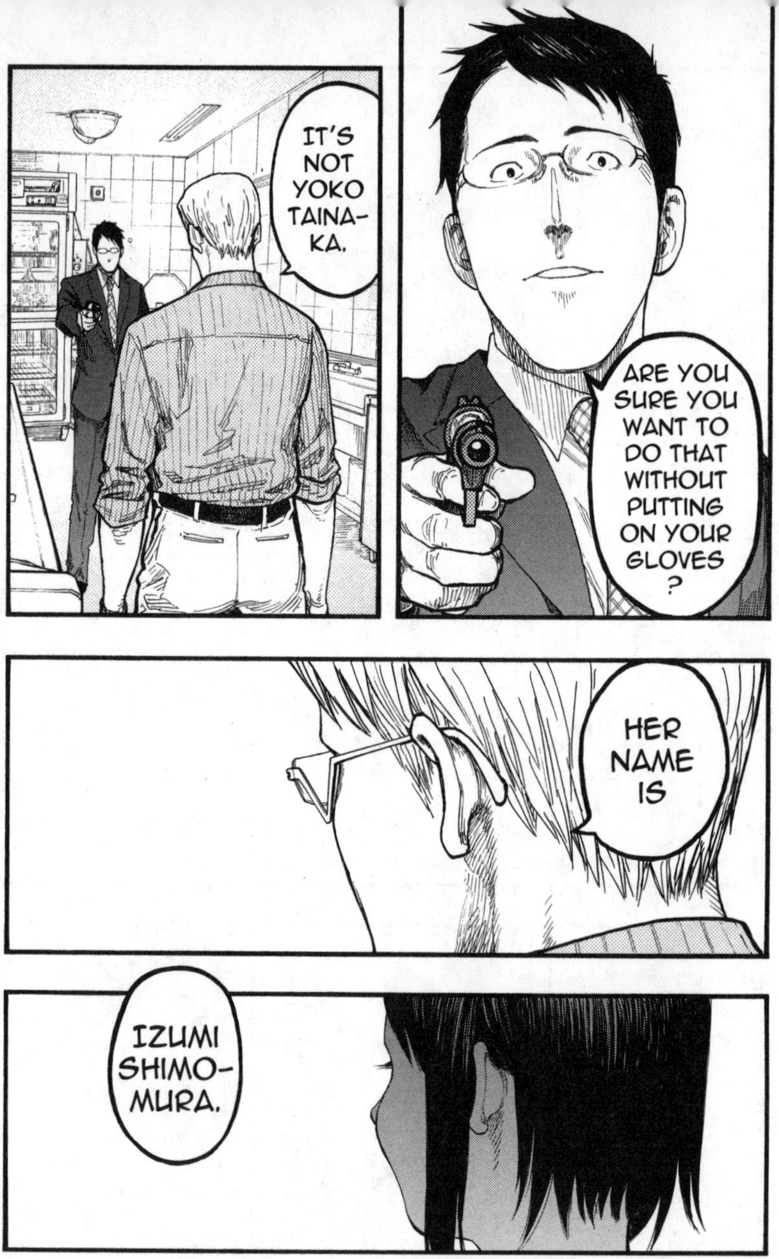
ARE YOU SURE YOU WANT TO DO THAT WITHOUT PUTTING ON YOUR GLOVES ?
IT'S NOT YOKO TAINA-KA.
HER NAME IS
IZUMI SHIMO-MURA.

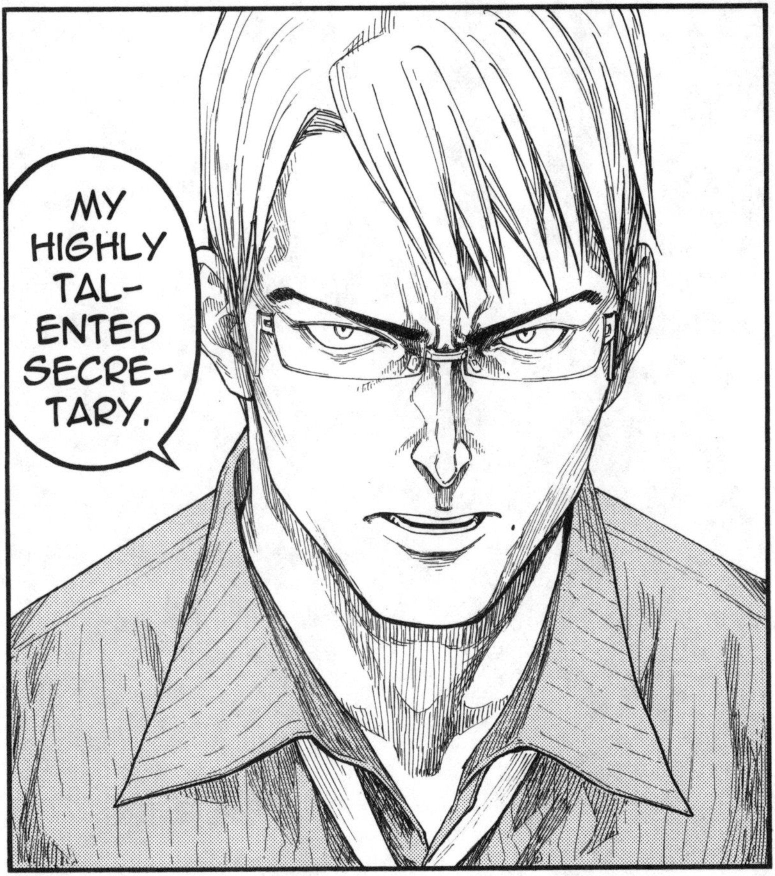
MY HIGHLY TAL-ENTED SECRE-TARY.

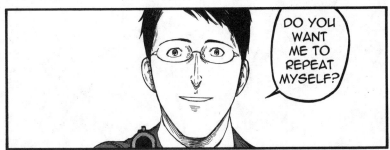

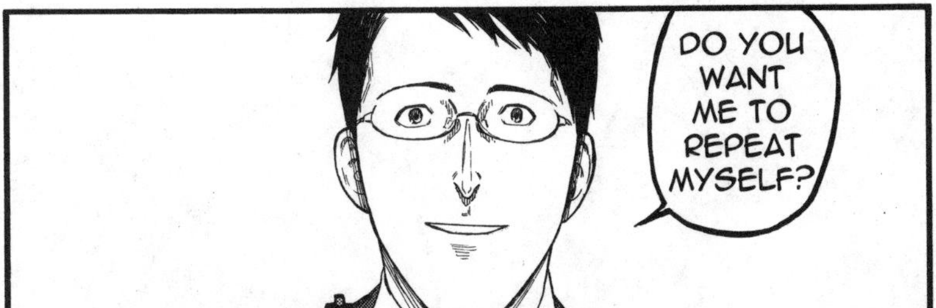
DO YOU WANT ME TO REPEAT MYSELF?

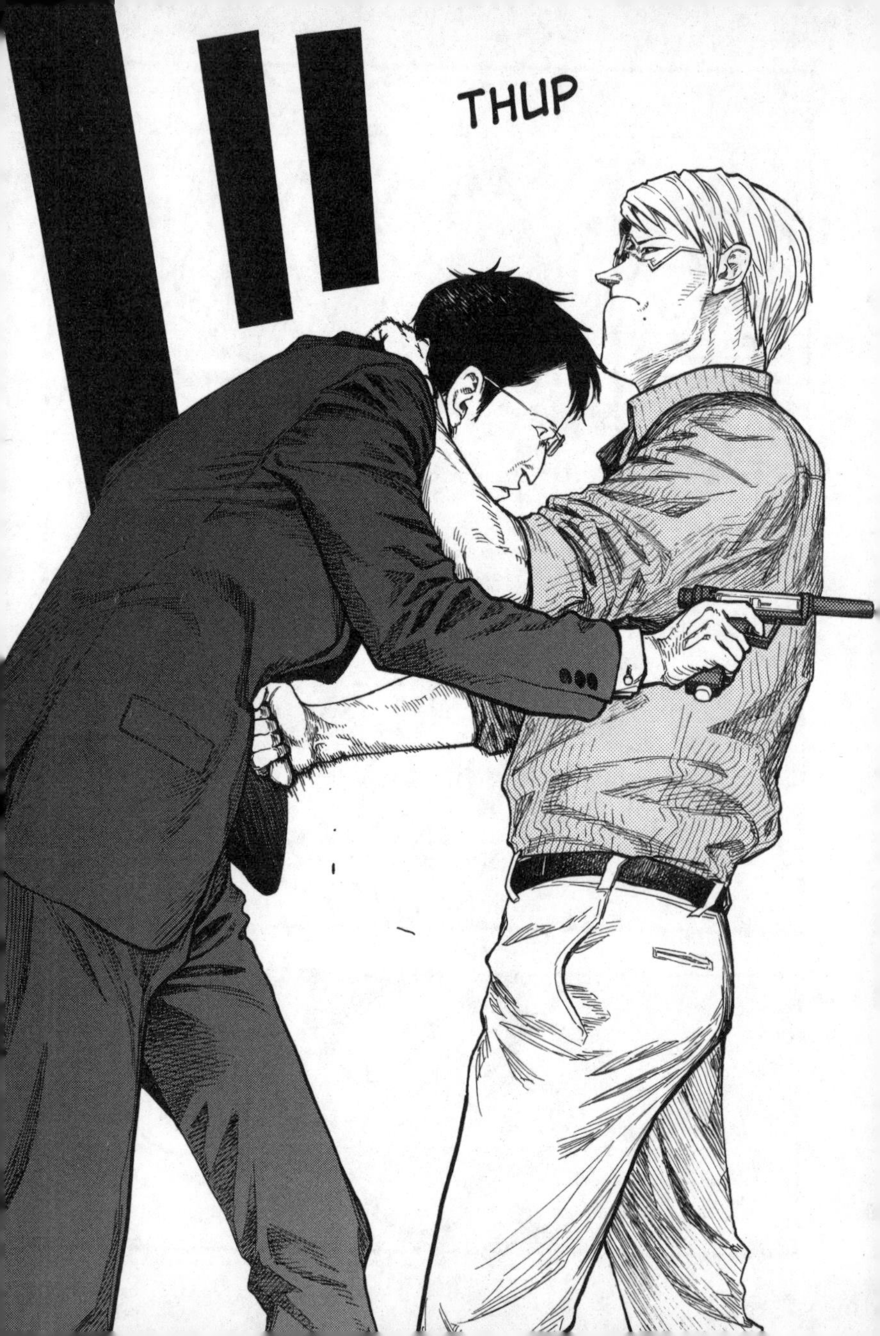
THUP

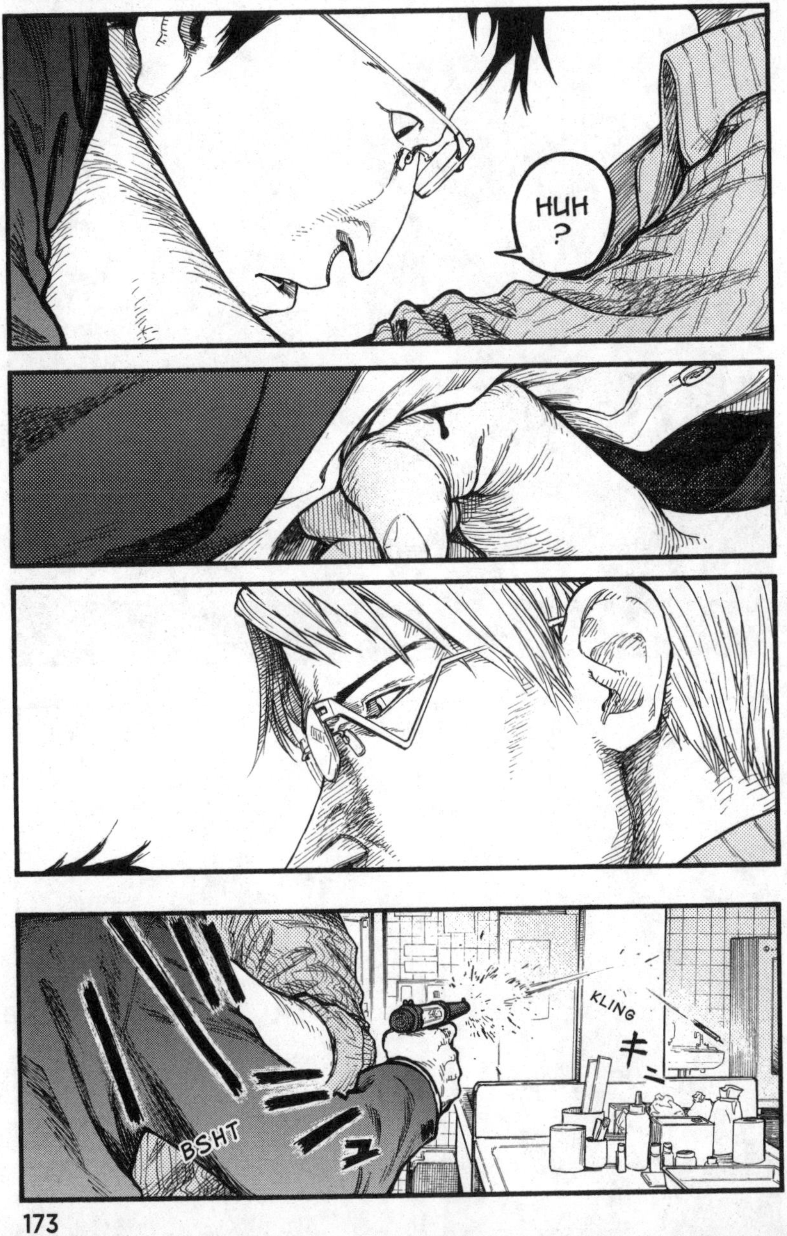
HUH
?
KLING
BSHT

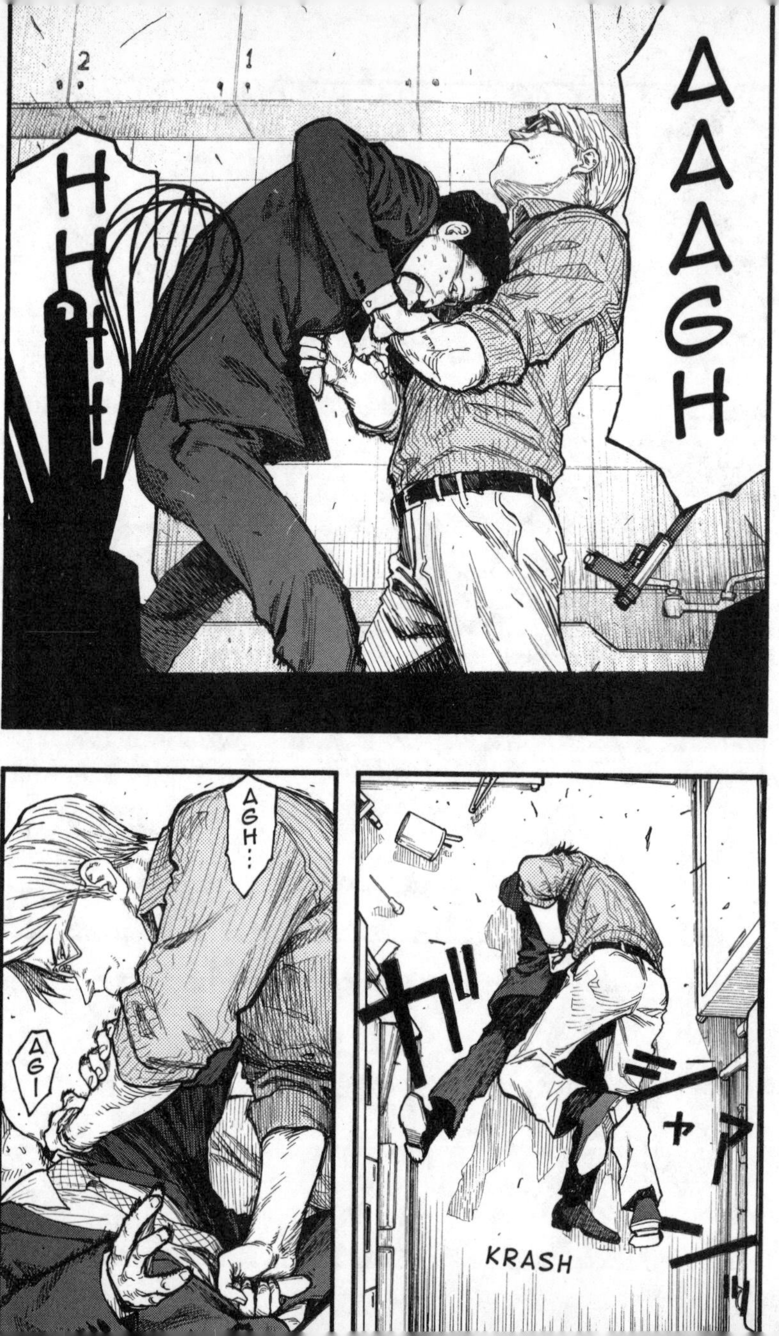
AAAGH
HHHHH
KRASH
AGH...
AGI

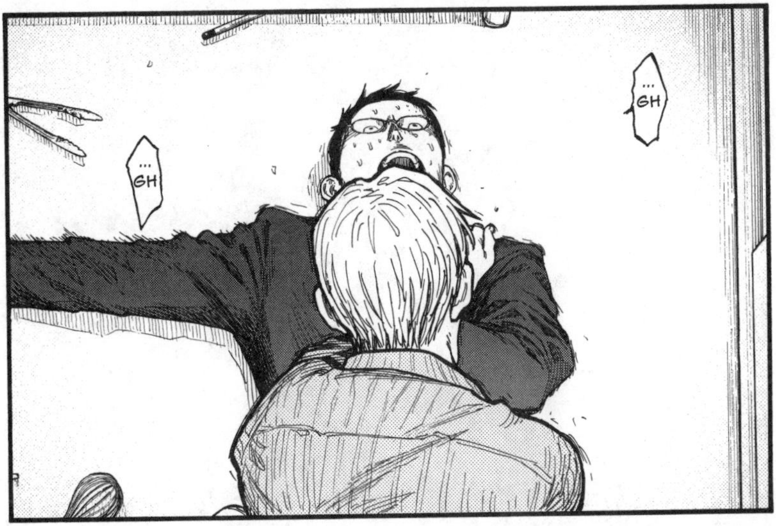
...GH
...GH
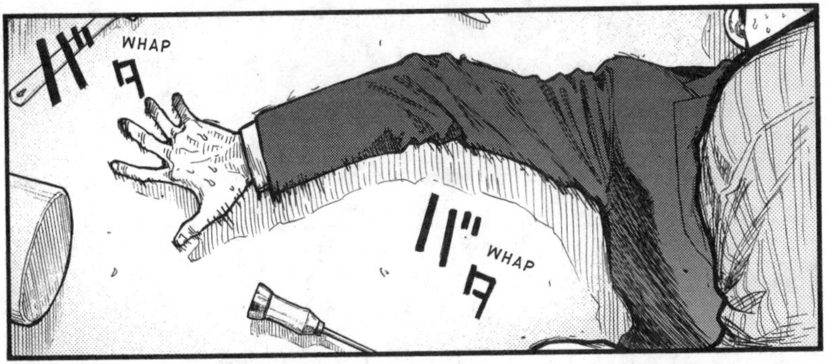
ガタ
WHAP
バタ
WHAP
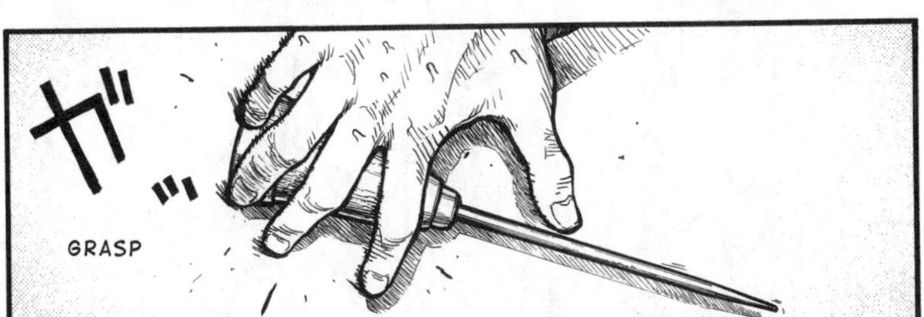
ガッ
GRASP

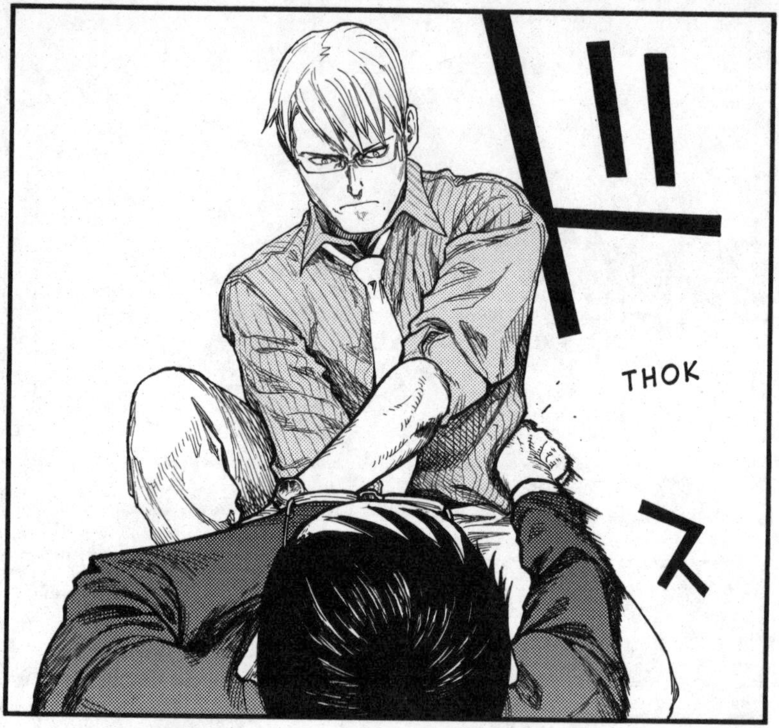
ドッ
THOK
ス
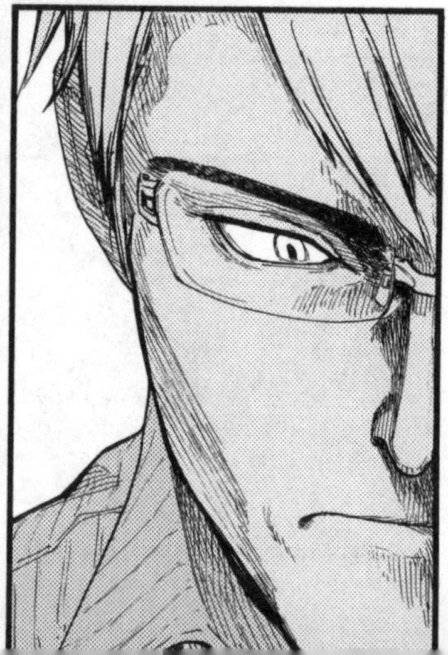
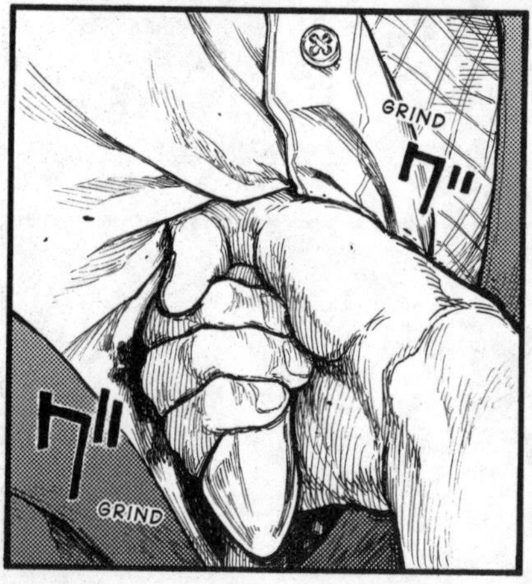
GRIND
グ
グ
GRIND

THOK
ド
ス

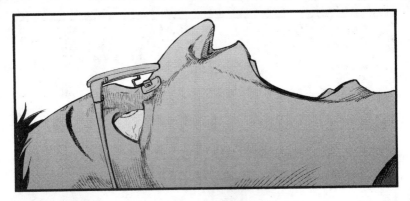

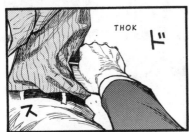

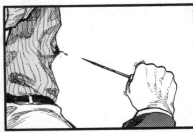

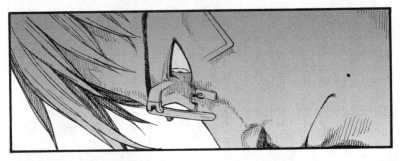

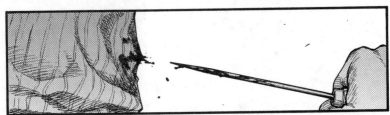

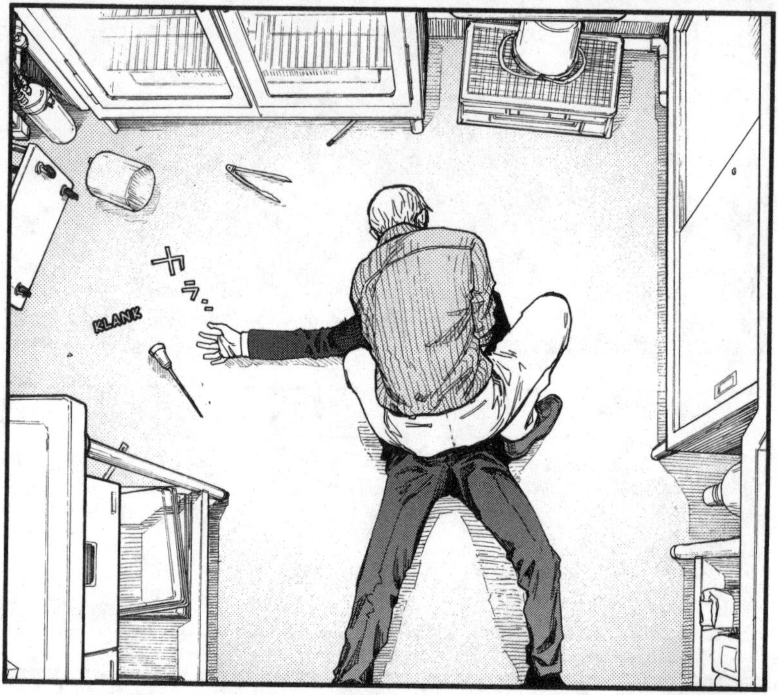
カラ…
KLANK
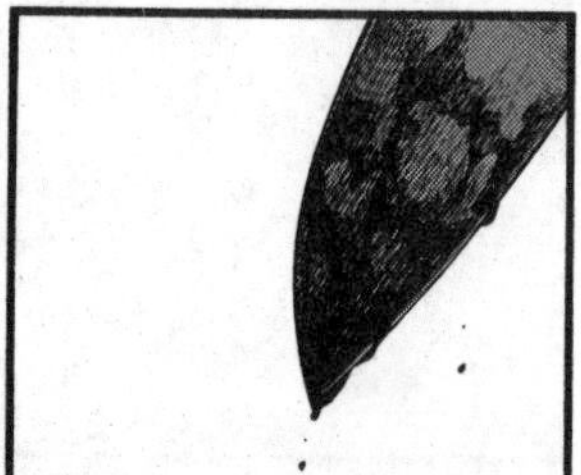
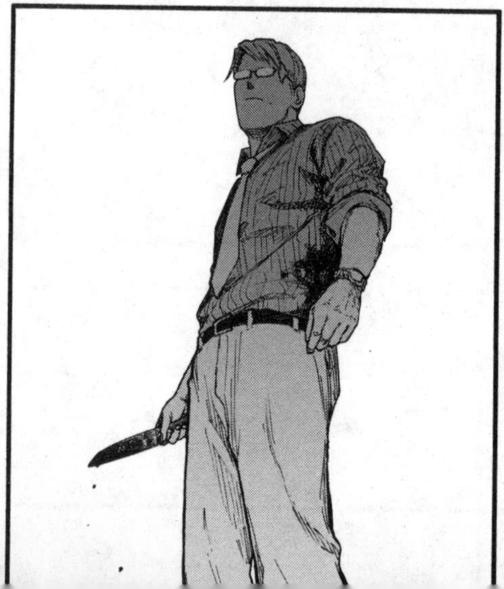

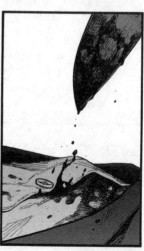

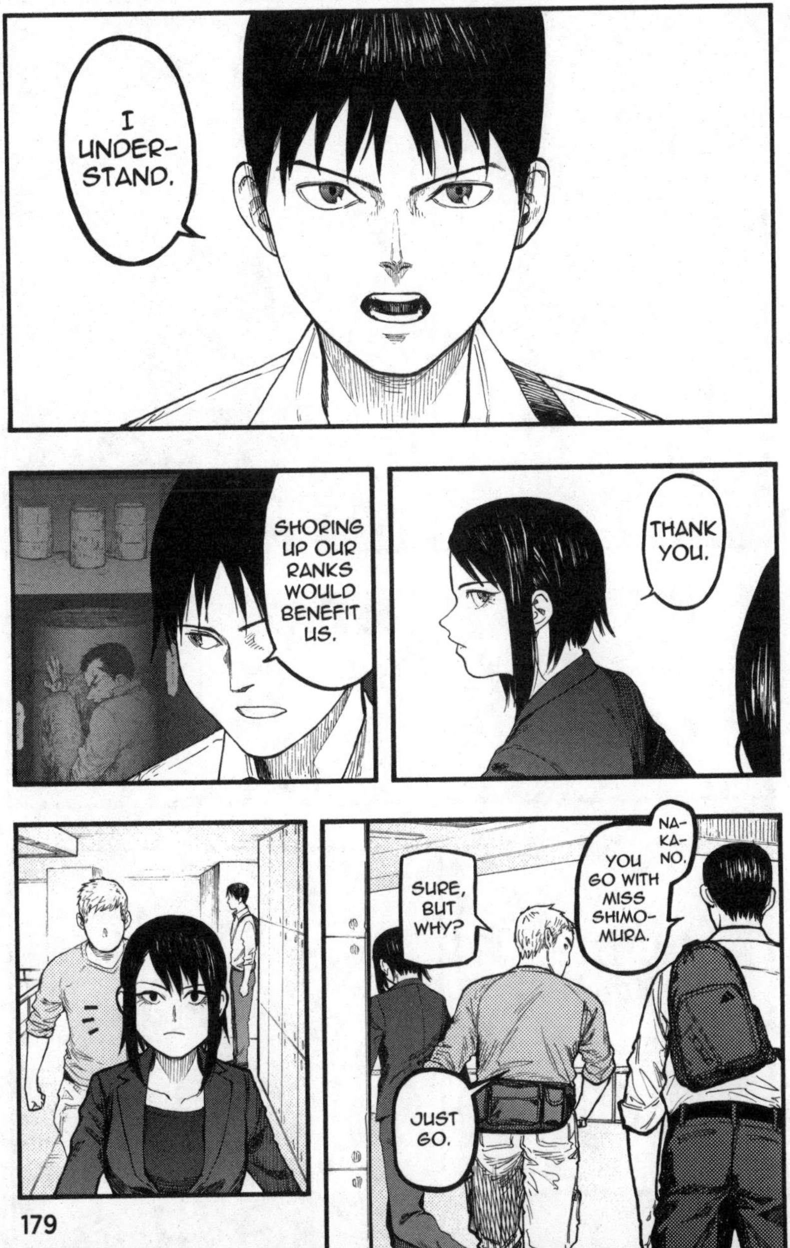
I UNDER-STAND.
THANK YOU.
SHORING UP OUR RANKS WOULD BENEFIT US.
NAKANO, YOU GO WITH MISS SHIMOMURA.
SURE, BUT WHY?
JUST GO.

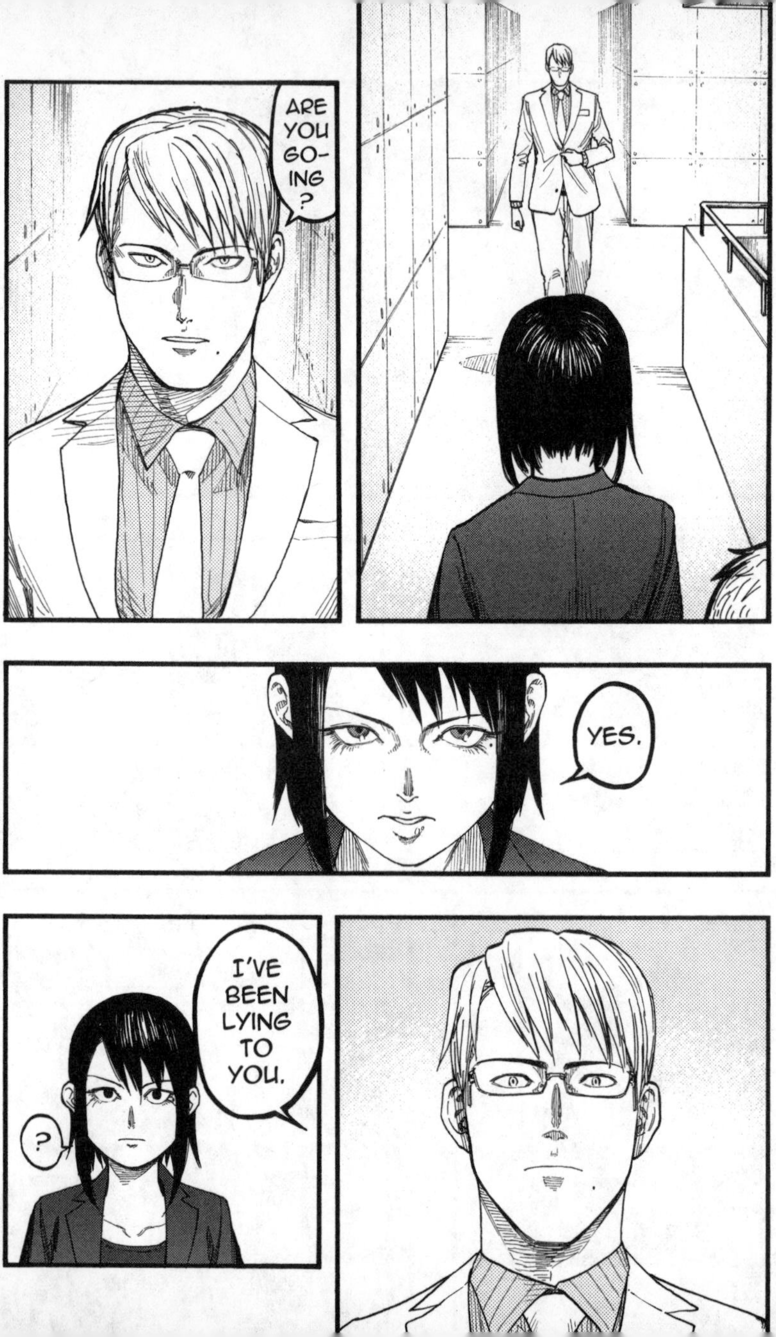
ARE YOU GOING?
YES.
I'VE BEEN LYING TO YOU.
?

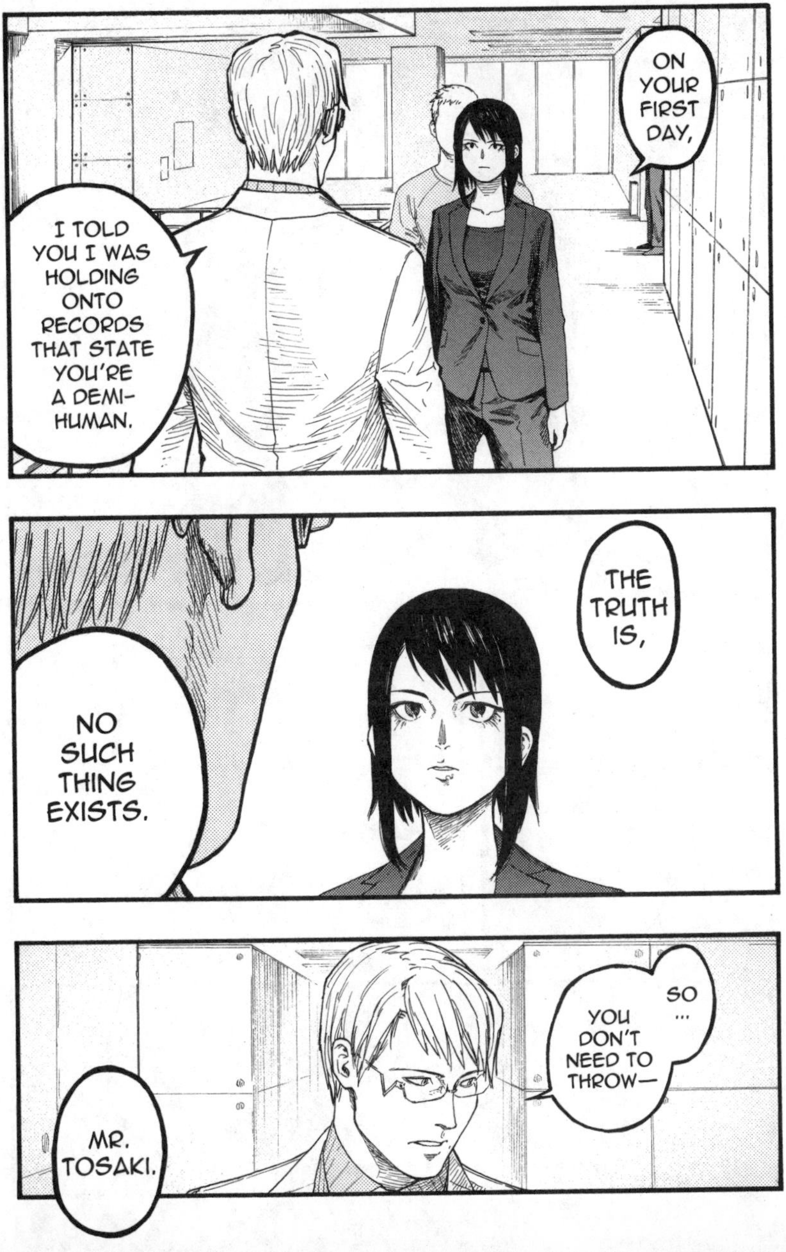
ON YOUR FIRST DAY,
I TOLD YOU I WAS HOLDING ONTO RECORDS THAT STATE YOU'RE A DEMI-HUMAN.
THE TRUTH IS,
NO SUCH THING EXISTS.
SO ...
YOU DON'T NEED TO THROW—
MR. TOSAKI.

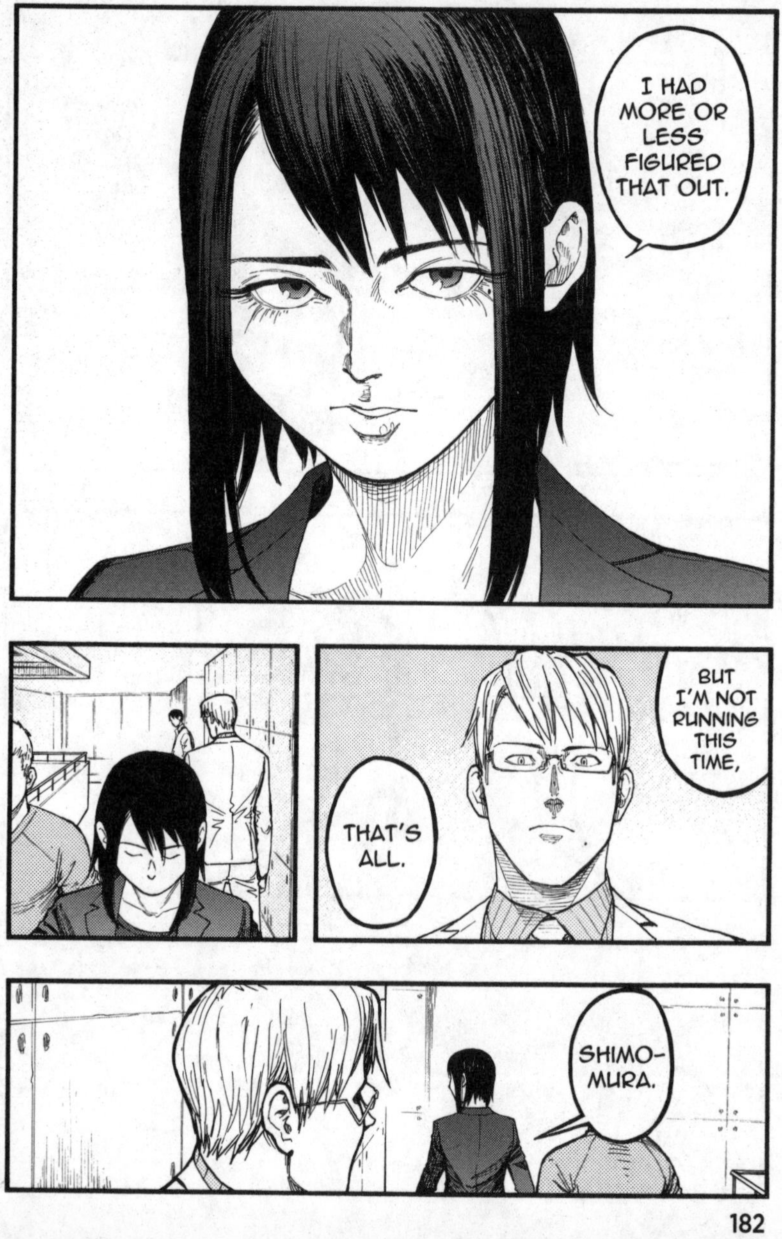
I HAD MORE OR LESS FIGURED THAT OUT.
BUT I'M NOT RUNNING THIS TIME,
THAT'S ALL.
SHIMO-MURA.

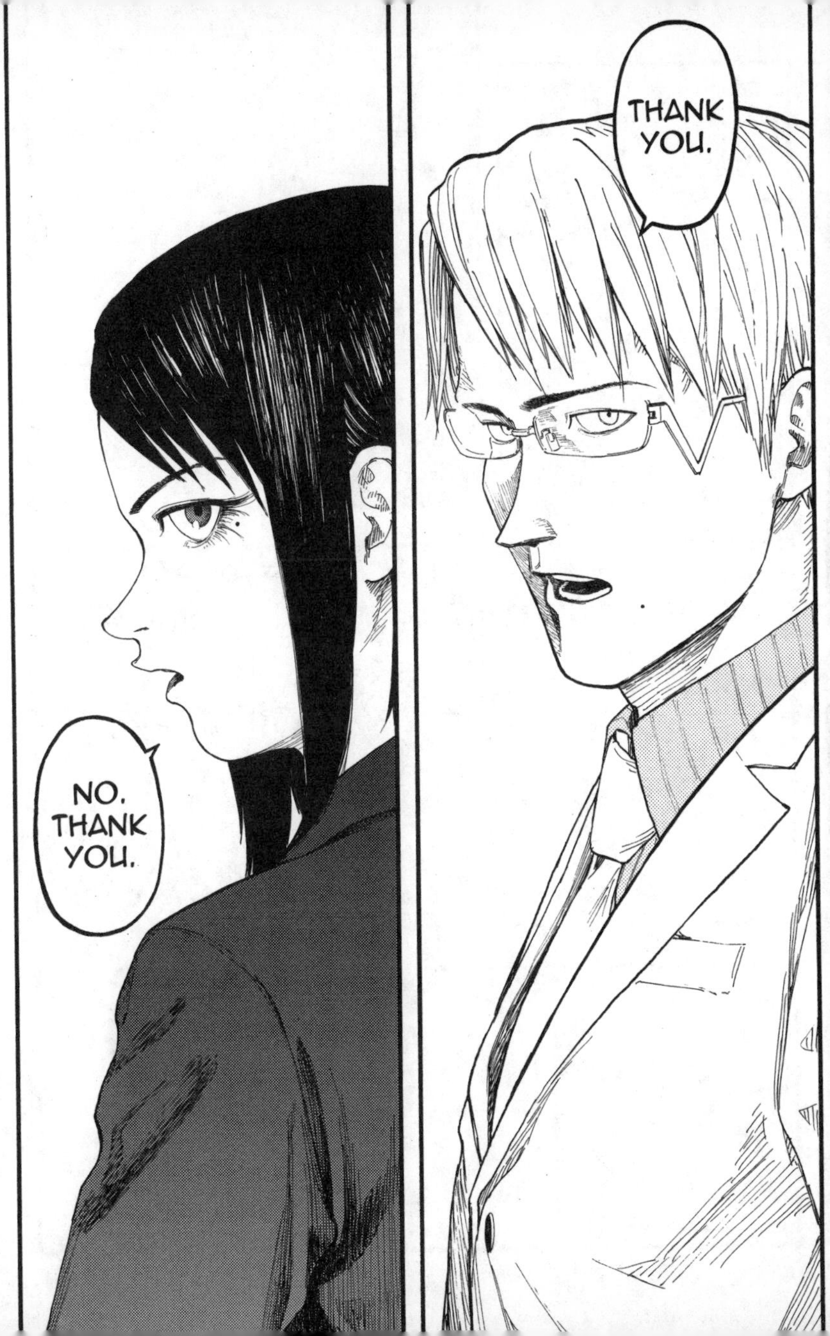
THANK YOU.
NO. THANK YOU.

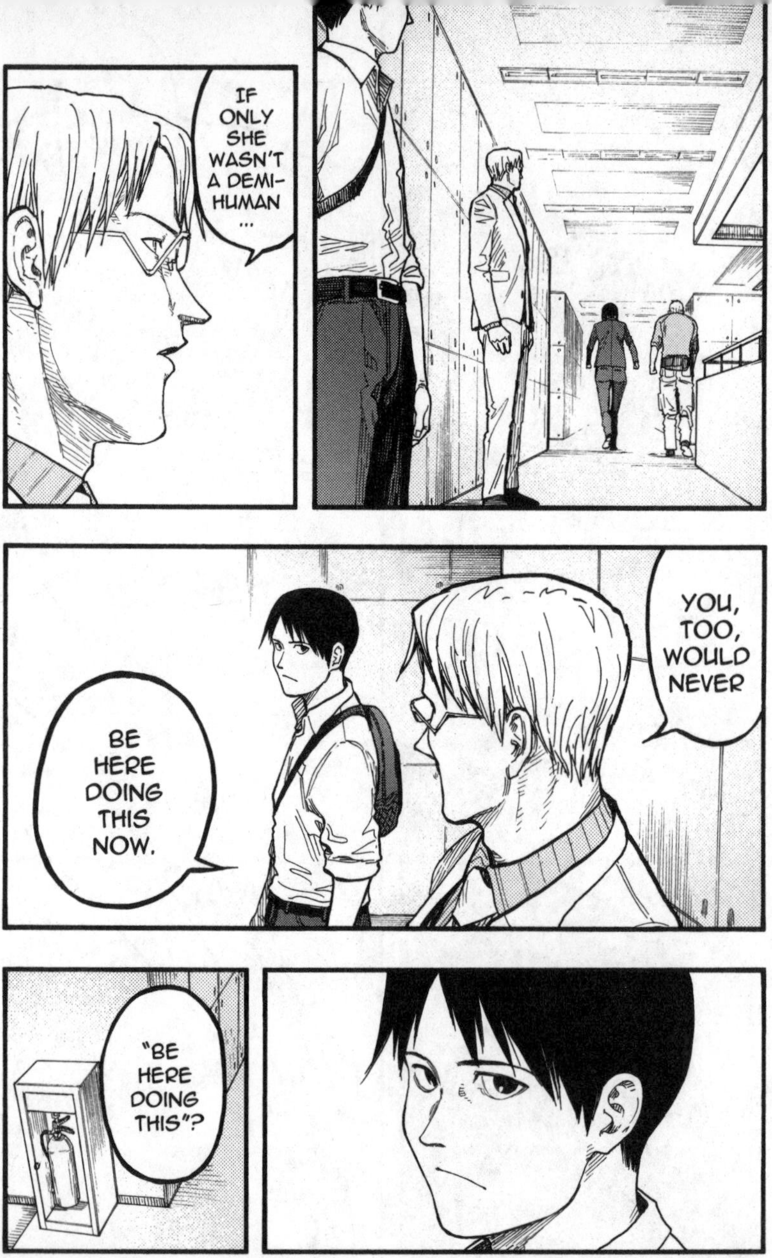
IF ONLY SHE WASN'T A DEMI-HUMAN ...
YOU, TOO, WOULD NEVER
BE HERE DOING THIS NOW.
"BE HERE DOING THIS"?

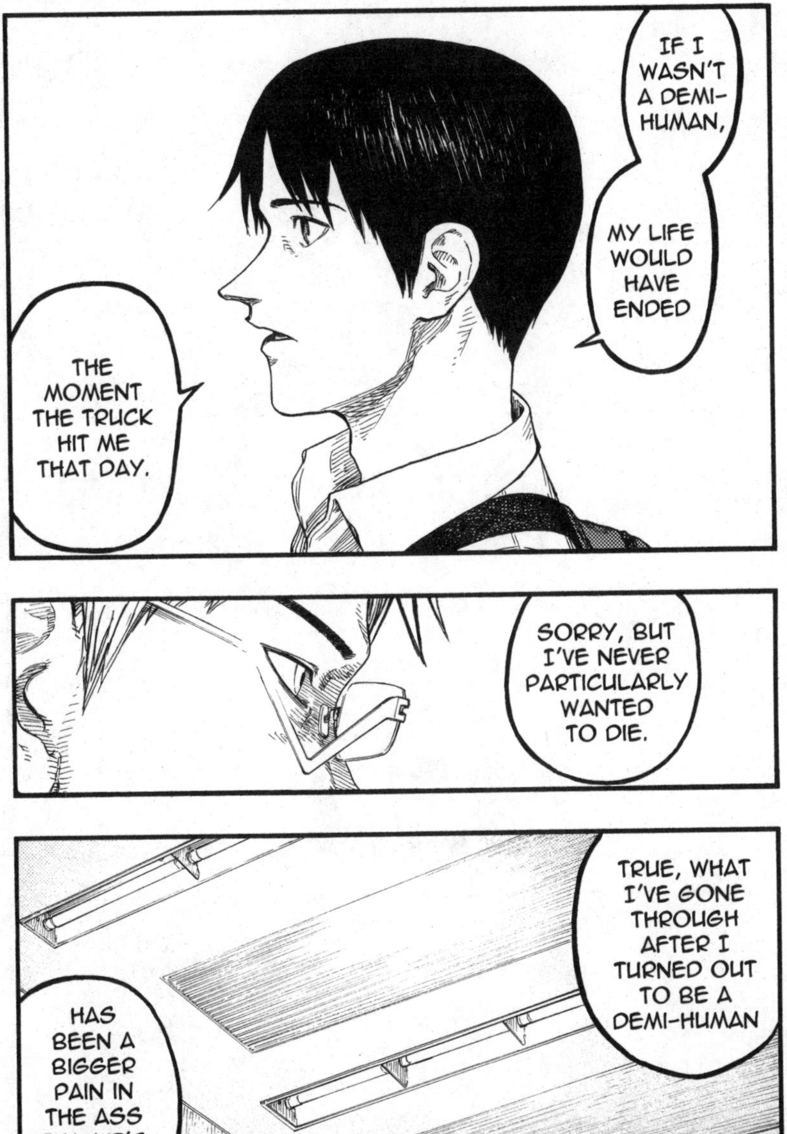
IF I WASN'T A DEMI-HUMAN,
MY LIFE WOULD HAVE ENDED
THE MOMENT THE TRUCK HIT ME THAT DAY.
SORRY, BUT I'VE NEVER PARTICULARLY WANTED TO DIE.
TRUE, WHAT I'VE GONE THROUGH AFTER I TURNED OUT TO BE A DEMI-HUMAN
HAS BEEN A BIGGER PAIN IN THE ASS THAN IT'S WORTH.

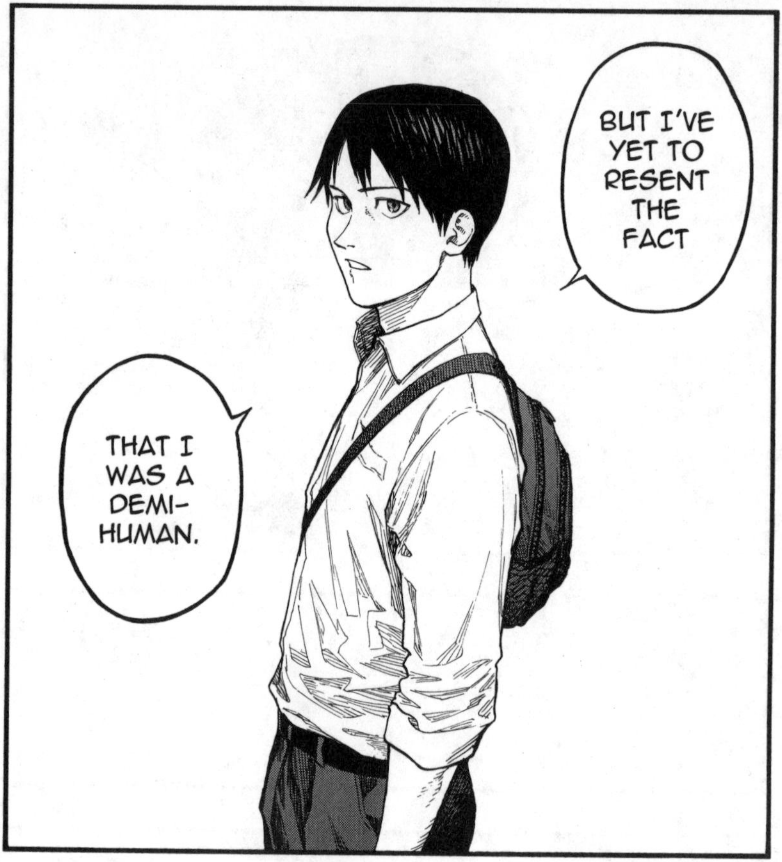
BUT I'VE YET TO RESENT THE FACT
THAT I WAS A DEMI-HUMAN.

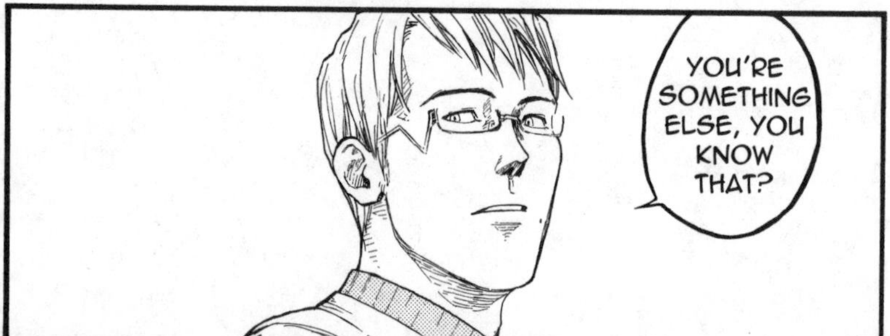
YOU'RE SOMETHING ELSE, YOU KNOW THAT?

IT'S ABOUT TIME FOR ME, TOO.

I'LL BE GOING.

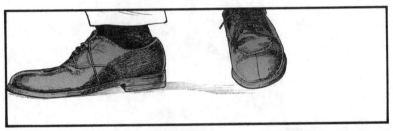

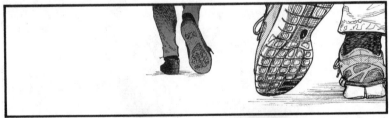

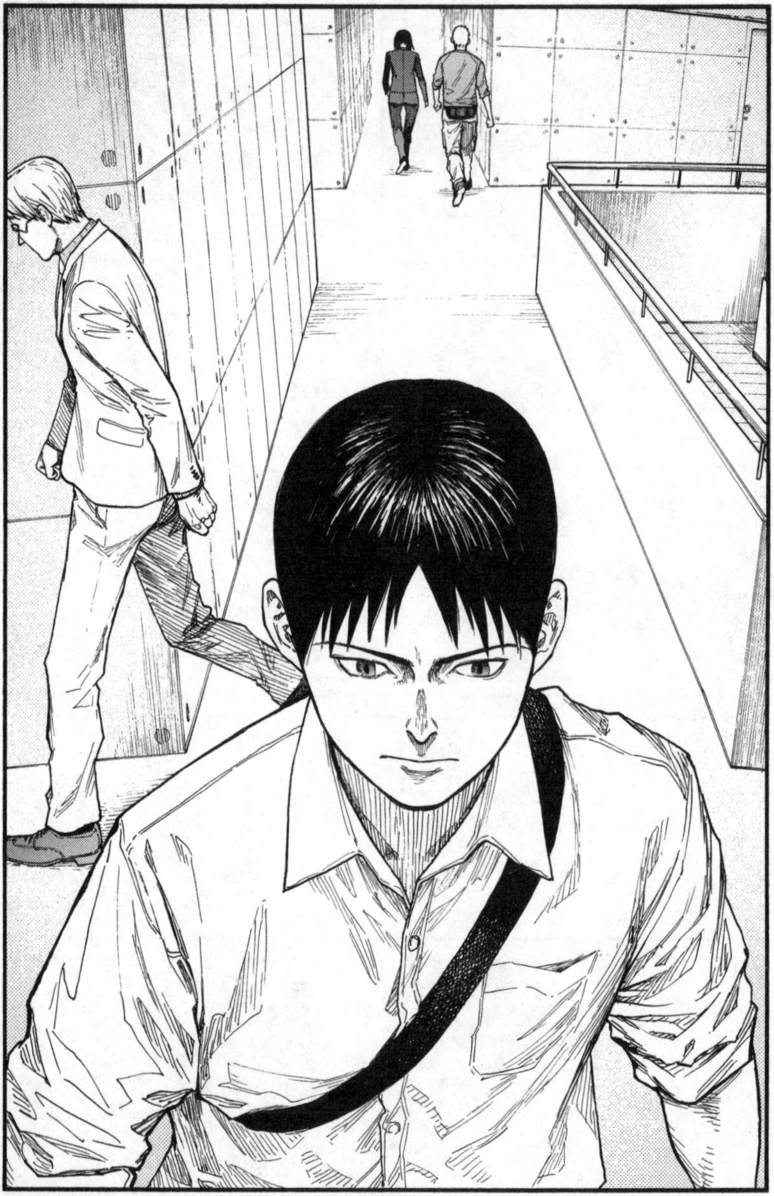

AJIN 11 End

DEMI-HUMAN

COMIC: GAMON SAKURAI

ASSISTANTS: CROUTON SANCHI (almost all tone range masking)

SAWANOSHOW (Line drawings)

[File 49: p. 24, panels 3, 4, 5; car: 91%] [File 49: p. 25, panels 1, 3, 4: car: 90%] [File 49: p. 25, panel 5: cigarette pack: 99%] [File 49: p. 26, panels 1, 2: phone booth: 99%]
[File 49: p. 28, panels 2, 3; phone booth: 95%] [File 49: p. 30, panel 1: tablet image: 25%] [File 49: p. 31, panels 1, 2, 3: car: 90%] [File 49: p. 32, panel 1: car: 85%]
[File 49: p. 33, panel 1: car: 85%] [File 49: p. 34, panel 1: car: 88%]

[File 50: p. 37, panels 1, 2, car: 95%] [File 50: p. 38, panels 1, 3: car: 85%] [File 50: p. 39, panel 4: car: 99%] [File 50: p. 40, panels 1, 2, car: 90%]
[File 50: p. 41, panels 1, 2, car: 88%] [File 50: p. 41, panels 1, 5: background: 95%] [File 50: p. 42, panels 2, 4: car: 98%] [File 50: p. 43, panel 4: car: 98%]
[File 50: p. 48, panels 2, 3: background: 95%] [File 50: p. 49, panel 2: background: 91%] [File 50: p. 51, panels 3, 5, 6; background: 95%] [File 50: p. 55, panel 4: car: 90%]
[File 50: p. 56, panels 1, 4: car: 90%] [File 50: p. 57, panels 1, 4: car: 91%] [File 50: p. 58, panel 1: car: 88%] [File 50: p. 61, panel 1: background: 90%]

[File 51: p. 67, panel 1: car: 96%] [File 51: p. 67, panels 2, 3, 4: Sato's car: 80%] [File 51: p. 66, panels 1, 2: background: 90%] [File 51: p. 69, panel 1: background: 95%]
[File 51: p. 70, panels 1, 3, 6: background: 95%] [File 51: p. 70, panel 2: car: 100%] [File 51: p. 71, panel 1: background: 94%] [File 51: p. 72, panels 4, 5: background: 94%]
[File 51: p. 73, panels 1, 6: background: 96%] [File 51: p. 78, panels 1, 2, 3: inside panel: 88%] [File 51: p. 79, panels 1, 2, 3: inside panel: 88%] [File 51: p. 81, panel 3: tripod: 85%]
[File 51: p. 83, panels 1, 3, 5: background: 87%] [File 51: p. 84, panels 1, 2: background: 70%] [File 51: p. 88, panel 4: license: 62%] [File 51: p. 90, panel 1: background: 90%]
[File 51: p. 91, panel 1: background: 95%] [File 51: p. 95, panel 2: vehicles: 98%] [File 51: p. 97, panel 2: vehicles: 95%] [File 51: p. 97, panel 4: mob: 91%]
[File 51: p. 101, panels 3, 5: background: 90%] [File 51: p. 107, panel 1: car: 95%] [File 51: p. 107, panels 2, 3: Sato's car: 99%] [File 51: p. 108, panel 2: background: 94%]

[File 52: p. 111, panel 2: vehicles: 100%] [File 52: p. 112, panel 2: shoes: 80%] [File 52: p. 114, panel 2: vehicles: 95%] [File 52: p. 120, panel 5: airplane: 95%]
[File 52: p. 121, panel 6: airplane: 85%] [File 52: p. 122, panel 3: airplane: 95%] [File 52: p. 125, panels 4, 5: car: 95%] [File 52: p. 126, panels 2, 4: vehicles: 90%]
[File 52: p. 127, panels 1, 2, 5, vehicles, driver: 95%] [File 52: p. 130, panels 1, 3, vehicles: 91%] [File 52: p. 131, panel 1: car, driver: 91%] [File 52: p. 132, panel 1: car: 90%]
[File 52: p. 134, panel 3: vehicles: 89%] [File 52: p. 135, panel 1: car: 97%] [File 52: p. 136, panel 1: background: 95%] [File 52: p. 138, panel 3: car: 94%]
[File 52: p. 142, panel 2: car: 80%] [File 52: p. 145, panel 3: tripod: 60%]

[File 53: p. 156, panel 1: background: 97%] [File 53: p. 157, panel 3: floor: 99%] [File 53: p. 158, panel 2: floor: 99%] [File 53: p. 166, panels 2, 3, 4: background: 91%]
[File 53: p. 167, panel 2: background: 95%] [File 53: p. 169, panel 1: background: 90%] [File 53: p. 170, panel 2: background: 89%] [File 53: p. 175, panels 1, 2, cookware: 70%]
[File 53: p. 187, panels 3, 4, 5; shoes: 70%])

KIMIYUKI MASAKI (Line drawings)

[File 49: p. 5, panel 1: background: 90%] [File 49: p. 11, panels 1, 2: background: 90%] [File 49: p. 17, panel 6: gun: 98%] [File 49: p. 18, panel 5: gun: 95%]
[File 49: p. 23, panel 1: background: 90%] [File 49: p. 26, panels 1, 2, background except booth: 80%] [File 49: p. 28, panel 3: background except booth: 85%]
[File 49: p. 30, panel 1: tablet image; 40%]

[File 50 security monitor images: 94%] [File 50: p. 40, panels 1, 4; background except car: 90%] [File 50: p. 42, panel 6: background: 80%] [File 50: p. 45, panel 6; background: 99%]
[File 50: p. 46, panels 1, 4: background: 95%] [File 50: p. 50, panel 2: background: 95%] [File 50: p. 51, panels 1, 4: background: 95%] [File 50: p. 56, panel 1: background: 90%]

[File 51: p. 70, panel 2: background: 90%] [File 51: p. 76, panels 1, 2: image except announcer: 96%] [File 51: p. 77, panel 1: image except announcer: 96%]
[File 51: p. 77, panels 2, 3: inside panel: 80%] [File 51: p. 80, panel 1: mob: 99%] [File 51: p. 81, panel 1: tripod: 95%] [File 51: p. 82, panel 1: camera, strap: 80%]
[File 51: p. 84, panel 2: Glock, hand: 95%] [File 51: p. 91, panel 2: background: 95%] [File 51: p. 92, panel 1: images: 90%] [File 51: p. 97, panel 2: mob: 88%]
[File 51: p. 98, panel 4: inside panel: 80%] [File 51: p. 102, panel 1: mob in image: 100%]

[File 52: p. 121, panel 3: SP badge: 98%] [File 52: p. 124, panel 4: Iruma Base aerial photo: 95%] [File 52: p. 125, panel 5: gun: 95%] [File 52: p. 127, panels 2, 4: gun: 95%]
[File 52: p. 128, panel 1: map, plan: 96%] [File 52: p. 133, panel 3: map, plan: 97%] [File 52: p. 145, panel 2: tripod: 60%] [File 52: p. 148, panel 1: gun: 79%]

[File 53: p. 153, panel 2: background: 80%] [File 53: p. 154, panels 1, 2: background: 98%] [File 53: p. 155, panel 1: background: 99%] [File 53: p. 157, panel 4: background: 97%]
[File 53: p. 159, panel 1: security monitors, images: 95%] [File 53: p. 160, panel 4: background: 98%] [File 53: p. 161, panel 3: background: 98%]
[File 53: p. 174, panel 1: cookware in foreground: 90%])

Ajin: Demi-Human, volume 11

Translation: Ko Ransom
Production: Risa Cho
        Hiroko Mizuno

First published in Japan in 2017 by Kodansha, Ltd., Tokyo
Publication for this English edition arranged through Kodansha, Ltd., Tokyo

Published by Vertical, Inc., New York, 2018

Originally published in Japanese as *Ajin 11* by Kodansha, Ltd.
Ajin first serialized in *good! Afternoon*, Kodansha, Ltd., 2012-

This is a work of fiction.

ISBN: 978-1-945054-69-3

Manufactured in the United States of America

First Edition

Vertical, Inc.
451 Park Avenue South
7th Floor
New York, NY 10016
www.vertical-inc.com